The Good, The Bad and The Gorgeous

THE GOOD, THE BAD
AND
THE GORGEOUS

♥

Popular Culture's Romance
with Lesbianism

Edited by
Diane Hamer and Belinda Budge

Pandora
An Imprint of HarperCollinsPublishers

Pandora
An Imprint of HarperCollins*Publishers*
77–85 Fulham Palace Road,
Hammersmith, London W6 8JB
1160 Battery Street,
San Francisco, California 94111–1213

Published by Pandora 1994
1   3   5   7   9   10   8   6   4   2

A catalogue record for this book
is available from the British Library

ISBN 0 04 440910 9

Typeset by Harper Phototypesetters Limited
Northampton, England
Printed in Great Britain by
Mackays of Chatham, Kent

CONTENTS

ACKNOWLEDGEMENTS

Thank you to all the contributors who have generously given their thoughts and their time to make this collection a reality. Thanks also to Vicky Wilson for her input into the early planning of the book; and to Sara Dunn for her editorial advice and nurturing through the final stages. And special thanks to Allegra Madgwick, Susan Ardill, Louise Anderson, Kay Ransome and Claire Relf, all of whom have read, questioned and discussed just about everything 'good, bad and gorgeous' in this book.

NOTES ON CONTRIBUTORS

ROSA AINLEY listens to country music in the company of other consenting adults and does not have big hair. She is currently writing a book about lesbians and identity from the 1950s to the 1990s.

SONYA ANDERMAHR teaches English and Women's Studies. She has recently completed a doctoral thesis on contemporary lesbian genre fiction.

SARAH COOPER lives in London with her guitar-shaped record collection and learnt everything she needed to know about life from the work of Gram Parsons and Hank Williams.

ANGELA GALVIN lives and works in Sheffield. She has a BA in Communication Studies and an MA in Film Studies. She spent five years as an economic researcher, and produced and presented video and radio for Women's Own Pictures, BBC Radio Sheffield and Radio 4. She has written for journals as diverse as *Spare Rib* and *When Saturday Comes*. Current work includes editing a bi-monthly supplement on community affairs for the *Sheffield Telegraph* and supporting the development of community initiatives around HIV. She also supports Sheffield Wednesday.

PAULA GRAHAM is working on a PhD at Sussex University on

lesbian film spectatorship, and teaches media and lesbian cultural studies in higher and adult education. She is currently writing a book on lesbians and popular cinema, and has contributed 'Girl's Camp: The Politics of Parody' to *Screening Out Women: Lesbians and Film*, edited by Tamsin Wilton.

JULIA HALLAM lectures in Communication Studies at Liverpool University. She has published articles on women and film and is currently writing a PhD on nursing and representation.

JENNY HARDING recently returned to live and work in London after spending several years in Sydney, where she completed her PhD on the regulation of sex in discourses on hormone replacement therapy. In the last fifteen years she has worked as a social researcher, taught cultural studies and has been variously involved, through writing and campaigning, in the politics of health, reproduction and sexuality.

ROSANNE KENNEDY teaches Women's Studies and English at the Australian National University. She is co-editor of *Feminist Legal Theory: Readings in Law and Gender* (Westview Press, 1991). She is currently working on a cultural study of evidential discourse in modern and contemporary culture.

MARGARET MARSHMENT lectures in Media and Cultural Studies at Liverpool John Moores University. She is co-editor of *The Female Gaze* (The Women's Press, 1988) and has published articles on feminism and representation.

ARLENE STEIN is currently visiting lecturer in Sociology at the University of Essex. She is editor of *Sisters, Sexperts, Queers: Beyond the Lesbian Nation* (Plume, 1993) and is the former editor of *Out/Look* Magazine. She writes and teaches about the sociology of sexuality, lesbian and gay identities and media and culture.

SUE O'SULLIVAN is a health educator and writer, and has written extensively on HIV/AIDS and women. She has worked as a researcher on British television's *Out on Tuesday* and is also a member of the editorial collective of *Feminist Review*.

YVONNE TASKER is a freelance writer and lecturer in Film and Media Studies.

CLARE WHATLING submitted her PhD thesis 'Configurations of sex, gender and sexuality: McCullers, butch/femme and Wittig' in the summer of 1994. She has published essays on Kristeva, Nestle and Califia.

GILLIAN WHITLOCK teaches at the Faculty of Humanities at Griffith University, Queensland, Australia. Feminist detective fiction is both a research interest and a pleasure activity.

INTRODUCTION

Within weeks of the publication of the August 1993 issue of *Vanity Fair*, the front cover – featuring cross-dressing k.d. lang being shaved by supermodel Cindy Crawford – became an internationally recognized symbol of the phenomenon of 'lesbian chic'. That cover-spread was both a symptom and culmination of a trend which had been gathering steam throughout the previous three years. For, in recent years, references to lesbianism have been making their way into mainstream culture in some surprising ways. Madonna has flirted with it, Martina Navratilova and k.d. lang openly admit it and the BBC makes costume dramas about it. Indeed, given the coverage in the popular media of late, it seems that everyone is now 'one of us' – or aspires to be ... It is this phenomenon which the contributors to this collection explore.

We began working on *The Good, The Bad and The Gorgeous* at the end of 1991. At that point, though there were early signs that the historical status of lesbianism was undergoing popular revision, there was no way we could have anticipated the *Vanity Fair* cover which appeared eighteen months later. Nor could the emergence of a wealth of other popular literary, filmic, televisual and musical products in which lesbianism has been brought into the mainstream have been predicted. So rapidly has the phenomenon gathered pace that it has been a challenge to keep this collection up to date.

Focusing on a variety of cultural 'moments', our contributors – some writers, some academics, all consumers of popular culture – investigate the meanings of popular cultural texts from a lesbian perspective; and explore the relationship between lesbianism and popular culture from a range of perspectives.

In different ways, each contribution explores why there seems to have been an opening up of possibilities for lesbian representation within popular culture, and also focuses on the limitations of lesbianism's acceptability within the mainstream.

DISTURBING PLEASURES

Popular culture has become an increasingly important discursive site for lesbian and feminist politics. Since political change centrally involves a struggle over meaning, it is not possible simply to dismiss popular culture as merely servicing the dual systems of patriarchy and capitalism. Rather, as Margaret Marshment and Julia Hallam show in their reading of the television version of Jeanette Winterson's *Oranges are Not the Only Fruit*, popular culture is a site where meanings can be contested, and where dominant ideologies can be disturbed. It is here, in television, magazines, films, books and music, that we are offered the culture's dominant definition of ourselves. We cannot dismiss the popular by always positioning ourselves outside it. Lesbians have now begun to look at how we can intervene in the mainstream, subverting hegemonic meanings and imposing our own in their place.

Popular culture has always been a source of great pleasure for individual lesbians, who have become skilled at challenging the dominant images of heterosexuality within it. As Clare Whatling argues in 'Fostering the illusion : stepping out with Jodie' lesbians have always found ways to 'read between the lines', projecting our fantasies of desire and identification onto heterosexual narratives and mainstream female icons. Whatling explores how a handful of films, with no obvious lesbian reference points, have been appropriated for a lesbian economy of desire as a result of what she terms 'extra-textual information' available about the films star or stars. Whether by rumour or gossip, the belief that a particular actor is a lesbian enables an appropriation of their films, regardless of the possibilities offered by the films themselves. Whatling demonstrates this by reference to a longstanding lesbian favourite, Jodie Foster.

In a similar vein, Yvonne Tasker's 'Pussy galore' examines how even the most apparently heterosexual of films can be appropriated by the lesbian spectator. She explores the pleasures available for lesbians in films as diverse as *Thelma and Louise*, *Black Widow*, *Silence of the Lambs* and *Basic Instinct*, and suggests that lesbians do not necessarily want a diet of 'positive images'. Instead, she argues, lesbian spectators can identify with heterosexual women, gay men and even straight men in their quest for cinematic pleasure.

These essays, along with several others in the collection, offer a challenge to contemporary feminist film criticism, which they argue is out of step with the viewing practices and strategies of a lesbian audience. Feminist film theorists such as Laura Mulvey and Mary Doane have argued that lesbian spectatorship is only possible when the spectator is positioned as a masculine subject. As Mandy Merck comments in her book *Perversions: Deviant Readings*, masculinization of the gaze has become one of feminism's most influential – and contested – premises. 'In particular . . . it has haunted descriptions of erotic looking by and between women' (p. 78).

In 'Looking lesbian: amazons and aliens in science fiction cinema', Paula Graham problematizes the notion that the lesbian spectator can only derive pleasure by taking up a masculine subject position.

Music is a hugely important popular cultural form, and pop stars such as Dusty Springfield, Joan Armatrading and Tracy Chapman have all been taken on by lesbian audiences as rumours of homosexuality have 'damaged' their careers. In 'Crossover dreams'

Arlene Stein looks at pop music since the 1970s and argues that the 'crossover artists' who embrace lesbianism while achieving mainstream success are a rare specimen indeed. But while images of heterosexuality dominate popular music, they do not go unchallenged. She argues that women have always found ways to 'read' pop music, by privately changing the pronouns of songs and by desiring apparently unreachable female stars. From Tracy Chapman, k.d. lang, Michelle Shocked, Phranc and the Indigo Girls, Stein looks at the pleasures of pop as well as lesbian efforts to influence pop music production.

The crime genre is one of the most popular for women readers, and one which lesbians in particular have appropriated. There has been an emergence of a number of private investigators who are articulate, independent women; from Sarah Paretsky's V.I. Warshawski and Sue Grafton's Kinsey Millhone to Katherine V. Forrest's cop Kate Delafield. In 'Cop it sweet' Gillian Whitlock looks at how the genre represents lesbians, arguing that crime fiction brings lesbians into popular culture in an unprecedented way. Acknowledging the wariness with which some lesbian feminist intellectuals have approached the dyke detective, she suggests that these widely-read novels intervene as agents of change, displacing and replacing negative representations of lesbians with other more positive ones and transforming dominant culture in the process.

LESBIAN CHIC

In the popular texts referred to so far, lesbian pleasures must be derived surreptitiously, in private and against the grain. But the rise and rise of lesbian chic enables a more public consumption. As consumers of popular culture ourselves, we personally enjoy and celebrate our newfound position at the cutting edge of fashion. Yet the profound reversal of lesbianism's traditional status, as a reviled and despised identity, and the sheer extent of recent mainstream references to our sexuality give pause for thought. It is important not to overstate the degree of popular acceptance, and we can only speculate on the likely long-term impact of this current popular fascination with lesbianism. We feel, however, that it is a subject worthy of deeper examination. A number of contributions to this collection consider possible explanations for the changing status of lesbianism, while others look at the terms of our inclusion into the mainstream.

In 'Making a drama out of difference' Jenny Harding critically examines BBC2's *Portrait of a Marriage*, one of the first mainstream drama series to show lesbian protagonists on television. Harding cites an early review of the series by Elizabeth Wilson, which had considered why lesbians were suddenly coming into vogue. Wilson wondered whether homosexuality was serving as a metaphor for heterosexuality's discontents and asked:

> Could it be that gay love is the lens through which heterosexual society is desperately peering at its own problematic practices? . . . Lesbian and gay love still struggling against prohibition, acts as a strange, illicit utopia of renewed desire by contrast with the clapped-out world of heterosexuality.

Harding takes up these ideas by asking whether *Portrait* threatened to unseat the norms of heterosexual marriage, or ultimately to make them safe. Was the series actually more about heterosexuality than homosexuality?

Wilson's early observations referred specifically to television, where representations of lesbianism seem to have the highest profile. In 'The gorgeous lesbian in *LA Law*: the present absence?' Rosanne Kennedy writes about the now famous 'lesbian kiss' episode. She asks why *LA Law* has achieved such cult status amongst lesbians despite the almost total absence of lesbian references in the series. She suggests that through the character of C.J. Lamb, played by Amanda Donohoe, lesbianism is maintained as a 'present absence' in *LA Law*, even though C.J. identifies as neither lesbian nor straight. Is she truly 'queer'? Or is she there merely to raise issues, not to be representative?

In 'From string of knots to orange box: lesbianism on prime time', Margaret Marshment and Julia Hallam examine *Oranges are Not the Only Fruit*, and argue that this realist television drama which 'naturalizes' lesbianism is a radical text. Diane Hamer is in conversation with producer Penny Ashbrook about the impact on mainstream television of the lesbian and gay series *Out on Tuesday*. Of course, there are many other lesbians on television; Sandra Bernhard's character in the American sitcom *Roseanne*; the lesbian storylines in British soaps, *Emmerdale* and *Brookside*, the fleeting lesbian subplots on soaps, like *Melrose Place* and *The Golden Girls*, and the British television version series of Armistead Maupin's book *Tales of the City*. All these are worthy of extended discussion in their own right, but sadly beyond the scope of this collection.

Wilson's insights about homosexuality as a lens for heterosexuality are not just limited to television products, but are capable of more general application. She gestures at two interconnected possibilities as to why dominant culture – whose privileged discourse has always been heterosexuality – has suddenly become obsessed with homosexuality. (Of course, in a sense, dominant culture has always been obsessed with homosexuality; what is different now is that homosexuality is being constructed as a glamorous, rather than a despised, identity). One possibility lies in the tired narratives of what Wilson refers to as 'the clapped-out world of heterosexuality'. Whether in television drama, film, or the world of women's magazines, storytelling relies on dramatic tension for its success. Drama requires conflict and prohibition. The attempt to find resolutions to that tension is what provides any good story with its narrative drive. Yet so few of the conventional representations of heterosexuality in film and television narratives now hold any dramatic tension. Sex outside marriage is no longer taboo, nor is adultery. Sex outside boundaries of class or race is becoming increasingly transparent as a device to enhance tension. So little is now forbidden within a heterosexual landscape that new metaphors must constantly be sought out. Homosexuality serves as a new and (still) shocking arena for the reworking of stories of sex and love, romance and desire.

The use of a lesbian character as narrative device is very transparent in films such as *Basic Instinct*, reviewed here by Angela Galvin. She teases apart the character of Catherine Tramell, played by Sharon Stone, and asks why this film was such a box office success. Was it the combination of elements – beautiful woman who sleeps with women and kills men – which made an otherwise badly scripted and rather predictable film such a big hit? Or was it the very fact of the gay lobby against it which boosted its popularity? If so, why did so many lesbians like it? Lesbianism as narrative tool is not a device confined to use in cinema; the lang/Crawford *Vanity Fair* photo spread achieved enormous sales to a predominantly heterosexual readership, precisely because of the frisson of lesbianism represented on its cover.

A second, related, possibility as to why homosexuality is in the ascendancy may be the anxiety about gender currently at large within mainstream culture. The artifice of conventional gender categories has been increasingly exposed by an active and assertive women's movement. Feminist critiques have, for the past two decades, sought to critique the nature of the relationship between women and men, and in particular have confronted the popular belief that women and men stand in a relationship of complementary opposition to each other. The result is that the difference between the two genders, once thought to be natural and inherent, no longer occupies such an unassailable position.

This gender anxiety is clearly finding expression in a popular fascination with homosexuality, recognized as a lifestyle in which gender roles are skewed. One pertinent illustration of both this anxiety and our culture's current obsession with homosexuality, was apparent on a recent edition of the *Phil Donahue Show*, an American daytime talk show: Martina Navratilova's ex-lover Judy Nelson, appeared as Donahue's special guest. With hair fashionably coiffed and makeup skilfully applied Judy, the ex-beauty queen, appeared to all the world as the archetypal feminine woman. The studio audience, predominantly women whose fashion styles mirrored Judy's own, looked on with horrified fascination as she described her love for Martina. In all respects she was a woman like themselves, whose glamour they could only aspire to – and yet she loved women! (That she announced on camera she was now having her second lesbian relationship only served to drive home their confusion). Diane Hamer's contribution to this volume examines how Martina and Judy's relationship – lived out in the glare of the public gaze – has confounded the tabloid press and popularly held beliefs that real lesbians are masculine. She argues that Judy Nelson's appearance on *Donahue* showed that dominant meanings can no longer be taken for granted. No longer does femininity automatically imply heterosexuality. The studio audience for the *Phil Donahue Show* that day was a study in gender anxiety.

This anxiety about gender and sexuality is further demonstrated by Cindy Crawford's claim, reported in the *National Enquirer*, that the reason she was photographed in sexually suggestive poses with self-proclaimed lesbian, k.d., was to *dispel* rumours that she (along with hubby Richard Gere) was gay. Whether the illogicality of this reasoning was hers or the *Enquirer*'s is immaterial; the lasting impression one is left with is of a world where sex and gender have been turned upside down.

The timing of lesbianism's appearance on centre stage is not solely the result of a heterosexual agenda. As Sue O'Sullivan argues in 'Girls who kiss girls and who cares?', it has been the unexpected catastrophe of AIDS which has prised apart the closed doors of mainstream culture to enable the representation of sexual diversity in a way previously unknown. This may also account for why lesbianism seems to be achieving prominence in a different way from the profile accorded to male homosexuality. It may just be that lesbianism is undergoing a 'catch-up' exercise; gay male sexuality has always been far more visible than lesbianism, and from at least the early 1980s male homoerotic imagery has successfully crossed over into the mainstream and been appropriated for a range of popular cultural texts.

However, the way in which lesbians and lesbianism are being embraced by popular culture is in some ways quite different from the terms of male homosexuality's incorporation. There have always been isolated examples of famous gay men, but more often than not their homosexuality has not been made public until their careers are on the wane. In the cases of Rock Hudson and Freddie Mercury their sexuality was not publicly acknowledged until their deaths.

In contrast, those famous women whose names have recently become associated with lesbianism – amongst whose number can be counted k.d. lang, Sandra Bernhard, Martina Navratilova, Melissa Etheridge, as well as apparent wannabes Madonna and Cindy Crawford – are women at the pinnacle of their careers. There is, it strikes us, no equivalent collection of male 'stars' able to take that very public step of identifying themselves as gay.

This difference is surely to do with AIDS and the meanings which attach to the HIV virus in popular discourse. The advent of AIDS has served to draw much public attention to homosexuality, and has rendered gay identities and communities far more visible than before, in a process which has encompassed both gay men and lesbians. And yet, simultaneously, the AIDS discourse does distinguish between gay sexuality and lesbianism.

Whether it is true in fact that lesbian sex is 'safe' from the virus is not our concern here; the important point is that unlike both gay sex and heterosexual sex, lesbian sexuality remains relatively free of the connotations of disease. By contrast, over the past decade a very rigid discursive connection has been constructed between gay sex, disease and death. Representations of gay men in popular culture inevitably now raise the spectre of AIDS, and in every attempt to represent gay sex the 'problem' of AIDS must necessarily be negotiated. (Hence, almost every mainstream film with a gay theme produced since the mid- 1980s seems to be about AIDS; *Longtime Companion, Parting Glances, Philadelphia, And the Band Played on,* and so on).

In this world where male sexuality – gay and also straight – has become hedged around with danger and with potentially life-threatening diseases, lesbian sex has surfaced as uniquely free from these connotations. Devoid of the grimly profound themes of sickness and death, lesbian sex has emerged as exciting, exploratory and glamorous.

The figure who perhaps best embodies the glamour and excitement of lesbian sexuality is Madonna. The most quintessentially female icon of the late twentieth century, Madonna's persona – though at times contradictory – serves to affirm an empowered female sexuality otherwise unseen in commercial pop. We were both very curious when, at the very beginning of the 1990s, Madonna started flirting with the idea of lesbian sex. She tantalized her public with hints of a lesbian affair with Sandra Bernhard, and incorporated lesbian imagery into her performances and videos, from 'Justify My Love' to her 1993 *Girlie Show* world tour and her album of photographs – *Sex*. In one sense the fact that she turned her attention to lesbianism is consistent with her constant search for new sexual boundaries to cross and new rebellious acts to perform. The result of Madonna's very public experimentation with lesbianism has been to lend to that identity a fashionableness it has never before enjoyed.

Yet Madonna's deployment of lesbian imagery as part of her sexual performance has been made possible only by a preceding struggle that has taken place over meanings. Could it be that what has made it possible for lesbianism to take on meaning as rebellious and exciting is the impact of gay liberation and lesbian-feminist politics? These movements have increasingly challenged the negative connotations associated with lesbianism. In so doing, they have produced, in the face of those overwhelmingly negative historical meanings, other more attractive possibilities.

It could be argued that in Foucault's terms a 'reverse discourse' has been created. The fact that Madonna can now play with lesbian imagery and promote the pleasures of lesbian sex suggests

Fair and *Elle*, originated. She chronicles how the meanings which circulate around lesbianism have changed and asks, what is the relationship between the meanings generated within popular culture, and the lived lives of lesbians? She argues that the existence of lesbianism and its subcultural manifestations was clearly a precondition of the lesbian images now appearing in the pages of glossy magazines; but which came first? Was it the chic lesbian in her natural habitat, or the chic lesbian in the pages of *Vanity Fair*? In this context, a further concern must surely be that, like any other popular fad, lesbianism is highly disposable and may soon become yesterday's news.

A most curious aspect of the current trend is how popularized the idea of the masculine-looking lesbian has become. The primary vehicle for this is, of course, k.d. lang, although in her butchness she is preceded by another famous lesbian, Martina Navratilova. In 'Netting the press' Diane Hamer argues that the figure of Martina served, for almost the whole of the 1980s, as the primary site for the articulation of popular ideas about lesbianism. One of the most pre-eminent of those ideas was the equation of lesbianism with masculinity – to a hostile tabloid press it was this which accounted for Martina's reign on the tennis court.

Martina's position as the world's most famous lesbian has been usurped by k.d. lang. Yet what is different now is that whereas Navratilova's perceived 'masculinity' was a source of ridicule and revulsion in the media, k.d. lang's is celebrated as glamorous. Unlike her predecessor, k.d.'s butch image seems only to add to her desirability in the popular imagination. Her *Vanity Fair* cover was a case in point. Dressed in ultra-male attire and reclining in a barber's chair, lang's face was covered in soap as she awaited a shave from the very feminine (barely clothed) Cindy Crawford. The clear invitation issued to readers by that cover image was to identify with Cindy Crawford in desiring the masculinized chanteuse. A year earlier the *Independent,* a British newspaper, had run a feature story on her which opened with a quote attributed to Madonna; 'Elvis is Alive – and She's Beautiful'. Again, k.d.'s attractiveness lay in her likeness to masculinity, this time embodied in the figure of Elvis Presley.

All of this signals to us that the historical status of 'butch' is shifting. Traditionally, because butch women have always been the most visible as lesbians, it is they who have been forced to carry the weight of dominant culture's disapproval. If one or two butch lesbians are now being celebrated, mustn't this be a good thing? In 'She thinks I still care', Rosa Ainley and Sarah Cooper examine the rise and rise of k.d. lang, and argue that to be less than totally enamoured by k.d. casts as much doubt on one's pride in identity as to have failed to be interested in tennis and Martina in the 80s. They credit k.d. with bringing country and western music – that last bastion of redneck male conservatism – to a lesbian audience, and at the same time taking lesbianism into the mainstream. The mainstream prominence of both Martina and k.d. signals that lesbian invisibility is now no longer de facto, something to be taken for granted. Rather, our icons are becoming public property on their own terms.

It is interesting to reflect on how those different audiences – lesbian and mainstream – read these icons. As Hamer argues, Martina's appeal to lesbians has been in the very knowledge that she is a lesbian, and as such she is both object of desire and bearer of a secret sexual knowledge. 'Somehow, when she wins her match, it is our sexual identity which is in the ascendancy; it is lesbianism which enjoys that brief moment of glory.' According to Ainley and Cooper k.d. is 'the stuff of which dyke dreams are made; androgynous towards butch, attractive, flirty, talented, and image conscious'.

But do the images of lesbianism now being reworked within popular culture say anything to lesbians? Or do they simply work on the level of heterosexual desire? *Vanity Fair* received an overwhelming amount of correspondence in response to 'that' cover. Much of it was from heterosexual women expressing their unqualified pleasure at the image and the article inside about k.d. There was just one letter – from a lesbian – who wrote to say the photo didn't do anything for her at all. Why should it? What does face shaving have to do with lesbian desire? As that one lone correspondent put it, it would have been much more exciting if Cindy had been shaving k.d.'s legs. . .

The very newness of 'lesbian chic' means that all our conclusions are necessarily speculative. However we cannot help but wonder if, despite all the positive pleasure this 'mainstreaming' of lesbianism has brought us, the images which finally get produced are ones which conform to a heterosexual economy of desire. Nonetheless, like lesbians always have done, we will take our good, bad and gorgeous, where we find it.

Belinda Budge and Diane Hamer

CROSSOVER DREAMS: LESBIANISM AND POPULAR MUSIC SINCE THE 1970s

Arlene Stein

Lesbians broadly constitute what Herbert Gans has called a 'taste public'.[1] We are a heterogeneous group of individuals who, like all members of society, wish to see aspects of our lives reflected in the films, books, music and other cultural goods we consume. We comprise a 'partial culture', that is, we share some basic interests that separate us from the rest of society, but we also belong to mainstream society.[2]

One would hardly know this from listening to popular music, however. Writing in 1990, pop critic Jon Savage noted that while 'popular music acknowledges the sign of "gayness", there is not yet a whisper of female sexual autonomy, of lesbianism'.[3] Because images of heterosexuality and, more specifically, female sexual accessibility, are central to pop music's appeal, out lesbians are not generally thought to be 'crossover' material. Driven by big hits and anticipating the spectre of meagre sales (or outraged moralists), commercial record companies steer away from potential controversy.

A performer who makes her lesbianism known typically becomes categorized as a 'lesbian artist', and is doomed to marginality. Consequently, performers, who labour under the competitive pressures of the market, engage in self-censorship, fashioning their words and images to achieve 'universal' appeal, or at least what they interpret as such. The 'crossover artist', who embraces lesbian identifications while achieving mainstream success, simultaneously acknowledging both lesbian marginality and membership in the dominant culture, is a rare specimen indeed.

But while images of heterosexuality dominate popular music, they do not go unchallenged. For example, women have always found ways to 'read' popular music against the grain, by changing the pronouns of songs in their heads and projecting their fantasies of identification and desire upon female icons. In addition, out lesbians have for at least twenty years struggled for greater participation in popular music production, both by explicitly encoding lesbian references into their music, and by using more implicit, ambiguous coding. In what follows, I look at lesbian efforts to influence popular music production, focusing upon recent experience in the United States.

SING THIS SONG ALL TOGETHER

Lesbian performers have long participated in the creation of popular music in North America. However, the social movements of the 1970s provided, for the first time, impetus for many women to openly incorporate their sexual identities into their creative work. In the early 1970s, young women who 'came out through feminism', as the saying went, attempted to transform lesbianism from a medical condition, or at best, a sexual 'preference', into a collective identity which transcended rampant individualism and its excesses, as well as compulsory sexual and gender roles. Central to this movement was a belief in what Michel Foucault and others have called 'reverse affirmation', the reclaiming and affirming of stigmatized identities, such as homosexuality.[4]

Lesbian feminism spawned the most vibrant and visible lesbian culture that had ever existed in the United States, or indeed the world. It encouraged women to develop their own fiction, visual art and music. 'Women's music' was an important product of this period of cultural innovation. Though usually not explicitly lesbian, women's music was created and performed primarily by lesbian/feminists. It defined itself as popular music which drew upon lesbian/feminist iconography and imagery, and dealt with themes which were of interest primarily to lesbian/feminists. Like other forms of women's culture at the time, women's music was imbued with a belief in a universal female sensibility, expressed in the idea of 'woman-identification'.[5]

This identity was defined, in large part, by its opposition to masculinist forms of culture, such as mainstream rock and roll – 'cock rock'. In 1974, *Ms.* magazine asked 'Can a Feminist Love the World's Greatest Rock and Roll Band?' and critic Robin Morgan replied with a resolute 'No!' She warned that lesbian feminists who listened to the Rolling Stones were no better than those who advocated non-monogamy and accepted transsexuals as allies: they had all adopted a 'male style' which would destroy the movement.

Women's music was also rooted in the populist tradition of social protest and in the belief that small and simple was best.[6] For the American Left, at least since the 1930s, folk music provided an antidote to an alienated mass culture in which cultural objects became isolated from the communities and traditions which initially gave them shape and meaning. Women's music, which grew partially out of this Left critique, sought to achieve a more authentic form of cultural expression for women, a goal which was embodied in the organization of the women's music industry itself. In addition to encouraging innovation in terms of musical content, women's music politicized the *process* of musical production.

Olivia, the pioneering women's record company formed in the early 1970s, comprised the backbone of the women's music industry. It, like most of the women's music industry, was founded on the belief that it was important to erase the distinctions between industry, performers and audience – distinctions which were central to commercial music.[7] Even more importantly, perhaps, women's music sought to redress the fact that women in general, and lesbians in particular, had been shut out of positions of power in commercial music. Within alternative music organizations such as Olivia, women were offered opportunities, as performers, singers, producers and promoters, never before available to them. As singer-songwriter Holly Near explained in retrospect:

> Women's music was not just music being done by women. It was music that was challenging the whole system, a little different from disco, a little different from David Bowie playing with androgyny . . . We were dealing with a lot of issues David Bowie wasn't dealing with, questions his management wasn't asking. So it was not just the music. It was like taking a whole look at systems and societies and letting a music rise out of those systems.[8]

The vision of women's music was an ambitious one. In positively valuing women's (and lesbian) lives and accomplishments, and serving as an organizing tool, it played an important role in the development of lesbian feminist culture. However, the narrow way in which women's music was defined – as music produced by, of, and for feminists – may have inadvertently limited its appeal.

Women of colour charged that women's music had become firmly entrenched in what was, for the most part, a European tradition. Confirming their suspicions was the fact that albums and tours by Black artists on women's music labels failed to attract much-needed sales. Criticism also came from women in punk, which like women's music, made a politics of disrupting gender and sexual codes, debunking 'male' technique and expertise and posing a critique of glamour.[9] But unlike women's music, punk refused to position itself as the affirmative expression of either feminism or gay liberation, and its brash style was at odds with the folkiness of women's music. As one of the founders of Boston's Rock Against Sexism, a cultural activist group comprised of 'closet rock-and-roll fans' in the women's community, explained: 'Women's music is really peaceful, not raunchy or angry; it doesn't really excite me or turn me on or get me energized'.[10]

In the 1980s, the viability of women's music was thrown into question by a crisis of identity. The 'decentring' of lesbian feminism, related at least in part to generational changes and to the critique posed by women of colour, called into question the prior belief that women's music could reflect an 'essential' femaleness. The notion of identity constructed by a century of scientific 'experts' implied that all lesbians were alike, united by a common deviance. Removing its basis in biology, lesbian feminists attempted to universalize the possibility of lesbian experience, but in its place they often created rigid ideological prescriptions about who belonged in the lesbian community, and what lesbian culture should look and sound like.[11]

In the end, women's music was revealed to be the expression of a particular generation of activist women. But its undercapitalization prevented it from branching out into other directions. Sales lagged, and many women's music producers responded by moving away from their lesbian-feminist roots.[12] In 1988, as Olivia Records celebrated its fifteenth anniversary with a series of concerts throughout the United States, its records languished in the 'women's music' section in the rear of record stores, if they were there at all. But at that very moment a new generation of women performers were entering the mainstream.

ANDROGYNY GOES POP

In 1988, American music journalists pronounced the arrival of a 'new breed of women' in popular music. Tracy Chapman, k.d. lang, Michelle Shocked, the Indigo Girls and Melissa Etheridge, among others, were noted for defying conventions of femininity in popular music, and moving 'back to the basics' away from artifice and role-playing into authenticity.[13]

It was a movement that confounded the critics. 'Neither their songs,' one critic wrote, 'nor the images they project, cater to stereotypical male fantasies of female pop singers.' Another proclaimed:

The most astounding thing of all is that Tracy Chapman *et al.*, even happened. Since when did the industry that insisted its strongest women play cartoon characters . . . allow a serious, powerful, flesh and blood female to stand firm on a concert stage?[14]

The answer, as any informed observer could say, was rather simple: the 'new breed' of pop women emerged once the industry was convinced that they were marketable. Tracy Chapman became a household name in 1988, selling more than ten million albums, because she was 'just so real', according to an Elektra Records executive.

Subcultures have long fuelled musical innovation: hugely successful commercial disco and house music, for example, had its origins in the Black gay dance floors of Chicago and New York. Likewise, on the heels of the feminist movement, female performers and fans became commercially important 'properties' and 'markets', giving them a new position of power to define what they did and demand what they wanted. The trail was blazed by such performers as Cyndi Lauper and Madonna – whose messages, though at times contradictory, affirmed an empowered female sexuality practically unseen in commercial pop. In 1983, Lauper released the single 'Girls Just Want to Have Fun', described by Lisa Lewis as a 'powerful cry for access to the privileged realm of male adolescent leisure and fun'.[15] Madonna, probably *the* most successful female star of the contemporary period, exuded sexual power and invincibility, at times making allusions to lesbianism, as on her 'Justify My Love' video, which was banned by MTV at the end of 1990.[16]

While there had been, at least since the early 1970s, women in popular music who defied conventions of femininity – Patti Smith, Pat Benatar, Janis Joplin, Annie Lennox were among the most central figures – what was new about the 1980s wave of androgyny was that its proponents, though not always lesbian-identified, tended to be rooted, at least partially, in lesbian subcultures. Tracy

Chapman made the rounds in women's music festivals in 1986 and 1987, while Melissa Etheridge, k.d. lang, Michelle Shocked and the others knocked around lesbian and 'alternative' clubs in Austin, Atlanta, San Francisco and New York City.

Though influenced by feminism, and frequently women's music, they were convinced that it was necessary to work within the constraints of the industry to get their message across, and saw mainstreaming as an act no less subversive than the feminist disaffection from the industry a decade earlier. Los Angeles based singer-songwriter, Phranc, whose 1989 album *I Enjoy Being a Girl*, sported her in a flat-top haircut (alongside a blurb that sang her prasies as a 'little daughter of bilitis'), toured as the opening act for the Smiths and other popular post-punk acts, playing for mixed audiences because, she said, 'It's important to reach out to the kids.' As a member of Austin, Texas' 2 Nice Girls, put it: 'We don't want to be found only in the speciality bin at the record store. We want to be in your face.'[17]

But the most ambitious of these performers carefully constructed their personae to assert a strong, sexually ambiguous female presence. Studiously avoiding male pronouns in romantic ballads, through the subtleties of self-presentation, which were often indecipherable to those who weren't cued into the codes, they made themselves objects of female as well as male desire. Swaggering in a man's western suit, k.d. lang proclaimed: 'Yeah, sure, the boys can be attracted to me, the girls can be attracted to me, your mother . . . your uncle, sure. It doesn't really matter to me.' On Michelle Shocked's 1989 album, *Captain Swing*, one had to listen closely to 'Sleep Keeps Me Awake' to make out the fact that it was a love song to a woman. Even as they were being applauded by the critics for their fresh, unencumbered simplicity and their return to 'honesty' and 'naturalness', many of these artists constructed their songs and their images with an ambiguity that at times verged on camp.

The arrival of the new breed of androgynous women in pop in the 1980s, propelled in large part by an increasingly self-conscious lesbian audience, evidenced the fact that some women could finally defy conventions of femininity in popular music and still achieve mainstream success. But the classic dilemma persisted: a performer either became known as a 'lesbian artist' and was doomed to marginality, or she watered down her lesbianism in order to appeal to a mass audience. Lesbian performers were only 'safe' (read: marketable) if their sexuality was muted – a woman singing a love song to another woman was still taboo.[18]

Some who had made an explicit politics of their lesbianism charged that the cultural revolution that had begun in the early 1970s had been stalled, gobbled up and incorporated by 'the industry'. As Phranc sang:

> Everybody wants to be a folk singer. They want to be hip and trendy. They want to make sensitive videos and sing about politics. Androgyny is the ticket or at least it seems to be. Just don't wear a flat-top and mention sexuality, and girl you'll go far, you'll get a record contract and be a star.[19]

Women's music, which was created in the context of lesbian institutions and communities, had linked lesbian/feminist authorship to feminist content and audience. With the arrival of the 'androgynous pop star', some argued that women's music had been replaced by music that blandly played with lesbian signifiers like clothes and hairstyle in order to gain commercial acceptance, but never really identified itself as lesbian.[20] While such criticisms were perhaps overstated, it was true that, shorn from its community base, lesbian music emerged in the mainstream as a series of floating signifiers, linked to feminist/lesbian sensibilities, but having no real loyalty or commitment to an organized subculture or movement.

Industry constraints were at least partially behind the apparent prohibition against 'speaking' lesbianism. In the 1980s, the belief in a undifferentiated mass market was replaced in favour of marketing appeals targeted to niches geared to specific racial, ethnic and 'lifestyle' groups of various sorts. Yet it was rare for a commercial record company to acknowledge the existence of the lesbian audience possessing a specific location and particular tastes. When record companies recognized the existence of such a market, they often saw it as a liability rather than as an asset. In marketing an out-lesbian musician such as Phranc, a spokesman for Island Records acknowledged that a performer who makes her lesbianism a central part of her act (that is, she mentions it at all) may have a 'limited consumer base'.[21]

But if many of these emerging performers were ambiguous about their identities, it was not simply because of industry constraints − it was also because, frequently, their identities *were* ambiguous. Historically, artists have often resisted the demands of identity politics, preferring instead to place their art above loyalties to any one particular group. In the 1980s, the 'decentring' of lesbian feminism called into question the tendency to make lesbianism a 'dominant' or 'master' identity. Audre Lorde wrote in 1979:

> As a Black lesbian feminist comfortable with the many different ingredients of my identity . . . I find I am constantly being encouraged to pluck out some one aspect of myself and present this as the meaningful whole, eclipsing or denying the other parts of self.[22]

Following from this, one can imagine that Tracy Chapman, a Black woman, is a complex personality, possessing commitments to more than just the lesbian community. So too is Michelle Shocked, who eventually became involved with a man. In the 1970s, Holly Near often hid her bisexuality in order to appeal to a women's audience, in the interest of providing a united front. Ten years later, there appeared to be greater tolerance for ambiguity, and even a certain attraction to *not* really knowing the 'truth'.

Anyway, what *was* the truth? The 1980s, after all, was a decade in which 'pleasure', said critic Larry Grossberg, 'was replacing understanding'.[23] David Letterman, the American baby boomers' late-night talk-show host of choice, celebrated alienation with a mocking self-referentiality, as MTV blurred the boundaries of pop music and advertising. Quick-change, recombinant pop jumped from style to style, integrating new sounds and textures, new identities and images and blurring cultural categories of all sorts. A rap song sampled the theme from the television series *Gilligan's Island*; Peter Gabriel and Paul Simon borrowed from African traditional music. Comedian Sandra Bernhard mixed and matched identities, alluding at times to her lesbianism without ever really embracing it. 'I would never make a declaration of anything', she proclaimed. 'It's so stupid. Who even cares? It's so presumptuous.'[24]

Indeed, for many audience members, particularly younger ones, it seemed, this ambiguity was part of the appeal. As one nineteen-year-old lesbian told me:

> I like 'cock rock' and women's music. I like both. But I like mainstream women's music the best. Music that speaks to women but isn't only of women . . . They don't use pronouns, proper nouns. To us that's cool. And we notice that men don't really listen to that music.

As Barbara Bradby has convincingly shown, the fantasies lesbians construct about particular performers' identities, and about themselves in relation to these performers, are a collectively shaped and shared part of lesbian experience.[25] Sexual ambiguity allows for the double appeal of the music – to the subculture, as well as to the mass audience. It allows performers to communicate with lesbian and feminist members of its audience without pledging allegiance to the norms of the subcultures, or becoming spokespersons for them. It allows audience members to listen to music which they consider, secretly, to be lesbian, with the knowledge that millions of other people are also listening to it.

In the end, perhaps it was a testimony to the maturity of feminist and lesbian culture that performers, as well as members of their audience, no longer saw it necessary to make their lesbianism the central overriding feature of their work. In the 1980s, as feminist styles were incorporated into popular culture, and the boundaries between the mainstream and women's culture blurred, some performers found an unprecedented degree of freedom to construct their images, and their music, as they pleased.

But this strategy also had its limitations. While the new wave of androgynous women in pop achieved mass appeal beyond the already-converted audience of women's music, they were reliant upon the existence of a savvy audience to read their codes. Young lesbians could finally see images in the mainstream that closely resembled them, but since lesbianism was still unspoken and since the vast majority lacked the necessary knowledge to cue into these codes, the heterosexual norm remained, for the most part, unchallenged.

CROSSOVER DREAMS, MARGINAL REALITIES?

In the early 1990s, a few women were able to 'cross over' and achieve mainstream success as out lesbians, integrating their sexuality into their art without allowing it to become either *the* salient fact, or else barely acknowledged. k.d. lang and Melissa Etheridge, who had previously coded their sexuality as androgyny, came out as lesbians, to great fanfare within lesbian/gay circles and even greater commercial success. Their coming out was highly significant, in part because it was certain to have a ripple effect, encouraging others to follow suit.

Still, it would be unwise to view this development as evidence of the unmitigated march of progress. While these artists were able to (partially) incorporate their lesbianism into their music and images, they did so only after they had achieved considerable commercial success. It was much more difficult, and perhaps even impossible, to do the opposite, to 'cross over' from margin to mainstream, and come out while one's career was still at the early stages of development.

Moreover, as I have tried to show, the representation of lesbianism in popular music is a far more complex matter than the sum of individuals who 'come out'. Lesbian representation in popular music has occurred through the interaction between performers, music industry and audiences. Artists attempt to achieve popularity while maximizing their creative autonomy, frequently against the imperatives of both the recording industry and a demanding public. The music industry, a source of both conservatism and innovation, tries to keep abreast of trends and emerging 'taste publics' without alienating existing audience members. Audiences are constantly in flux, shaped by cultural trends and social movements (such as feminism and gay liberation) which create subcultures that in turn influence popular tastes.[26]

Furthermore, lesbian representation is not simply a matter of making lesbianism visible. Increasingly, as Biddy Martin has argued, the 'irreducibly complex and contested nature of identity has itself been made more visible'.[27] Women of the baby-boom generation, the founders of women's music and culture, believed that they could construct a collective sense of what it meant to be a lesbian, and also develop representations of that collective identity. Today's emergent generation, much more aware of the limitations of identity politics, seemingly does not. While this indeterminacy is deeply troubling to many women, particularly those who once held the hope of constructing a lesbian-feminist movement that was culturally and ideologically unified, a 'decentred' lesbian identity and culture may present new democratic potential. For one thing, many women who felt excluded by an earlier model of identity and cultured now feel that they can finally participate on their own terms.

During the last two decades, female pop stars, a good number of whom are lesbians, have worked within these constraints, utilizing different strategies to bring their message to an increasingly self-conscious and sophisticated female audience. The influence of feminism upon mainstream culture has meant that many performers are able to exercise a greater degree of control over their image and their music. Popular music is today performed by self-identified lesbians and sympathetic others, drawing upon lesbian iconography and/or subcultural sensibilities, and addressing an audience which at least partially consists of lesbians. And while the dream of a body of music and art that expresses lesbian experience(s) openly and honestly has not yet come to pass in the mainstream, in the meantime, lesbian performers and audiences are struggling in various ways to construct positions from which to speak that acknowledge both lesbian marginality *and* membership in the dominant culture.

A QUEER LOVE AFFAIR?:
MADONNA AND LESBIAN
AND GAY CULTURE

Sonya Andermahr

MATERIAL GIRL :
REINVENTING THE FEMALE ICON

When I started to think about the relationship between mainstream popular culture and lesbian and gay subcultures, I kept confronting the image of Madonna: the quintessential female icon of the 1980s. Madonna has achieved archetypal status; nothing can be said about the image of woman in the last decade without reference to her. She has transcended her particular roles as popstar, dancer, actress, and now, with the publication of *Sex*, porn queen, and captured the popular imagination in a way no woman has achieved since Marilyn Monroe. Her image has barely been out of public circulation since the mid 1980s, and millions of words have been spoken and written about her, in biographies, magazines, newspapers and, as here, in academic papers. She is a major discursive event, meriting endless public speculation and serious study on cultural studies courses.[1]

Central to all these discourses is the question of what makes her special. How does she differ from the pantheon of female icons, from Helen of Troy to Bardot and Monroe, with which mainstream culture has always abounded? One answer is that although there is no shortage of attractive images of powerful sexual women, these images are largely products of male imaginations with male pleasures in mind, whereas central to the Madonna myth is the idea that she possesses an autonomy and self-determination they lack: Madonna is now her own (re)invention. Certainly, unlike the majority of women in the entertainment industry, past and present, Madonna calls her own shots. And, although she can no more control the ways in which her image is read than can the page three pin-up, she exercises more power and control over the production, marketing and financial value of that image than any female icon before her. She has never been content to be the face that launched a thousand record covers; she has to be the helmswoman too. She is that rare thing, a woman who has beaten the boys at their own capitalist game. She may sell herself, the traditional prerogative of women, but she does it for big bucks.

One of the major achievements of her ten-year career is, I would argue (apart from making millions of dollars) to have redefined female sexuality, within mainstream popular culture, as both power and pleasure *for women*. As Suzanne Moore comments, Madonna's sexuality is essentially selfish, an auto-erotic self-pleasuring, which sometimes invites but does not require male assistance.[2] Moore describes Madonna as part 1980s material girl, with a head for business, and part 1960s sexual swinger with a curiously old-fashioned philosophy of liberation through sex. But whereas 1960s liberation was driven by a phallic imperative, Madonna's fantasies are centred around the 'insatiable clitoris'. It is this insistence on the dynamic female body and female sexual pleasure that explains Madonna's special appeal for women. Rather than rejecting gender binarism, the tropes of masculinity and femininity, she challenges dominant sexual forms from within by exploiting their rich sexual language to create an aggressive femininity which, above all, is about female pleasure. Typically, she takes traditional, easily recognizable, dominant images of woman, such as the 'virgin/whore' dichotomy and pushes them to their limits, often in a single representation as in her 'Like a Virgin' video. Simultaneously virgin and whore, she shows both the artifice of such cultural clichés and their sexual force: rather than allowing them to frighten her, she luxuriates in them, relishing the power of trespass they give her.

Her power as icon resides in her ability to both insist on her femininity and yet transcend narrow gender definitions. She presents female sexuality as a kind of radical transvestism as she raids the visual vocabulary of sexual difference to create her own display of sexuality. Adopting a masculine style here, a feminine pose there, substituting sexual object choices as the fancy takes her, she is simultaneously butch and femme, both gay and straight. The term 'gender fuck' could have been coined especially for her. Always out to shock, she represents a sexual scandal, epitomized by her *Blonde Ambition Tour* garb of pink corsets over a man's suit, and the infamous Jean-Paul Gaultier cone-shaped bra which reference both the breasts and the phallus. Above all, she presents sexuality as a performance, as a game or joke; a set of pleasurable pick-and-mix roles which can be adopted and discarded as the desire moves her. To quote one of her biggest fans, Camille Paglia, celebrating 'the dazzling profusion of her mercurial sexual personae':

> Madonna . . . sees both the animality and the artifice [of sex]. Changing her costume style and hair colour virtually every month, Madonna embodies the eternal values of beauty and pleasure. Feminism says 'No more masks'. Madonna says we are nothing but masks.

Paglia's provocative reference to 'feminism' sharply focuses the epistemological debate *within* feminism between modernist and postmodernist narratives of sexual identity. Whereas modernist feminism seeks to assert an integrated, authentic female identity as the basis of a female gender class, postmodernist feminism stresses the multiple, inauthentic and provisional nature of gender, and indeed of all, identity. Whereas to the former Madonna's multiple identities make her a confused and inappropriate role model, in postmodernist terms she exposes gender as the fiction it 'really' is. In one account Madonna wittily deconstructs sexual difference, in the other she perpetuates the objectification of women. I don't have space here to comment further on this debate; instead I would like to argue that Madonna's gender simulations and foregrounding of inauthenticity open up a space for those traditionally deemed sexually inauthentic and transgressive: lesbians and gay men.[3]

JUSTIFY OUR LOVE: MADONNA AS GAY ICON

Madonna registers the crossover between the mainstream and subcultures which was an unprecedented feature of the 1980s. She traverses the space between the sexual mainstream and the sexual fringes of culture. In addition to its woman-centred message, Madonna's work speaks to and about a variety of other 'minority' constituencies: African Americans, Hispanics, lesbians and gay men, and sexual interest groups such as SMers. For many lesbians and gay men she has come closer than any other celebrity figure to being an out gay icon. While other stars, such as Diana Ross and Joan Armatrading, share her icon appeal, Madonna is unique in openly and explicitly courting her gay fans. In consciously referencing gay discourses and culture in her work (especially the later work: 'Express Yourself'; 'Vogue'; 'Justify My Love'; the *Blonde Ambition Tour*; and *In Bed with Madonna*), in working with gay people, as dancers, choreographers, and so on, and in speaking up publicly against homophobia, she signifies both an appropriation and an affirmation of lesbian and gay lifestyles, and makes a significant contribution to the politics of queer sex.

Madonna borrows shamelessly from gay male and lesbian subcultural styles; dressing up in our clothes and replicating our constant self-reinvention. She saturates her work with homoeroticism, such as in her use of gay art and porn iconography in her stage shows, videos and her book of erotic fantasies, *Sex*, and in the latter's references to gay practices such as cruising and cottaging. Paying homage also to the homoerotic Hollywood tradition represented by Dietrich, Garbo and Louise Brooks,

Madonna is the first major mainstream artist to give gay images and themes explicit mass treatment and exposure. Whereas, in this tradition, gayness was a subtextual phenomenon, Madonna insists, *pace* ActUp and Outrage, on 'outing', promoting and flaunting homo- and bisexuality in her work. Where else, apart from a Madonna video, can millions of viewers see two women kissing on prime-time television? Like Dietrich's before her, Madonna's lesbian image aims to titillate the heterosexual audience but, in consciously addressing women as sexual agents and in staging the desiring 'gaze' – not to mention touch – between women in videos such as 'Justify My Love', Madonna also acknowledges and encourages lesbians as sexual consumers of her image.

'Justify My Love' is, if not her best, one of her music videos which is most infused with a gay sensibility. Evoking a European sexual demi-monde, reminiscent of Dietrich's own *The Blue Angel* and Isherwood's *Goodbye to Berlin*, populated by a similar cast of prostitutes, lesbians and pretty boys, 'Justify My Love' is a fantasy of euphoric, polymorphous sexuality. Made up of a series of camp, erotic tableaux, its androgynous, sexually and racially varied figures almost float through the scene, coming together to touch, kiss and flirt and move gracefully apart. And, for those in the know, there is the treat of Madonna's embrace with gay male porn star Tony Ward. Through its use of androgyny and drag and its tantalizing sexual indeterminacy, 'Justify My Love' confounds the rigid gender definitions and clear-cut categories of sexual attraction codified in mainstream music culture. This record, whose lyrics signify a disregard to official sanctioning of sexual non-conformism, and demand only its self-justification, became something of a gay anthem in the clubs and bars of Britain and the United States.

Within the context of lesbian and gay culture, Madonna's 'inauthenticity', her deployment of simulation and artifice, seems less like a political liability and more like an opening up of other ways to envision sex in popular culture. It also has an affinity with the gay cultural practice of camp. Camp is an act, a disguise that is not so much a concealment (passing) as a revelation of artifice. Madonna's many disguises work in exactly the same way: talking on the phone in a shower cap and vest while eating cabbage soup in *In Bed with Madonna*, Madonna is no more 'truly herself' than she is on stage. Her wardrobe of personae, as Lisa Henderson argues, encapsulates the essence of camp:

> cracking the mirror, dressing up and acting out to *expose* the constructedness of what in other settings passes as 'natural' male, female, or heterosexual (p. 122).

Dressing-up is fun, and a campy, parodic humour is central to Madonna's self-representation; a humour encapsulated by Madonna 'wannabe' Cyndi Lauper's 1980s hit 'Girls Just Wanna Have Fun' or her own 'Material Girl' in which she parodied a 1950s image of the glamourous gold-digging female with an adoring male entourage. This kind of humour also characterizes Madonna's public flirtation with lesbianism which she presented and presumably experienced as an enjoyable erotic joke (one which turned sour for 'girlfriend' Sandra Bernhard) or, more recently, in *Sex*, as an erotic fantasy. Precisely because of the instability of sexual signifiers which make up 'Madonna', she is able to act the dyke and retain her pre-eminent position in mainstream culture.

This positioning of herself both inside and outside the mainstream, of it yet against it, explains the controversy around her and why she provokes such contradictory responses from feminists and radicals as well as from sexual conservatives. She refuses to be wholly assimilated into the dominant culture, continually moving (from) the margins to the centre, but she also resists full identification with oppositional and identity politics. Her contradictoriness is not, in my opinion, a failure to put her message across, but part and parcel of her message: Madonna articulates the contradictions of feminine pleasure in particular, and of sexual identity in general, constantly negotiating the borders between power and powerlessness, proper and improper, male and female, straight and gay.

'BUTCH GIRLS': THE LESBIANIZATION OF THE FEMALE ICON

In promoting lesbian styles and images in her work, Madonna has participated in what could be called a lesbianization of the female icon in the 1980s, a process which embraces both an aesthetic and a politics of the body. It implies not merely the adoption of a masculine 'look', but also the assumption of masculine prerogative and agency. The masculinized female body asserts not only its right to be sexual but its autonomy, its physical integrity. This butch figure has also materialized in the new screen heras of the 1980s, such as Linda Hamilton in the *Terminator* films and Sigourney Weaver in the *Alien* trilogy. In these films lesbian signifiers – muscles, cropped hair, sexual independence from men – are used to denote agency, activity and toughness. This strategy was pushed to parodic limits in *Aliens* in the character of the Chicana soldier; unambiguously butch, she worked out, flexed her muscles, loaded an outrageously sized machine gun, and jockied with the male jocks, braver and meaner than the lot of them. Yet despite depending on lesbian signs, these representations largely resist explicit lesbian identification – by the absence of other women or, in the case of *Aliens*, by maternalizing Weaver's image.[4] Nevertheless, these films invite women as well as men to both identify with and desire the particular combination of masculine beauty in female form embodied by their strong, self-determining heroines. Their huge popularity with female, not to mention lesbian, audiences is a measure of the appeal of the butch figure and the desire for such female role models and heras amongst women.

A parallel trend can be observed in lesbian subculture of the 1980s. Just as femininity in mainstream cultural images has been inflected by butch, producing a 'dykey het' image, so in lesbian subculture lesbian sexual identities have been re-eroticized by a reappropriation of femininity, producing the 'femme dyke' and the 'lipstick lesbian'. A recent article in the *Guardian*'s Women's Page identified this trend, contrasting the stereotypical image of political and desexualized 'rad les fems' of the 1970s with the new femme fatales and 'nubile nude vixens' of the late 1980s.[5] The comeback of the femme and the reincorporation of gender difference into lesbian identities suggests a rejection of 1970s feminist androgyny and certain of its feminist orthodoxies around the body and self-presentation: the injunction against feminine adornment and its oppressive signifiers – makeup, high heels, skirts, long hair and so on – became oppressive and trapping in itself.

If the emergence of these sexual styles was partly a reaction to prescriptive forms of feminism, it is also true to say that in the mid and late 1980s a space opened up, within and outside feminism, for women to speak about and embody sex in ways which hadn't been possible since the early days of women's liberation, when all aspects of sexuality were open to question and nothing was seen as fixed or taken for granted. Many women started to rethink the relationship between gender and sexual identity, to talk about what turned them on, and to shift the focus from men's back to women's desire in its heterogeneous forms. Joan Nestle's publication in the mid 1980s of her collection of essays *A Restricted Country* was an important part of the rehabilitation of the 'femme' in lesbian subculture. The book took on iconic status in the lesbian community, as a symbol of either the sexual integrity of butch/femme identities or reactionary role-playing depending on one's political point of view. For Nestle the 1980s emphasis on subversive gender performance, symbolized by Madonna, provided a context in which to articulate her experience in the 1950s of the simultaneously sexual and political nature of role-playing, and thereby connect up her 'pre-' and 'post'- feminist identities.

Elsewhere in the lesbian community self-proclaimed 'sexpert' Susie Bright proselytized about lesbian sex to rapt audiences, photographers such as Della Grace and Tessa Boffin produced erotic fantasy images, and a variety of lesbian sexual fiction, answering a need for glamour, sexiness and frivolity, appeared on the bookshelves.

TRUTH OR DARE?
LESBIAN ICONS AND REAL LESBIAN ICONS

If Madonna is the first among equals, the major female icon of the moment, she now has competition for dykon status in k.d. lang, who to many lesbians represents their very own 'real life' lesbian hera. With a record in the pop charts, lang has move out of the C&W, minority music scene and into the big time of the popular mainstream. Interestingly, and to the joy of many lesbians, lang's mainstream success coincided with her disclosure, in 1992 in interviews and on stage, of her lesbianism. lang's appeal for lesbians, apart from her vocal and physical attractiveness, is rooted in her identifiable and stated gayness. With her cropped hair, sharp baggy suits, masculine stance and pinkie ring, all signifiers of lesbian butch, lang was out even before she was out. Now doubly out, it is her 'authenticity' and butchness which ensure her rapturous lesbian following. In some quarters, lang is the 'real' lesbian's lesbian icon, whereas Madonna is the pseudo-dyke, the bisexual cop-out. I partly concur with this designation: lang's uncompromising butchness (which did indeed threaten her early C&W career) is arguably more challenging than Madonna's lipstick lesbianism which is always open to (male) heterosexual co-option in a way lang's style resists.[6] But there are horses for courses: some of us identify with/desire lang, some of us identify with/desire Madonna, and some of us cross the lines. Moreover, lesbian identity and desire, as both Madonna's aggressive femininity and lang's butch womanliness show, exceed the oppositions of real/pseudo and butch/femme. Madonna, I would argue, has particular resonance for femme dykes, those of us who negotiate a femininity constructed by patriarchy as heterosexual and male-oriented. Whereas butch dykes reject the feminine masquerade, Madonna teaches us how to enjoy its pleasures and make it woman-centred. If she isn't a 'real' pussy-licker, then never mind, she talks enough about her pussy in a way which speaks to our desires and, now and again, she acknowledges that we're out there.

The arrival of k.d. lang highlights the debate in the lesbian and gay communities about our representation in the mainstream. This debate, as I have suggested, has come to centre around the issue of 'authenticity', and it structures the lesbian and gay reception of Madonna in terms of appropriation and exploitation. It raises the question of the relation between Madonna's postmodern play and our real lives, between her queer thrills and our survival. Is it truth, or dare? Lesbians and gay men have always partly acknowledged that the Madonna phenomenon is a double-edged sword, and that she is both champion and pirate of our lifestyle. Michael Musto, a gay critic in the *Village Voice*, beautifully states the ambivalence felt by many lesbians and gay men towards Madonna:

> She shimmies into our fag imagination, spreads her legs for our dyke approbation [and] grabs us by the pudenda . . . After an hour's private session with her, we're aroused but wearing condoms, mad at her for ripping us off, but somehow thanking her for noticing us, legitimizing us, pulling us up . . . out of hiding and into the public pleasuredome of scrutiny and success (p. 122).

The debate was brought into sharper focus for me during a London ICA conference on Madonna's *Sex*. One of the speakers was the British lesbian photographer, self-styled 'pussy-licking sodomite', Della Grace. Her critique of Madonna's lesbian images, delivered with discernible indignation and some resentment, made fascinating listening.[7] Like many gay cultural producers, Grace feels that Madonna has ripped off her style of lesbian representation. She argues, with justification, that Madonna, by virtue of her power and status, has a licence to exhibit lesbian outlawry which is denied to lesbian artists and performers, who find it difficult to get any publicity for their work, never mind making millions from it. While Grace's complaint began to sound like a 'me-first' self-regarding whine, rather than the defence of the organic lesbian art it ostensibly was, her argument about the dangers of mainstream appropriation of minority styles and images is a powerful one.

While the mainstream more or less happily accommodates Madonna's gender-bending antics, it overwhelmingly refuses to acknowledge, encourage or support lesbian and gay artists and art *per se*. It might like Madonna's gay effects, but it doesn't care at all about their gay sources.

On one hand Grace's argument is a valid criticism of the problems posed by subcultural appropriation, on the other it leads to the paradox that whereas Madonna's interventions are merely playing with the perverse, Grace's own work is authentically/ *seriously* (?) playing with it. If, as Grace maintains her images explore lesbian fantasy through play, irony and artifice, then why can't Madonna? Grace's work positions itself within postmodern discourses about the constructedness of gendered identity and desire, but for Grace the success or validity of the work is dependent on its prior inscription as *lesbian* through the authenticating presence of the lesbian author. Despite the flaunted constructedness of her images therefore, Grace locates their rationale in identity politics. Where her work is authentic, Madonna's is all simulacra. There is additional irony in the fact that while Madonna rips off lesbian and gay styles, Grace, in common with lesbian sex activists of the late 1980s, borrows from gay male subcultural style, in her 'lesbian boys and other inverts' series for example, in order to eroticize lesbianism. Does this make some of Grace's work inauthentically lesbian? Of course, what is at stake in the authentic/inauthentic debate is the sexual visibility of lesbianism as a lived experience rather than as a mere spectacle for mainstream consumption. While some would argue that the distinction is discernible in the work itself – Grace's 'realistic' though posed images, versus Madonna's 'obviously' faked gay ecstasy in *Sex*, it is ultimately context and signature which mark the difference between Grace's 'real thing' and Madonna's 'sexual tourism'. And, of course, a hell of a lot of money.

AFTERWORD: LIFE AFTER MADONNA

When I started this essay I was an ardent Madonna fan, with the fan's unconditional allegiance to, and refusal to brook criticism of, their icon. Having to provide theoretical justification for my lesbian love affair with Madonna caused me to view Madonna in a less one-sided light and to acknowledge some of the contradictions she poses as a *lesbian* and *feminist* icon. Finding those contradictions productive of lesbian meanings and signs represents, perhaps, partly a justification of my original, more visceral hera-worship. If Madonna flirted with, but never *identified* herself with, lesbianism, if she borrowed its styles, but didn't live its lifestyle, she nevertheless made same-sex desire visible for those who could see.

Since I've been working on this piece, however, the passage of time and two events in Madonna's career have combined to lessen my ardour. These are the publication in December 1992 of her collection of erotic fantasies, *Sex*, and the release, in April 1993, of her film *Body of Evidence*. Although I was looking forward to the former, and liked some of the images, I found it largely lacklustre and uninspiring, lacking the vibrancy of her music videos. As for the film, to my eyes, Madonna looked jaded, haggard and totally without sex-appeal. I felt it would have been improved if almost any other actress had been in the lead role. Could I possibly have fallen out of love with my hera? Yes, it seems I'm bored by Madonna. Part of the problem relates to overexposure; the old chestnut that a glimpse is better than a full-frontal. This applies to Madonna's flirtation with lesbianism as well as to her breasts: if everything was suggested but never ultimately disclosed in a Madonna video, I rather liked it that way. I'm not sure how to rationalize this disillusion, or how it connects to my analysis of both her appeal and significance to lesbian and gay audiences, and the importance of her sexual interventions in popular culture. Madonna remains the major female icon of the last decade, with a radical and challenging body of work to her name, capable of appealing to sexual and social minorities beyond popular culture's usual mainstream heterosexual constituency. It's just that she's no longer the icon I love to love.

SHE THINKS I STILL CARE: LESBIANS AND COUNTRY MUSIC

Rosa Ainley and Sarah Cooper

These days, to be less than totally enamoured by k.d. lang casts as much doubt on your pride in your lesbian identity as it did in the 1980s to have failed to be interested in tennis and Martina Navratilova (how convenient when the two of them were allegedly an item). Not having tickets for k.d.'s Hammersmith concerts in 1992 was the equivalent of missing Pride.

There seems to be an idea that k.d. lang represents the tip of the iceberg of a burgeoning lesbian country music scene. Worldwide, country is one of the biggest-selling musical forms, even if the statistics use a limited idea of what constitutes the world. It is country music which has delivered lesbians with the 'pop world's first honest lesbian icon' (*Vox*, April 1993), and at the time of writing k.d. is probably the most famous lesbian in the world. Ironically, as the idea of a lesbian country scene became a reality – a feature on lesbians and country music on *OUT* from 1991 was repeated in the 1992 series and several lesbian country bands and a lesbian country bar have appeared on the scene – k.d. herself has moved away from country into the mainstream, yet closer to the collective lesbian bosom.

At first glance, lesbian and country may seem like a contradiction in terms, and publicly at least, anathema to lesbians influenced by feminism. Lesbians have always taken what they can from popular culture, but country music has always been seen as the last, unassailable, bastion of the mainstream. In the late 1980s, two things have happened to change this: the rise and rise of k.d. lang and the diversification of lesbian style and cultural consumption.

'THIS WOMEN'S LIBERATION HONEY IS GONNA START RIGHT HERE'

In the 1970s and 1980s lesbianism and feminism came together to create a critical community which, on examination of popular culture in its many manifestations, found it politically wanting. In response lesbian feminists formed subcultures which supposedly rejected and were free of the taint of the mainstream, which they regarded as under patriarchal control. Without exploring in any detail the shifts in thinking of lesbian feminism through the 1980s here, we need to examine the hold it had on lesbian subcultures and, though this, lesbians' cultural choices. It is here that lesbians' traditional political resistance to country music is located.

Feminism tried to create an autonomous subculture in which cultural products – whether music, theatre or literature – were created for women by women, and informed by feminist ideology. Feminism's artistic vision for many years lay in the creation of a separate and superior culture. In music there were attempts to create an arena where the artist and the audience, in sharing a common political vision, not only broke down the hierarchical relationship that existed within mainstream performance but also sought to demystify and de-talent art, in an any-woman-can sort of way. In this refusal to elevate performers to star status it reduced them to being 'just another sister', and in the process inhibited any investment of fantasy in them by the audience.

Fashion also came to lesbian feminism's critical attention and was thrown out along with other constraining symbols of conventional femininity. The only time lesbian feminism took notice of fashion was when there was a knitting pattern in *Spare*

Rib for a jumper with women's symbols.

> Some of us demonstrate our opposition to what is considered the 'ideal' female appearance by wearing clothes and hairstyles which are deliberate attempts to show men we are not interested in them. This is not because we want to appear masculine, but because we reject the consumerism of fashion pressures and the artificiality and constraint imposed by commercially propagandized notions of beauty.[1]

Paradoxically, however, as Lillian Faderman has noted, although 'butch-and-fem were "politically incorrect" in the lesbian-feminist community, everyone looked butch'.[2]

The k.d. lang convention in London in 1993 would never have existed in those days. Nor would the k.d. fanzines now advertising in the lesbian press. All those feelings of star-struck admiration and the fantasizing about popstars, film actors, whoever, were totally unacceptable. Olivia Records, a women-only label, presented their artists in a clean-cut, worthy, outdoorsy way – no pin-ups for the sisters, please. Fantasizing about real-life girlfriends (or lovers to use more contemporary terminology) was in itself insulting and demeaning, in a climate when fancying someone was – really and truly – supposed to be about admiring their politics. Day-dreaming about such ephemera as popstars remained a secret indulgence.

YOUR GOOD GIRL'S GONNA GO BAD . . .

The 1980s welcomed a more assertive articulation of identity politics which stratified and polarized what had strenuously attempted to present itself as a unified lesbian community. Somewhere along the line, lesbians started wearing lipstick and dresses, liking popstars (though some had never stopped) and doing things that would have been an outrage to lesbian feminism in the 1970s and early 1980s. This diversification in lesbian dress and social pursuits was both a reaction to, and an expression of, identity politics. Simultaneously, lesbians were also caught up in the obsession with the designer lifestyles that were popular before the current recession. Part of the visual diversification of lesbian culture in the 1980s reflected the influence of the style decade, even amongst a group supposedly above the sartorial imperative. But it was also a reaction to lesbian-feminist dress codes. Lesbians stopped looking like lesbians a long time ago, and increasingly butch and femme roles were reinvested as boastable lifestyle items where they had previously been sneered at.

By 1991 lesbians were discussing their haircuts on TV; in 1992 lesbians became queer (along with everyone else apparently) and got interviewed about their favourite dildoes. You've come a long way baby. None of these changes are unimportant, from the small details like wearing lipstick to the more controversial public display of the insignia of s&m sex. The role of fantasy in our lives was 'reclaimed' too, and with that a spotlight was placed on lesbian sex and sexual practices, triggering long-running battles about the representation of lesbian sexuality, porn and erotica. This resiting of fantasy also allowed us to go public about our enjoyment of women performers, especially those who represented our social and sexual aspirations – k.d. being the most obvious example. It is not insignificant that it is during this period that country music has shed some of its infamy on the playlist of the lesbian nation.

'YOU'RE THE REASON GOD MADE OKLAHOMA'

Country music is camp, sentimental (read masochistic?), has 'spunky' women performers, and great clothes. These are qualities which, in any other form, would have great appeal to the average lesbian. But country has also attracted an enormous amount of censure: it has remained largely unacceptable to the right-thinking or right-listening lesbian, as though it were a music apart, unrecuperably reactionary and anyway just plain ridiculous.

But you can look at country in two ways. The majority view is that country is a music bogged down in its history, epitomizing and even celebrating a place with a past where God, white America and the family rule supreme. It would be naïve to deny that some performers and their audiences exemplify this. It is no doubt true that the majority of country music performers and audiences are white, and some undoubtedly are racist.

But it would also be wrong to assume all country fans share these values or look to country for a reaffirmation of racism. Country music was not created to be simply a vehicle for reactionary attitudes. It grew out of what was essentially a regional folk music, just like blues, merengue, calypso, which, like all folk music, express the experiences of particular groups. In the case of country, this was originally the rural white working class in America. Just like other folk musics which have persisted and survived, country music has been influenced by and influenced in turn, many other types of music, including blues, r & b, various European folk musics and Tex-Mex.

The appeal of music, and indeed that of other forms of cultural and artistic expression, is not solely dependent on the politics and sentiments it articulates. Music isn't meant to be entirely cerebral – whatever happened to enjoyment? Politically-correct culture doesn't exist, which isn't to say that listeners should fail to be critical about what they listen to. But fulfilling some spurious notion of right-on-ness isn't what music is for. And anyway, one woman's Holly Near is another's Tanya Tucker. Assessing music in this way is a reductive approach that generalizes about the attitudes that are found within it – as though country music were some monolithic entity in which all performers held and expounded the same values, regardless of their own experience or beliefs. This approach generalizes about the attitudes found within country, eroding its own specific form of expression. It is also dismissive of country's strength in portraying very real experiences such as rural recession, for example, 'Trouble in the Fields' (Nanci Griffith), 'Wild Horses' (Garth Brooks).

Very few forms of popular culture could be examined critically by the standards that are brought to bear on country music, and still come off well. There's no disingenuousness intended here – there are still a lot of reasons why lesbians might find country music politically unacceptable . . . just like any other kind of music in fact. Certainly country has its share of reactionary, racist, homophobic practitioners – but hey, this is the music industry, and so far as we can discover, there's nothing unusual about that. Like the rest of the entertainment industry, the music business is subject to all the worst excesses of late-twentieth-century capitalism. It is, after all, driven solely by profit, the considerations of anti-racism, anti-sexism and general exploitation only becoming pertinent where units can be shifted and money made. What else can explain the enthusiastic marketing of someone like Tracy Chapman by her multinational label? WEA execs are unlikely to be found sitting around 'talkin' 'bout a revolution'. Not the one that she means, anyway.

'I WAS COUNTRY WHEN COUNTRY WASN'T COOL'

There have, of course, always been lesbians who have resisted peer group pressure or social mores and who have continued to like country music, no matter how surreptitiously. For some older lesbians who always liked country music, pre-New Country, it was the complementary attractions of Patsy Cline's torch songs and Calamity Jane's sassy appearance: tough dykes can have a heart. *Desert Hearts* arrived neatly at a time in the mid 1980s when it was able to tap into both that tradition and the emerging redefinition of lesbian taste(s), but the clothes also accentuated the camp appeal of country while the look and demeanour of the lead characters ideally matched the rise of the lipstick lesbian, the tough femme.

At the same time, the emergence and popularization of New Country offered an alternative updated image to the tackiness (alternatively read camp) of the Nashville sound through the 1960s and 1970s, by returning country to its roots. The boys and girls of

New Country disowned the strings and schmaltz arrangements that had dragged down great singers like Tammy Wynette for more rootsy types of song, some made great by country music's traditional heroes.

They looked roots as well – New Country saw the return of work shirts, cowboy boots and hats, jeans and waistcoats with a vengeance, men and women alike. But New Country was not just a repackaging exercise; while the look and musical style might be traditional, the attitudes of its practitioners were not so predictably caught up in the traditional values of the rural white South. Although country's more explicitly political rebels still tend to come from its older generations - such as Johnny Cash and Willie Nelson, artists such as Mary-Chapin Carpenter, Lyle Lovett, Garth Brooks, project a more urbane and sophisticated image which can also appeal to a more liberal urban young audience. At the same time aspects of country, such as bluegrass and western swing, can now be reassessed as a folk music form, as another world music, through the re-emergence of abandoned instruments like the fiddle and dobro.

New Country, a cool, credible and less politically contentious music than ever before, has opened up huge new and different audiences. Its political attitudes reflected more contemporary themes: the women updated the cowgirl brand of feminism that was first seen in numbers like Dolly Parton's 'Dumb Blonde', with songs such as 'He Thinks He'll Keep Her' (Mary-Chapin Carpenter) and 'Ford Econoline' (Nanci Griffith). At the same time the boys were articulating sentiments totally in conflict with the Nashville old school. Camp is too mild and understated a description of Lyle Lovett's reading of the infamous 'Stand By Your Man' while Garth Brooks sings 'when we are free to love anyone we choose, then we shall be free'. Currently one of the world's top ten earning performers (*Vox*, January 1993), ahead of Prince and U2, Garth Brooks can be credited with widening the interpretation of that ol' country mainstay, traditional family values as 'encouraging children to be the best they can. If your parents are black or white, if your parents are the same sex, that's still traditional family values to me.' Country with a conscience. It is also rumoured that his sister, who sometimes plays guitar in his band, is a lesbian.

'OUT OF MY HEAD AND BACK IN MY BED'

There is an enormous amount of kudos attached to being one of those lesbians who saw k.d. perform before she made it big. It has become the equivalent – in a different social scene and some seventeen years later – of having seen the Sex Pistols play at the Screen on the Green. In 1993 k.d. lang had the music world at her feet. She has achieved unique status – being both popular, and out. The amount of press coverage in the so-called quality music and daily papers has been enormous, and what is interesting is that her sexuality, though not glossed over, is rarely treated with any particular prurience. She is in this sense a bit of gift to the liberal journalists; the token lesbian entertainer. The British *Independent*'s article on k.d. began: 'I would rather be seen as a professional artist than as a professional lesbian.' Her country music past is treated by journalists as an amusing irony, rather in the same way that it has been gratefully forgotten by many of her lesbian fans. For it is not as a country singer that she has achieved fame and press approval. *Ingénue* showed a marked change of direction for her, from twang to torchsong, from country to pop, while retaining some of its country influences, notably its extreme sentimentality and over-the-top delivery. Indeed, '*Even Cowgirls Get the Blues*' is a neat dove-tailing of *Ingénue*'s swoon with yodel of *Shadowland*, and sees something of a return to country and k.d.'s claim for a stake in the revisionist western scene as represented by *The Ballad of Little Joe*, *Unforgiven, Posse,* and so on.

'DON'T LET THE STARS GET IN YOUR EYES'

k.d. is a musical icon for lesbians in a way different to any previous performer, because she's so dykey, and out. Her attractions are not just confined to a lesbian audience, Madonna has already produced the perfect quote: 'Elvis is alive – and she is beautiful', indicating that lang-fancying is not the legitimate provenance only of lesbians. Indeed, a quote from *Vox*, a straight mainstream music paper, confirms this: 'Every woman I know fancies k.d. lang.' But as an out and famous dyke, k.d. has a devoted lesbian following, the like of which it was impossible to predict any lesbian star generating.

But the k.d. phenomenon has always been more about who she is than what she does. k.d.'s country, best represented by *Shadowland*, demonstrated a conservatism not mirrored in her dress sense. But her clothes were acceptable in a post-*Desert Hearts* culture, where cowgirls wore bootlace ties and seduced divorcees. Add to this her androgyny, her sentimentality, her lyrics endlessly discussing beginnings, endings and totally thwarted relationships . . . and you're talking dyke delight.

Lesbian nation is beside itself, at k.d.'s feet. Possibly the most extreme example of this so far was the k.d. lang convention held in London in February 1993. Four hundred lesbians met to indulge in k.d. karaoke, lookalike competitions, swoon over videoed footage and talk to other devotees. The convention was an almost religious experience, in spite of the fun side of it. Certainly not everyone there was a totally committed fan – tongues in cheeks were spotted – but the overall atmosphere was one of reverence and devotion. Wesley House, the London Women's Centre which was the venue for the occasion, reeked care and concern – commonly associated with very different types of events. And all this for a popstar. With langmuzak playing all day throughout the building, a total press ban, pictures of Herself used as signposts for the different convention activities, and even a helpfully marked-up reproduction of a map of Alberta (k.d.'s home province), parallels with more sinister shades of religious cult practices were difficult to avoid.

There was another interesting, though less surprising, phenomenon in terms of fan behaviour. In the video about 'what k.d. means to you' she was described by interviewees as if each had just fallen in love with their latest flame, with body language to suit. It was coy, liplicking stuff, behaviour more usually associated with teenage Take That fans than from thirty-something lesbians.

In 1992 k.d. did two nights at London's Hammersmith Odeon to audience acclaim that has been accurately described as equivalent to a Beatles concert. But while Beatles concerts were characterized by the sheer volume of audience noise – girls screaming and singing and crying – k.d.'s show saw more of a hushed reverence, with occasional shouts of 'I love you' and 'Lesbians are everywhere' (certainly they were that night.)

'BOY NAMED SUE'?

In 1991 k.d. appeared on a Gap advert, in a series of about-to-be-very-famous-stars portraits by Herb Ritts. Whether a real Canadian country girl would wear Gap jeans is a moot point, but there's no doubt that it was a smart move on Gap's part. Gap are well-known for making lightweight urbanized and competitively priced versions of workwear classics, as worn by, yes you guessed it, real cowboys and real dykes. Featuring in the Gap promotion made a certain kind of popular sense – there was a fit between her appeal, and Gap's.

This is not to suggest that if you like wearing the clothes you should like the music – but lesbians have always been conscious of the meaning of clothes, if not always fashion-conscious. No one would reasonably complain that a dyke wearing jeans, a workshirt and blanket jacket was a redneck. This is widely-made fashion choice not a statement of politics. Lesbians who become rabid at the very mention of country music will happily clothe themselves in garments whose origins are in western workwear and, contrary to popular assumption, wearing cowboy clothes is not an essential part of liking country music. k.d.'s outfits have also always been an important part of her act, and certainly one that has not been lost on lesbians. Her change of musical direction also seemed to result in an alarming change of dress judging by her video for 'Miss Chatelaine'. It is worth noting that this cross-dressing (although not the first time she's done it, only the most extreme) has happened at the point of her crossover from cult starlet to megastar; it also possibly enhanced it. It is interesting to see how popular her new image as a lipstick lesbian in a dress is amongst her dyke audiences, judging by the positive reaction at the convention. Again, a quote from the *Independent* article speaks volumes: 'She stopped acting like a masculine woman, and became like a *feminine man*. It looked much better' (their italics, their problem).

'COUNTRY GIRL WITH HOT PANTS ON'

k.d.'s initial fan base was the largely straight country (albeit New) audience. A few of these are still to be seen, somewhat bemusedly, at her concerts. That her country audience may not be tempted to cross over with her is anticipated in *Nashville Babylon*, a book devoted to the exhibiting of country's dirty linen. There Randall Reise hails her as 'the most stunning explosion of talent to emerge from Nashville in decades', then adds coyly, 'but her decidedly androgynous look might be too off-putting to too many.' And apparently it was, to many straight country fans, or perhaps more to the point, to the country music establishment, not known for its liberal views. k.d. herself has said, 'Winning a Grammy and yet not getting any airplay was an obvious sign to me that I'd gone as far as I could.' In fact it was actually her anti-meat commercial that probably did her country career more damage than her sexuality.

The advent of k.d. lang in the late 1980s had a massive influence on the visibility of the lesbian country fan, whether as k.d. fancier or original country fan coming out of the closet. If the media were looking for a marketing concept to attract lesbians, could they have dreamt up k.d. lang? And while there will be some women who liked k.d.'s music and explored further into country music and liked that too, the reaction to *Ingénue* strongly suggests that there will be far more who thought of her as an exception – she's gorgeous even if she does play that redneck music – and have been relieved at the release of *Ingénue*. Nevertheless it is likely that country's attractions for a lot of other lesbians will persist, even if the voice that played over a thousand broken hearts, the face that launched countless crushes has decamped to less problematic pastures. k.d. lang will remain a subcultural crush object, every dyke's wank fantasy, whether she's singing or acting or posing for advertising shots or wearing a dress. It probably doesn't much matter which.

'IT'S A GOOD THING I WAS BORN A WOMAN OR ELSE I'D HAVE BEEN A DRAG QUEEN'
Dolly Parton

Country, with all its contradictions, has tremendous appeal for lesbians, and provides an interesting illustration of how lesbians find meaning in forms of popular culture ostensibly imbued with heterosexual and conservative values. While it may dent some lesbians' fondly held prejudices about country music, it does have a strong tradition of women retaining some semblance of control (which, given how the music industry works, is the best that can be achieved) of their music or production, playing their own instruments. There's no, one unequivocal reading of any type of music or of particular songs, a fact evidently true of country as well as other forms. What is cherished as downhome-ness, upholding family values and domesticity for some country fans is high camp for others.

The camp in country is undeniable – the outrageous clothes, the posturing, the rampant sentimentality – but it's also accompanied by country's basic domesticity. This complicates the messages. Unravelling these is revealing work, shedding light on why lesbians might be attracted to country. There *are* a lot of songs about housework, farming, dogs – and why wouldn't there be? Do people complain about the blues being too depressing, or soca [soul/calypso] being too cheerful? In any case 'domestic' doesn't just mean housework: country lyrics also concern themselves with the minutiae of relationships. And not just limited to sexual or potentially sexual relationships – country takes the wider view and includes parents, employers, god, cousins, siblings, grandparents, friends and pets. Pretend families all over again really. And as we all know, lesbians are notoriously obsessed with their relationships, their lack of them, their brevity, their longevity . . .

'I'VE GOT GEORGE JONES ON THE JUKEBOX, AND YOU ON MY MIND'

Some of us actually take country music lyrics to heart . . . for all the validity of claims for country music's campness and its potential to subvert, behind closed doors it gives a lesbian with girl trouble the opportunity to wallow in countless songs depicting broken relationships (self-indulgent misery?). Lyrically, pop music has moved on little from Tin Pan Alley's 'moon in June' preoccupations, and most modern songwriters still rely heavily on a very limited rhyming dictionary. In contrast, country music is very adult in its lyrical concerns, depicting a wider range of scenarios: emotional and economic. While problems with your tractor may not have an enormous relevance for the urban lesbian, infidelity, non-monogamy and general all-round heartbreak do. So when your girlfriend goes off with your best friend, what else can you play but 'She's Got You' or '(I Never Promised You a) Rosegarden'?

Dolly Parton and Tammy Wynette are the indisputable queens of country, and camp queens they are too. Dolly Parton in particular is upfront and fully conscious of what she's up to. There was a time when lesbians considered her as a woman with internalized sexism of outstanding proportion – what was she doing with that hairdo, that bust, those outfits? Like a Sindy doll who ate Eve's original apple in fact – and hadn't she heard of feminism? Whether she had or not, she was deftly managing her career (which as well as 'Jolene', that classic cry on non-monogamy, has included some very un-Bimbo-like songs like 'Harper Valley PTA', 'Dumb Blonde') and stage-managing her image, to great effect.

But what about Tammy Wynette; quite apart from the obvious camp classics of domesticity like 'Stand by Your Man' and 'No Charge' ('For the toys, food and clothes, for wiping your nose, No charge . . .'), she recorded 'Cowboys Don't Shoot Straight Like They Used To'. Could a woman who we know to be as wordly wise as Tammy Wynette be unaware of the innuendo of a title like that? Tammy's material is mainly rubbish, but her voice is great. Could that even be seen as a hallmark of much country, or indeed most music: great voices, strong women, lousy material? Popular culture forces us to contrive meaning where we can after all. With her talent for transforming personal adversity into good publicity, Tammy Wynette has achieved a sort of camp appeal through her emphasis, on record and in interviews, on the sheer awfulness of her life. Her act – on stage and elsewhere – is a strange mixture of the dangerously mundane and over-the-top performance – but is her, and other performers', down-to-earth domesticity only seen as exaggerated because cool urban and urbane lesbians can't believe any of it could possibly be real?

Patsy Cline too has always been a favourite, helped along somewhat by the *Desert Hearts* soundtrack: kitsch, sentimental love songs and tragic death to boot. k.d.'s band The Reclines, were named as a homage to her. You only have to see *Sweet Dreams*, featuring Jessica Lange, to realize she was a hard-working woman with a very unappealing husband problem. Domestic violence isn't camp. It's worth noting that Lange's appearance in the film, another lesbian favourite, probably helped popularize Patsy Cline even more. Patsy Cline is one of those artists whose untimely death was a great career move: she had the luck to escape both the excessive glitzy period of country and the crossover pressures that accompanied it, leading to some very embarrassing cuts. Her material combines simple sentimentality with a strong unashamed sexuality. This, her unadorned look, together with the knowledge that here was a woman running her own career is very seductive to a lesbian audience.

Once explored, the question 'why do lesbians like country music' flips over to ask instead 'why not?' In our previous lives as right-on dykes country was seen to represent everything that lesbianism as a political identity was sworn to challenge. Along with lipstick and lingerie, Loretta Lynn became a forbidden pleasure. It's an irony that it's from country that the first lesbian star emerged, even if she was just passing through.

The 1980s saw a questioning and reassessment of what it meant to be a lesbian. Issues of race and class were already raising major questions around lesbian identity and its relationship to feminism. With the designer decade as backdrop this spilled over into issues around lesbian dress, style and tastes. Part of the reassessment of lesbian identity and its expression was an exploration of areas previously considered taboo and transgressive. Some of these tastes provoked considerable controversy, for example the discussions that have taken place around lesbian s&m and representations of lesbian sexuality.

Challenges were made to lesbian and feminist assumptions that the only cultural expressions to be enjoyed without guilt were those that reflected the prevailing political ethos. In some ways country represents a similar deviance from the lesbian-feminist line, were it not that the music's camp maudlin and masochistic side is almost perfectly balanced by strong women performers and worthy songs. There is no doubt that country represents some sort of rebellion against right-on-ness and an opportunity to express lesbian camp. Whatever your views are on the disentangling of lesbianism and feminism, there has been a freeing up and opening out of cultural choices which has allowed lesbians to enjoy new experiences: fancying popstars and country music to name but two. These clearly have their attractions even if, as we have pointed out, our enjoyment of them may be complex, and not unproblematic.

To sneer at the reality of it (domesticity) and then transform it into something more exaggerated and indulgent (camp) is not an unprecedented response to other aspects of the culture that lesbians have salvaged and taken as their own. But it's a disturbing response, reflecting a dearth of mainstream culture which does not need to be remoulded or transformed for our consumption (but we know this already). This either bespeaks a lack of available culture for lesbians to own, or that lesbians' requirements are too stringent to be easily met. It also suggests an inability to accept or enjoy what does not in some way, no matter how contrived, reflect your own experience. Which is of course what popular culture is all about, reflecting some kind of normalized (read heterosexual) existence, thus ensuring that lesbians are unlikely to see many representations of their lives unless purged of any threatening sexual connotations. It becomes even clearer how important the character behind the product is for lesbian audiences, perhaps as much as the product itself. Enter Ms lang.

k.d. lang highlighted for lesbians the music's visual potential for camp while *Shadowland* offers an album-worth of songs to break up with your girlfriend to. After *Ingénue* it seemed that country was something k.d. was just visiting, but *Even Cowgirls Get the Blues* may have allayed those fears for the country inclined fan. While for many lesbians k.d. will represent the only acceptable face of country, others will continue to enjoy country music as we do other areas of popular culture: taking what we can that speaks to us. Filtering out and sifting through popular culture to see what's in it for us may seem ultimately unsatisfying, suggesting as it does that we will always feel excluded, made 'other' by popular culture. But then who does it really represent anyway – idealized couples in coffee ads?

NETTING THE PRESS: PLAYING WITH MARTINA

Diane Hamer

> Martina Navratilova has ended her relationship with champion skier Cindy Nelson for singing star k.d. lang. The match makes them the highest-profile lesbian couple in the world. *Pink Paper,* 21 March 1993.

> Tennis great Martina Navratilova has a new woman in her life – Grammy Award-winning singer k.d. lang. Although the openly lesbian superstars have denied they are dating, we have the first exclusive picture of them out on the town together. *Woman's Day,* 17 May 1993

Since these headlines hit the news-stands in early 1993 it has been a matter of intense debate whether or not the tennis star and the singer – both lesbian icons in their own right – ever *actually* had an affair. But the rumour itself – unthinkable ten years ago – is interesting to speculate on. Why? Because it is premised on the existence of not just one, but two, famous lesbians. Even more interesting is the fact that not only the gay press reported the alleged affair. Around the world, mainstream publications carried the story. In Australia, it appeared in *Woman's Day* and *New Idea*. In Britain, even the *Guardian* gave it passing mention, while in the United States every glossy magazine seemed to have something to say about it. What all this signifies is that lesbian invisibility is no longer something we can take for granted. Our status is shifting: our icons are now public property. Martina Navratilova is one such icon.

For a long time, Martina Navratilova has been a figure whose presence has served as a site for the articulation of popular ideas about lesbianism. Most frequently the vehicle has been the tabloid press, who snatch every available opportunity to exercise their prejudices about lesbians. The young Czech's aberrant sexuality was first a source of public fascination in the early 1980s. Since then Martina has continued to bear the weight of popular attempts to come to grips with lesbianism. In this process, Martina Navratilova herself has been increasingly active, inserting herself into discourse in a way which has transcended popular attempts to define her and which has left even lesbian fans speechless. Nowadays, Martina Navratilova is as likely to find her way into the papers for her views on AIDS and homophobia or on the Colorado anti-gay legislation as she is for her tennis victories. Just as it seemed she could not get any more public, she pulled off another ace, with her 'love match' to rising C&W star, k.d. lang.

It seems apt then, to use this moment to reflect on the decade in which Martina Navratilova rose to fame, not only as the world's leading tennis player but also as the most public lesbian since (and perhaps even including) Radclyffe Hall. It is here that Martina Navratilova's importance lies in any study of lesbianism and popular culture. Because she has served as the most sustained lesbian presence in the media over the past ten years, she is also the most consistent popular signifier of lesbianism to date. Whether we love her or hate her, as a repository for popular ideas about lesbianism, Martina is part of a lesbian politic. We might question Martina's politics or personality – I've certainly questioned her choice of lovers – but her enduring contribution has been to put lesbianism on the popular cultural map. For a decade, news of Martina's 'marriages' – affairs, expensive-gift-giving, and spectacular breakups have repeatedly made their way into the national and international press. Whenever Martina steps onto centre court at the Wimbledon women's final, the whole world is watching, in the knowledge that she is a *lesbian*.

PUBLIC PROPERTY

Many discourses have coalesced around the figure of Martina. Some of these are familiar – the masculine lesbian, the lesbian as predator, the lesbian as loner, the lesbian as *other* to normal womanhood. They are the residues of earlier historical discourses which have defined lesbianism from the late-nineteenth century on. But ideas about lesbianism have not remained static over the period of Martina's reign. Gradual changes in the way Martina's sexual identity has been portrayed in the tabloids signal incremental shifts in the status of lesbianism within popular culture. In the early 1980s, reports of her lesbianism were met with scandalized disbelief that she could embody such a vilified identity. This was the period of Martina's relationship with lesbian activist and author Rita Mae Brown. That lesbianism was something shameful was confirmed by Martina's own disavowals, and her retreat into bisexuality in her autobiography *Being Myself.*

By the late 1980s, there was an identifiable shift towards the sanitization of her sexuality, aided by her own attempts to feminize herself (not hugely successful). This was the period of 'former beauty queen and mother-of-two' Judy Nelson, whose impeccable heterosexual credentials also, bizarrely, cleansed Martina of the taint of lesbianism in the eyes of the tabloid press.

In 1990 however, with the very public breakup of Martina and Judy it was impossible for the press to pretend the two had not been lovers. This was the year of Margaret Court's denunciation of Martina's 'corrupting influence' and of Martina's emergence into a politicized identity. It was a period of backlash, but also a time when Martina most vigorously transcended the categories created for her within dominant culture.

In all these different moments, tabloid discourses of Martina's lesbianism have not been without internal contradictions. At times the press has refused even the most obvious meanings their own words convey in order to confirm historical precedent or popular prejudice. This is most glaringly illustrated in the tabloid's erasure of Martina's lesbianism while she was lovers with Judy Nelson. Nor have the shifts in representation happened evenly. As recently as late 1993 it was possible to read John Junor in the *Mail on Sunday* express his relief thus:

> Isn't it heart-lifting to have at the very top of women's tennis two ladies who both look as if they might actually use perfume and wear frilly panties and not, like so many of their rivals, aftershave and calico drawers? Quoted in the *Pink Paper*, 17 September 1993

THE LESBIAN IN TENNIS

The popular press has always had a problem with Martina. Ever since hints of her unorthodox sexuality entered the public domain she has presented a contradiction which the tabloid press have had to grapple with. In a sense she embodies a problem which runs right through women's professional tennis – the threat of lesbianism which casts a shadow over the international game. The sportswomen who participate in international competition are at the top of their profession, and as such are highly newsworthy. They serve as role models for girls and women throughout the western world, and are the subjects of public spectacle every June as they compete at Wimbledon. Yet for over a decade rumours have circulated that some of the top players are lesbians, an identity which has always been regarded as a monstrous deviation and something to be vilified rather than lauded, in the eyes of the popular press. For years the press have struggled to negotiate this tension between tennis champion as popular heroine and tennis champion as lesbian, a problem embodied not only by Martina but by Billie Jean King before her. A report in the *People* in 1986 neatly states the problem which Martina's dual status poses: 'More than anyone else it is Martina who has made lesbianism almost acceptable in the public eye.' *People*, 22 June 1986

It is not only the lesbian champion who presents a conflict of representation. To some degree, all top sportswomen are a 'problem' for the popular media. In *Grace Under Pressure*, Adrianne Blue notes the opposition between what she identifies as two exclusive categories; the sporting hero, and the woman (p.9). Conventionally, women's success is measured according to their possession of feminine skills and virtues which marks them out as different to men. *Sports*women, by contrast, sweat, grunt, groan and display a physical strength and dexterity which far outstrips that of an ordinary man. For this reason, successful athletes are often regarded as failures as women. Blue also suggests the slur of lesbianism has been used by the media as a punitive device against women who buck notions of femininity by entering professional sport (p. 41).

The earliest rumours of Martina's lesbianism were reported in this vein. At the beginning of the 1980s headlines like 'Sex smear on tennis star Martina' (*Sunday People*, 15 June 1980), 'Girl tennis star tells of sex life "dilemma" ' (*Sun*, 31 July 1981) and 'My love affair with Rita' (*Daily Mirror*, 31 July 1981) began to appear. The *Daily Mirror* followed their headline with a telling commentary:

> Tennis star Martina Navratilova has revealed she is a lesbian. But she is frightened to discuss her love life in detail in case it harms the game . . . Her admission confirms what has long been suspected – that lesbianism is rife on the international circuit.

It was clear from the reportage that the charge of lesbianism was a damning indictment. The press quoted sources who talked about the threat it posed to the women's tennis circuit, which relied on sponsorship to provide prize money for the game. According to the *Daily Telegraph* (6 May 1981) Billie Jean King had been dropped from a pharmaceutical company's advertisements after her palimony suit and Avon, at the time the biggest sponsor of women's tennis, contemplated pulling out of the game if any other top player talked about her lesbian life (*Daily Mirror*, 31 July 1981). Navratilova worried about the effect of the charge on her own endorsements, and on her application for United States' citizenship (*Daily Star*, 16 June 1980). Martina and Rita Mae Brown denied they were lovers. Martina was quoted in the *Daily Star* : 'I find it offensive and ridiculous that anybody should think that I am gay' (*Daily Star*, 16 June 1980).

More than one commentator voiced concerns about the corrupting influence of the tennis circuit. Major 'Mr Wimbledon' Mills reported, in the *People*, how:

> The mother of one American tennis debutante confessed to me that her daughter suffered the unwelcome and disgusting overtures of several hardbitten lesbian tennis players who refused to take 'No' for an answer . . . I told her that unless her daughter had a definite possibility of making the world's top eight she should quit the circuit and content herself with playing in lesser tournaments. She took my advice and got out and a year later she was a changed person – confident and happy and engaged to marry a home-town boy. *People*, 22 June 1986

PLAYING LIKE MEN

As a professional sport, tennis occupies a unique position in the relationship of women to athletic achievement. It was the game which inaugurated women's entry into top-level competition and has remained prominent as *the* sport in which women have excelled (Blue, p. xv). In tennis history it has often been considered that top women players play like men, a belief which began with French champion Suzanne Lenglen in 1919 (Blue; p. 4). The ambiguous gender status of these women has been compounded by the women themselves who have donned increasingly less feminine modes of dress for play. Lenglen abandoned the full-length skirt and petticoats for knee-length culottes, a move which spectators and commentators watched with horrified fascination. In 1993, in an equivalent gesture, Martina Navratilova became the first woman to play in international competition in shorts.

If women tennis players have come to be regarded as masculine it is not surprising that the equation has been made between women's tennis and lesbianism. The history of lesbianism is now well-documented (see, for example, Lillian Faderman). One of the most enduring ideas about lesbians is that they are not truly women. As an identity lesbianism has been masculinized and equated with heterosexual male sexuality – active, predatory, in pursuit of the 'feminine' woman. These ideas can be traced through the literature of nineteenth-century sexology, through early- and mid-twentieth-century lesbian writing (from the work of Radclyffe Hall to Ann Bannon) and persists today in many of the popular representations of lesbianism (illustrated by tabloid coverage of the Jennifer Saunders case; see also Hamer, 1992).

Throughout her career Martina has been dogged by charges of masculinity. As the attention of the media became focused on Navratilova, whose game was unrivalled during most of the 1980s, the slippages in popular discourses between tennis, masculinity and lesbianism have become transparent. Her skills and triumphs on the tennis court became wedded to her sexual identity. An article in *The Sun* newspaper, headed 'Don't call me Mister' reported:

> Mighty Martina muscled her way though a centre court opener yesterday. Then she laughed off suggestions that she is more suited to the men's singles [when] challenged afterwards that her new coach was getting her to perform more like a man. *The Sun*, 22 June 1988

'LOCKER ROOM LESBIANS'

Other themes, consistent with historical ideas about lesbians, are apparent in the press coverage of Martina's lesbianism in the early 1980s. One is the predatory nature of lesbians, represented in headlines like the *Daily Telegraph* 'Tracy Austin had to fend off locker lesbians':

> Tracy Austin, who burst into international tennis at the age of 15 had to have a bodyguard to protect her from lesbian advances in locker rooms, it was reported yesterday. *Daily Telegraph*, 6 May 1981

According to the press, Austin was not the only young and vulnerable girl to require protection. The *Sunday Mirror* (10 May 1981) reported that two other girls had complained of sexual approaches. Both were chaperoned by their mothers; one commenting 'I must watch the girls around Bettina more than the boys'. And the *Daily Star* reported Linda Geeves, former English captain, complaining that 'If I had £1 for every time I have been propositioned by a woman I'd be almost as rich as Bjorn Borg.'

The *People* surmised that:

> No pretty young player is safe when the butch battalions are prowling the locker rooms . . . The lonely nights and lack of male company make inexperienced girls easy prey for the randy predators of the women's circuit . . . Barricaded doors are often the only way of keeping the amorous amazons at bay. *People*, 22 June 1986

The author of the article makes no attempt to hide his 'distaste for any kind of sexual deviation' – lesbians in tennis were an 'unsavoury spectre'. It was, he says, 'more like Sodom and Gomorrah than the Wimbledon I loved'. One of his fears was that these monstrous women would be held in admiration by spectators. 'The public should know because they hold these creatures up on a pedestal and try to emulate them.'

The power of homosexuals to corrupt the young has been a constant theme since the turn of the century – it was one of the stated reasons for the censorship of Radclyffe Hall's *Well of*

Loneliness and almost sixty years later was what drove the advocates of Section 28 of the UK Local Government Act to initiate legislation prohibiting positive images of gay sexuality. Corruption of the young also emerges as a theme around the spectre of lesbians in women's tennis. Linda Geeves is again credited as an authoritative source, in the *Daily Star*:

> Many of today's top women players are homosexual and a good percentage of them are actively recruiting new talent . . . I've been downright disgusted as one of my all-time heroines has repeatedly chatted me up with more lecherous looks than any man has ever given me. Two women who specialize in wolf-whistling prospective recruits in broad daylight, parade around Wimbledon changing rooms in men's Y-fronts. *Daily Star*, 21 May 1981

Linda Geeves' imaginative account displays a deep-seated anxiety that she too could be implicated in sexual attraction between women ('It could have been me. It was all so plausible and attractive') – an anxiety which is at times overt.

In the tabloids' characterization of the predatory 'locker-room lesbian' Martina is at once the predator and the victim. Her friend (sic) Nancy Lieberman was quoted in *News of the World* on 2 August 1981:

> I want to give her a chance of changing. I'm not here to force guys on her, but just to help her get out of that environment.

The search for explanations for same-sex desire has been a constant preoccupation within popular culture. The *Sunday Mirror* discovers that:

> The loneliness of the long-distance tennis circuit is the reason that some women tennis stars are driven into lesbian love affairs. *Sunday Mirror*, 10 May 1981

Separated from friends and family, living in hotel rooms, out of suitcases, these lonely girls get 'caught in a sex trap'. It is a theme reiterated throughout the tabloid press.

Additionally, the *Daily Star* reasons that the absence of men is responsible for turning women into lesbians. Again the authoritative Linda Geeves proffers her opinion:

> When I started playing . . . it used to be fun to go to tournaments. They would be mixed affairs with plenty of eligible attractive young men to socialize with between matches. These days, with the growth of the lonely women-only circuit it is a profession I would think twice about before allowing a daughter of mine to follow. *Daily Star*, 21 May 1981

British xenophobia is rife within these accounts. It is always English players who are cited as authorities on the perversions of women at Wimbledon and the damage to the game. And it was always those from other countries – the United States or the former Soviet bloc – who manifested this monstrous deviation. Martina's strangeness as a sombre and rather heavy-set Czech woman reinforced her sexual strangeness.

ALL EYES ON MARTINA

In the early 1980s Martina's sexuality was seen as part of a larger problem, which also included Billie Jean King and, it seemed, hundreds of unnamed other women players in the tennis world. In this early period, the ideas about lesbianism produced in the tabloid press were the historical residues of early-twentieth-century discourses. By the mid 1980s, Billie Jean King had dropped out of the tournament and Martina was going from strength to strength. It was then that she became the exclusive focus of media attention.

This moment marks the beginning of the most interesting attempts by the tabloid press to negotiate around Martina's lesbianism. It is a period in which the contradictions between earlier historical discourses and newer meanings become most apparent. Heralded by the *Daily Express* serialization of the sexier parts of her autobiography, *Being Myself*[1] in the summer of 1985, the period is one of extraordinary inconsistencies and reversals.

Martina's autobiography makes her sexual preferences abundantly clear. She openly discusses her initiation into lesbianism, her relationship with Rita Mae Brown and current lover Judy Nelson. Any remaining doubt is dispelled by a *Daily Star* headline 'My love for the girls' (16 June 1987), followed by an article lauding her honesty and acknowledging she has borne the brunt of the criticism of lesbianism in women's tennis.

The *People* accepts her lesbianism as a given in their headline 'Martina will wed Judy' (21 June 1987). The article details the support with which Judy's family regards their relationship, which they represent as a settled, domestic relationship. The *Daily Star* (16 June 1987) examines Martina's own claims of bisexuality in her autobiography, published in 1985. It is clear, the article states, that the label of bisexual was simply a way of making her sexual preferences for women palatable. That she could call herself *bi*sexual, they joke, was on the basis of only one or two (unsuccessful) relationships with men.

In a curious way the effect of these reports, from roughly 1985 on, is to give credibility and emotional content to Martina's sexuality. The references to family life, domesticity, in-laws and pets normalize her relationship with Judy Nelson as something akin to heterosexuality.

MARTINA AND JUDY

However, in the same moment that Martina's lesbianism is normalized within the tabloid press, her relationship with Judy is sanitized and desexualized and heterosexuality upheld as the privileged regime within which their relationship is explained. This occurs through the erasure of the sexual implications of the relationship. That they were in a *sexual* union was a fact occluded by the constant signifiers of heterosexual normality that circulate around Judy Nelson in these texts.

The phrases that were constantly employed to describe Martina's lover were a continual reminder of her prior heterosexual status; 'mother of two', 'formerly married', 'ex-beauty-queen':

> Dallas born Judy, a mother of two who is married to a Texan lawyer. *Today*, 1 July 1986

> Live-in companion blonde mother-of-two, former beauty queen, divorced . . . *Daily Star*, 16 June 1987

> Live-in lover, blonde mother of two Judy Nelson, ex-beauty queen. *People*, 21 June 1987

The use of 'blonde' here clearly signifies Nelson's heterosexual attractiveness. Note that Martina is never described as blonde. Clearly a quintessential femininity, signified by blondeness, does not fit the description of Martina the lesbian.

The cumulative effect of these tabloid descriptions of Judy Nelson's heterosexuality is to cancel out Martina's lesbianism. Proof of Judy's past purges Martina of the taint of lesbianism – or at least testifies to some desexualized standard in her relationship with Judy. From the descriptions of their relationship in the press – 'great pals', 'constant companions' – one could be forgiven for assuming the relationship was entirely platonic. The effect is to desexualize the relationship with Judy even while Martina's own lesbianism is being named more explicitly. Martina might be a lesbian but Judy Nelson never could be – not a blonde with two children and ex-husband. Despite the texts' own anxiety that lesbians in tennis locker rooms might pervert innocent young women, there is nevertheless a wilful resistance to believe that women can and do change their sexuality or that a mature woman with a heterosexual past might prefer another woman over a man.

The most transparent illustration of this contradiction is represented by an article in *Today* newspaper (29 June 1989). Judy is predictably billed as 'former Dallas beauty queen, now a 43-

year-old mother of two'. She is credited as being Martina's constant companion, having 'left her wealthy vet [elsewhere a lawyer and a gynaecologist!] husband Edward and two sons five years ago to join Martina on the tennis circuit'. Judy, the article reports, provides Martina with 'emotional stability, support and encouragement' and Judy's parents have 'shown their approval of the relationship' by staying with Martina and Judy during the Wimbledon fortnight. It is difficult to read this as anything other than a description of a stable, long-term lesbian couple. Somehow, however, *Today* manages to do just this. Note how the following passages manage to locate the relationship in a dominant heterosexual paradigm in which the implication of lesbianism is shifted from the relationship itself to Martina alone. Judy's mother, Francis, is quoted: 'When Judy left Ed she wasn't ready to date or anything like that. Martina was and is of enormous support and help to her.'

The implication seems to be that when Judy, now out of the sexual fray, is ready to 'date' again, it will not be with Martina, or any other woman. Completely absent is the small detail – that Judy actually left Ed *for* Martina. Thus their relationship is read as a narrative of heterosexual restoration. Any lesbian signifiers slide away from the relationship and onto Martina alone. Again we hear the authoritative voice of Judy's mother who: 'Thoroughly approves of her daughter's *friendship* with the star who *once* confessed to lesbian *affairs*' [my emphasis].

The effect of all this is heightened by Martina's own increasing feminization at the hands of Judy. The central image accompanying the article in *Today* is of Judy and a male hairstylist (obviously gay) fussing over Martina, who sits at a makeup table, looking into a vanity mirror, her hair teased and sprayed into a fluffy bouffant, pink eye-shadow and matching lipstick. The caption reads:

Close friend Judy Nelson holds the lipstick and looks on approvingly as a hairstylist puts the finishing touches to Martina's softer, more feminine look.

It has often been said privately amongst lesbians that Martina in women's clothes looks like a man in drag. The irony of the visual image of a tall, athletic woman in feminine dress is not lost on a *Sunday Mirror* reporter, who comments on her new exercise video:

> Tennis ace Martina Navratilova reckons her rippling body is a turn-on for both men and women. The Wimbledon champion adds as she flexes her muscles: 'I am told that some women and men would give their arms to have these legs.' [Martina] appears heavily made-up and with coiffured hair. At times the veins can be seen standing out starkly in her strong arms. *Sunday Mirror*, 10 April 1988

Yet the feminization and desexualization of Martina is not quite successful. The meaning of Martina and Judy's relationship escapes even the tabloid's attempts to erase them.

> The boys [Judy's children] like her and she loves being with them. She is like a father and plays volleyball and soccer with them. *Today*, 29 June 1989

> Martina's relationship with Judy's sons is strong. 'She plays football and basketball with them' said [Judy's mother]. 'It's absolutely fantastic, she's more like a father to my grandsons'. *People*, 21 June 1987

These texts do allow for Martina to be like a father to Judy's sons. Why is it that they so wilfully resist the analogy, that she is like a husband to Judy?

THE FEMME FIGHTS BACK

The prevailing account of Martina and Judy's relationship in the tabloid press is not really surprising. In fact it is entirely consistent with how lesbian relationships have been represented historically. Always, it has been the butch woman who is constructed as the authentic lesbian; rarely is the femme seen as such. Traditionally, the femme has been constructed as essentially feminine and heterosexual; her lesbianism at most a passing phase, resulting from seduction by a predatory butch or a temporary retreat from men after some damaging experience. Both these meanings have been evident in the tabloids' readings of the 'blonde ex-beauty-queen's' 'friendship' with Martina.

But now, using her breakup with Martina in 1991 and the resulting 'galimony' suit as a vehicle, Judy has become extremely outspoken about her former love. Now it is her, rather than Martina, who is beginning to bear the popular meanings of lesbianism, in a manner unprecedented for a femme. Her public statements have included numerous press interviews (see for example, the British *Daily Mirror*, 16/17 Sept 1991; *Sunday Mirror*, 29 March 1992; *Observer*, 27 June 1993 and the Australian *Sunday Telegraph*, 27 June 1993), the publication of a book based on her relationship with Martina (*Love Match: Nelson vs Navratilova*), and an appearance on the *Phil Donahue Show* (shown in Australia in the last week of June 1993) on a programme about women who leave men for other women. She also made the news when she started a new relationship – with Martina's ex-lover Rita Mae Brown, (*Daily Mirror*, 18 May 1993)! That Judy has moved out of her relationship with Martina and into one with another *woman* blows apart the myth of her essential heterosexuality. Moreover, precisely *because* she is so feminine, and was formerly heterosexual, she represents the embodiment of feminism's catch-cry, 'Any woman can be . . .'

Judy's public statements actively emphasize the quality of difference being with a woman offers, evident in the headline from the *Sunday Mirror*, 'There's an intimacy you can get with two women that you can't have with a man'. In the accompanying article she says:

> I spent the happiest seven years of my life with her. I found the equality that was missing in my marriage. *Sunday Mirror*, 29 March 1992

It is via Judy that details of the 'marriage' with Martina, in a private ceremony in Australia, have become widely known (*New Idea*, 13 March 1993). It is also Judy who has made the sexual nature of their relationship explicit, in her own descriptions of her love for Martina as a 'confusing kind of excitement', as 'electricity' (*Sunday Telegraph*, 27 June 1993), and as a 'compulsive attraction' (*New Idea,* 13 March 1993). According to sources close to Judy: 'Sex kept Judy and Martina together during the affair which rocked the world' (*New Idea*, 13 March 1993). Judy spares us nothing, including overt statements of physical lust which gesture towards the unthinkable – the butch lesbian as object of desire for the 'essentially heterosexual' femme:

> Her body was the best I'd ever seen. It was not the sleek body that epitomizes the 'southern beauty queen' but a slender, athletic body with well-defined muscles, smooth and tight . . . Her legs were to die for and she had the prettiest hands I had ever seen. *Sunday Telegraph,* 27 June 1993

Judy's public statements have effectively silenced the tabloid press. Because they had constructed Judy as essentially heterosexual, and had played on her status as a successful feminine woman to sanitize and desexualize her relationship with Martina, the press are now incapable of responding to Judy's own very clear assertions of the passionate and intimate quality of their relationship. That a formerly heterosexual, feminine woman could embrace a lesbian identity is beyond the comprehension of the tabloid imagination. It remains scandalous, and therefore worthy of reportage, but inexplicable, and so beyond comment by these same sources. Judy's behaviour exceeds the discursive categories that the press have previously deployed to explain her position.

FLAUNTING IT

While ex-girlfriend Judy has stepped into the identity of the lesbian, to become the voice of lesbian love and a lesbian lifestyle,

Martina, meanwhile, has shifted into a more political discourse. The early 1990s, the period roughly coinciding with the ending of her relationship with Judy Nelson, has signalled the beginning of Martina's own inscriptions into the discourses generated about her within popular culture. Until now Martina had been an object invested by the discursive manoeuvring of the tabloid press. But now a shift occurs, in which Martina begins to make her own interventions into these tired scripts; and begins to write her own narratives of sexual identity which eclipse those provided by the popular press.

There are a number of key moments which signal what I call Martina's 'excesses'. They are excesses in a literal sense, because they are often manifest in overblown emotion and high drama, but they are also excessive in the sense that they exceed the image of Martina's lesbianism endorsed by the tabloids.

The first moment occurs in the late 1980s. It is the point at which she employs transsexual Renee Richards as her new coach; a move which is wilfully provocative and which confirms her own position within dominant discourse as sexual deviant. What this represents is a refusal of the respectability which mainstream culture is conditionally prepared to grant her in exchange for her complicity with their silence around the *sexual* aspects of her sexuality. As 'Mr Wimbledon' David Mills notes in the *People*, under the heading 'Wimbledon sodom', Renee Richards is a bizarre choice for Martina, and one which 'does her no great service':

> When I discovered that this person had been taken on by Martina Navratilova as a coach my mind simply boggled at the kind of gossip such an association would inevitably lead to. *People*, 26 June 1986

He means, of course, that choosing Renee Richards, formerly Richard Raskind, a post-operative transsexual who was once winner of the United States' Junior men's titles, could only serve to draw attention to Martina's own sexual difference. Martina's choice reads as a signal of her willingness to defy, rather than pander to, the demands of a media critical of her sexuality. What is brave about her choice is that, in a world in which she is already labelled a sexual freak, she chooses another who is more 'freakish' than herself. In this period she begins to embrace notions of outsiderness, rather than struggle to fit into a conventional schema.

Far from discreetly leading a private lesbian life, Martina and Judy's relationship also constantly produced moments of excess through the late 1980s and into the 1990s. This was manifest in extravagant public gift-giving normally the prerogative of rich glamorous heterosexual couples, and in their well-advertised 'marriage' which provocatively usurped heterosexual privilege.

A further moment of overt defiance and public flaunting of a despised identity was in the famous hug with Judy Nelson, after Martina's ninth Wimbledon title win in the summer of 1990. It was a significant moment for her and a thrilling one for every lesbian viewer around the world. The title, a result of her victory over Zina Garrison, represented the pinnacle of sporting achievement for Martina. No other player, male or female, had ever won as many Wimbledon tournaments in the history of the competition. It was the apotheosis of her career. After the winning game, and in a move which echoed Pat Cash's triumphant dash through the spectators to hug his wife three years before, Martina leapt through the crowds to embrace each member of her entourage in turn. Viewing this spectacle on my television the anticipation was excruciating as I waited for her to reach her lover, Judy. I was not disappointed as the two clung together in a passionate embrace which filled the whole screen. I thrilled to the knowledge that tens of millions of viewers around the world were at that moment watching two lesbians publicly display their love for each other.

But although the whole world had seen the embrace live on television, no one would ever see it repeated on any sporting round-ups. Punishment for Martina's transgressive behaviour was swift and damning. Every newspaper in Britain carried the story of Margaret Court, former tennis champion and respectable churchgoing mother of four, denouncing Martina. Under headings like 'Martina turns girls into gays' (*Sun*, 12 July 1990) and 'Martina love-game blasted by ex-champ' (*Daily Star*, 12 July 1990) all the tabloids reported Margaret Court's fears for young girls at the bad example being set by Martina.

But for Martina, the moment seemed to mark a departure. Any attempt to contain her lesbianism within a notion of 'private life' was now abandoned in favour of a more self-conscious political identity. It signalled her refusal to disguise any longer the nature of her relationship with Judy or to compromise about the meanings surrounding her sexuality. In short, she began to flaunt it.

The openness with which Martina has, in the 1990s, embraced her lesbianism had already been anticipated in 1985 with the publication of her autobiography. There she had made statements about her sexual preferences as representing her independence as a woman, about her passion for Rita Mae Brown who was 'open and proud as a gay woman', and had described her conflict with her parents who clung to the notion that lesbianism was a form of sickness. All these statements are consistent with a liberal agenda, which asserts the right to individual choice and tolerance. But in the 1990s Martina's voice takes on a new critical and angry note.

This is manifest first around basketballer Magic Johnson's revelations about being HIV-positive, late in 1991. Martina used the opportunity of a post-match press conference to attack the hypocrisy and double standards that allowed Magic Johnson, 'heterosexual stud', to be seen as a popular hero as a result of his openness. Martina accurately pointed out to a startled press that, had Magic been infected through gay sex, or had a woman athlete of Magic's stature contracted the virus as a result of sexual contact with many partners, they would have been pilloried, not glorified, by public and press opinion (*Guardian*, 21 November 1991). The following year she appeared on the *Phil Donahue Show*, again defending her position regarding Magic, as well as more personal challenges from the audience to her sexual preferences.

In 1993 Martina was vocal on lesbian and gay rights in her opposition to the anti-gay legislation in Colorado. Threatening to withdraw one's patronage from the ski fields of Aspen is a political gesture only the super-rich could aspire to – but it did serve to draw international attention to the Colorado legislation. And in April 1993 she appeared as a speaker at the lesbian and gay march on Washington. And her identification with a lesbian and gay *politics* looks like it is here to stay – it is rumoured she will also open the gay games in the United States in 1994.

MARTINA–WATCHING

What I want to explore finally is the intersection between the meanings Martina has been ascribed within popular culture and lesbian readings of her identity. Tabloid coverage of Martina's exploits through the 1980s, no matter how prejudiced in form, has served a purpose for lesbians. In demonstration of her status as a lesbian, and as if it served further proof of the fact, her popularity amongst lesbians has been repeatedly noted by the tabloids. There is a fascination, for example, with the number of lesbian fans who turn up to watch her pre-Wimbledon, Pilkington Cup matches at Eastbourne. Such references, while possibly intended to bring Martina herself into further disrepute, are one of the few ways the existence of a lesbian community was acknowledged at all during the period.

In *Grace Under Pressure*, Adrianne Blue has identified a phenomenon common to women's tennis but unknown to men's, that once they become best in their field, women players become figures of hate in the media. Nowhere has this been more true than for Navratilova, who has carried the double burden of being both champion *and* self-confessed lesbian. But while the media might control the *forms* of representation, they cannot guarantee how those representations are read by their audience or readership. I personally have thrilled to the media's horrified fascination with her sexuality. Reading behind the derogatory intentions of the press, I nurse a secret belief that her excellence as a player surely reflects on her choice of women as lovers.

Martina has two desiring audiences, fulfils two sets of desires. For mainstream audiences she embodies in her butchness and masculinity the horror and fascination of deviance; they enjoy her demonization. For a lesbian audience and for me as a lesbian viewer, the pleasures she offers are clearly different. She serves not only as an object of desire, but also as the bearer of a secret sexual knowledge. When I see her on centre court, I am thrilled by the realization that she too has experienced the pleasures of fucking a woman. This is not simply fandom or the search for 'positive role models'; it is a moment in which private passions are given a collective focus. Somehow, when she wins her match, it is our sexual identity which is in ascendancy; it is lesbianism which enjoys that brief moment of glory.

The mainstream press are obsessed with lesbianism. For the past decade this obsession has coalesced around the phenomenon of Martina Navratilova. Despite the confused, contradictory and often pathologizing meanings generated by this attention, the implications for a lesbian audience are that we have been offered a popular signifier of our sexuality. Martina has served as a point of unprecedented public recognition of a still largely invisible identity. References to this high public profile as a lesbian were playfully made in the title sequence of Channel Four's lesbian and gay series *Out on Tuesday*. What all this suggests is that Martina is a prefigurative icon who marks the insertion of lesbianism into the glamorous lifestyle of the rich and famous. By breathing emotional life into a monstrous category, Martina has made lesbianism into an identity that women might aspire to, rather than despise.

All thanks to Allegra Madgwick for inspiration and press cuttings; to Belinda Budge for editorial advice.

GIRLS WHO KISS GIRLS
AND WHO CARES?

Sue O'Sullivan

A mature woman sits down at her computer and stares into space. A lesbian contemplates her place in different mainstream cultural representations. A fifty-something fashion freak peruses a magazine. A mature lesbian feminist experiences the world as pleasurable, painful, difficult and easy. A woman remembers her childhood after a night of dreams. All of these women are part of me. Swarms of words and thoughts buzz around busily. Identity versus diversity. Flux and flow opposed to inner truth. Lesbianism as a major political statement, or sex acts between women as part of a smorgasbord of trendy sexual possibilities. Politics versus pleasure. The politics of pleasure. Contested power or contested sites? Polarizations of imagination and fantasy with real people and practice. The appeal of the outlawed, the naughty. The idea of transgression as an advertising tool. Once the wickedness is recognized and aspired to by others is it really wicked? Reality in the 1990s or opportunism at the edge of the century?

I want to look at and try to fasten down ever so tentatively the way in which lesbianism has surfaced as a fashion item and as a part of what's naughty and trendy in the 1990s by being brazenly selective about the mainstream British, American and Australian magazines I look at. I see a series of shifting sexual contradictions taking place, well mixed-up with co-options, ruptures, spaces, possibilities and marketing techniques. I want to understand better what is going on! As an avid consumer of magazines (my popular culture of choice) and as a self-consciously political creature, I'm tantalized. However, before speculating a popular culture's eye view of lesbianism, I want to set the scene, sift through a few bits of history, look at some of the different players.

In the 1970s what *challenged* mainstream media were the militant demands of feminism, demands which rocked any easy older certainty about women's place in the world. Even if popular media reacted with hostility to women's liberation, react and write about it they did. What *titillated* the media during the same period was the imagined connections between women's liberation and lesbianism. After all, it was 'common knowledge' that women's liberationists hated men. What else could they be but a bunch of 'hairy dykes'? Their accusations conveniently framed an attack on the politics of early feminists.

After the movement's first shameful (and defensive) response that its adherents were 'ordinary women', attitudes changed in fits and starts as lesbianism was accepted (sometimes grudgingly) into a line-up of politicized identities *within* feminism and gay politics. By the early part of the 1980s the fear emanating from *within* feminism that its demands would be dismissed as the mad-hatter rantings of man-hating lesbians had abated, largely because lesbians has forced the issue into the political arena. However, the media have continued to spit out their ignorant loathing and stereotyping of lesbians. Today the so-called loony, ugly (read not stereotypically feminine) lesbian, increasingly designated as an arbiter of rigid political correctness, remains a figure for derision and hatred, especially whenever the *politics* of feminism or lesbian feminism become a contentious issue in the larger society.

However, at some point during the mid to late 1980s something shifted in popular media's representations of lesbianism. An erotically charged image of a completely different lesbian began to materialize, coinciding with the older caricatured portrayal. k.d. lang and Cindy Crawford's now famous 1993 *Vanity Fair* lesbian-fantasy-come-true cover and the eulogistic article inside was perhaps this trend's culmination. The development of this new dynamic is what I'm interested in here, particularly in the way it has shown up in magazines, although I will allow my glance to wander to the pages of newspapers from time to time. Where did these images come from? How have meanings about lesbianism changed and where are the interchanges between those meanings in popular culture and the lived lives of lesbians? Clearly the existence of lesbianism and its subcultural manifestations is a precondition for the lesbian images appearing in glossy and not so glossy magazines. But what came first? The chic lesbian in her natural habitat or the chic lesbian in the pages of the media?

I remember an early 1980s issue of *Tatler* magazine which featured a gorgeous sailor girl model on the cover. The fashion spread inside was all about sailor fashions for women, and some of the layouts were suggestive of an erotic tension between the female models. An accompanying article covered real-life lipstick lesbians, clubbing in London. In the 1980s, British magazines like *Tatler* flirted more than once with lesbianism in their fashion layouts, once camping up a 1980s version of the upper-class country-weekend set, complete with languishing lesbians à la Vita Sackville West.

The point is that in the magazines' terms these were attractive and seductive images whose main purpose (outside of advertising and selling!) was neither straightforward pornographic arousal nor putdown. For the knowing reader of the time, however, magazines like *Tatler, British Elle* and *Vogue* appeared as if compelled to reflect a fascination with all things sexually strange – but – only if they were stylishly dressed. These included vaguely s&m images, direct from or influenced by Helmut Newton, and fashion spreads peopled by effete young men and languid ladies draped and intertwined together, but desiring who?

Women posing in these magazines were also wearing men's suits, playing with images of maleness and borrowing from an ongoing lesbian cross-dressing tradition. In the mid 1980s, when

Princess Di turned up at a star-studded event in a tuxedo, she was ensuring the public's interest in and acceptance of these new, slightly ambiguous ways some heterosexual women were choosing to dress. Although lesbianism was not overtly named in most of the magazine fashion features of the mid 1980s, its presence flirted around the edges outrageously.

Of course there have been other ways in which lesbianism has been inserted into magazines or the news media during the past ten or fifteen years. This often has occurred through a media eye view of the political agendas and campaigns of lesbian and/or gay groups, and through struggles around HIV and AIDS, although the odd lesbian sex scandal might occasionally surface. (Stor-oriented tabloids such as the *National Enquirer* often seem obsessed with the existence of lesbians and gay men. What a hoot it is to read their gasping stories on the shock/horror world of TV/screen/sport star gay sex, right alongside the more usual tales of monster babies and UFO sightings). Lesbians, for instance, might appear in the media through stories on lesbian headteachers, gays in the military, lesbians having babies, domestic partnership campaigns, lesbian and gay pride celebrations, Clause 28 demonstrators involvement in local or national Government, or supporting gay men with AIDS.

However, these are more news-based stories; their presence serves to make homosexuality, both female and male, less hidden and more a part of popular discourse around sexual identity. But I would argue that this type of story does not have the effect of creating a desirable lesbian object, nor of appealing directly to the woman who lusts after women. As well, the effect of such stories does not necessarily challenge the derisive way in which the character of the strident, 'ugly' lesbian continues to be used to attack feminist and/or lesbian-feminist supposed excesses; in other words, their militancy and the articulation of lesbianism's challenge to male-defined heterosexuality.

Musing over the possible underpinnings of lesbian chic and the continuing contradiction posed to it by an older lesbian feminism, leads me to think about shake-ups which might have altered how lesbianism is currently perceived. The first thing that comes to mind is the continuing SF scenario of AIDS. What makes it different from other frightening diseases of the late twentieth century is its real and imagined connections to assumed forms of heterosexual and gay male sexual practices. It's the historical timing of HIV which creates its difference from previous diseases linked to sex; making its first appearance at a particular point of sexual flux, when there was a lot of old unfinished sexual business around, but also new and energetic things happening, including significant numbers of women asserting themselves with men, demandingly saying, 'I want my pleasure too.' As well, more lesbians were branching out, tentatively exploring a more open approach to sex, kicking over the careful traces which previously had been maintained in a hostile yet perving world.

Since the 1970s, feminists have been actively criticizing and attacking popular women's magazines for their refusal to budge on the assumed heterosexuality of their readers, a heterosexuality which positioned the woman as eternally wanting to please her man, the man she was so lucky to have caught. Sex-obsessed magazines of the 1970s and early 1980s like *Cosmopolitan* ran never-ending stories (and still do) on how to catch, keep and please a man sexually. Although many women's magazines had moved towards incorporating aspects of feminism by the late 1970s, especially around notions of equality, heterosexuality still ruled the roost. It was the unexpected, the wild card of AIDS, which I suggest served to prise open the magazines' covers slightly and allowed sexual diversity to seize some space within their pages. AIDS forced a recognition that sexual diversity existed and it did it relatively quickly. However, this sideways recognition did not mean that news-stand magazines took on the radical political position which posed lesbianism as a challenge to assumed or compulsory heterosexuality.

AIDS' imprint on various sexual discourses has been immense, recasting the debates and sexual politics of the 1960s, 1970s and

1980s in its light. It is commonplace to refer to the way in which AIDS has forced a more public and mainstream recognition of gay male sexuality in countries where homosexuals were the first and hardest hit by the virus. At the same time, a concurrent but more oblique recognition of gay male desire has crept in. In a narrative filled with ironies, one is the way in which gay men, now associated in mainstream culture with AIDS and death, at the same time have surfaced more openly as sexual, sexy people. Whether it is drag queens in Sydney's Mardi Gras, fabulously muscled bodies at the club or gym, or fashion freaks in the more bohemian parts of town, it's clear that gay men conjure up more than the ravages of AIDS.

One spin-off of this opened space has been the different way in which lesbianism is also signified. At first, lesbians are implicated in the AIDS tragedy by virtue of their perverse same-sex desire and practice. They are perceived as a 'danger' because they too are homosexual. Later, and in ways too complicated and varied to go into here, lesbian and gay coalition politics around a range of issues, including AIDS but perhaps more accurately described as 'gay and lesbian rights', assures the linkage between the two in the media and the public. Lesbians have grown in confidence and visibility in proportion to how strongly they've pushed for recognition and equality in the wider society, *and* expanded the boundaries of their own developing social networks and cultural representations.

The initial aspect of the heightened awareness of gays and lesbians in the media continues today but is not the *only* way AIDS has affected the attitudes displayed in the media. A decade later, different layers of lesbian and gay identities and lives have permeated, mixed it up with other cultural developments and produced for instance, AIDS activists, queer theory and queers, and 'outing' as a significant event in some countries – all of which have been covered in the media. There is a more general recognition, as famous people announce their HIV status or become ill with AIDS, that homosexuals really are 'everywhere' and that these deviant men have sisters. 'We are everywhere!' the rallying cry of the 1970s gay and lesbian activist, becomes a bizarre and poignant reality within the context of AIDS in the 1980s and 1990s for both gay men and lesbians, when they are *seen* to be everywhere.

But AIDS is only part of the explanation of why images of real-life lesbians like k.d. lang and the fantasy lesbians acted out by models in magazines have emerged as desirable objects on their own terms, while different images of lesbians continue to serve as the target for denunciations whenever any form of radical feminist politics is floated. Even the term 'lipstick lesbian' indirectly signals that there is another lesbian who overtly shuns makeup in the name of a political rejection of male dominated notions of femininity. Yet in previous eras of lesbian style, lipstick was accepted. One has only to think of the French salon of Natalie Barney or the more recent western traditions of butch and femme.

A recent American anthology edited by Joan Nestle, *The Persistent Desire*, focused on butch/femme historically and in the present. Many of the older writers in it refer angrily to the rules and regulations of the women's movement of the 1970s which they say denied their experiences and desires. However, since the mid 1980s, many younger lesbians have been eager to rediscover and play with aspects of butch/femme. These women look upon the 1970s as *passé* and rigidly politically correct. Initially they materialized at the end of the 1970s on the lesbian and/or gay scenes of cities like London, New York, San Francisco and Sydney, attending women's balls dressed in tuxedos and ball gowns, well before Princess Di ever dreamt of cross-dressing.

I bring up those dim and seemingly superseded days of the 1970s, ones which the neo-butch/femme *aficionados* of the 1990s now regard so grimly, because they do have a bearing on how lesbianism is now being touted (or ridiculed) in the media. In fact, the pastiche of retro styles and culture which many younger lesbians and gay men have favoured in the past five years or so are in sync with a more generalized cultural appreciation of those styles by other groups of young people, young designers – straight or gay. The currently favoured butch/femme look and flavour is located in a reinvention of the styles of the 1940s, 1950s and 1960s. These neo-butch/femme styles of urban western life are titillating *and* complimentary to current straight fashions, styles and attitudes which many magazines are covering and creating a wider interest in.

Reflecting on the ephemeral nature of what is 'in style' and what is not, what is retro and what is considered *passé*, and what meanings are attached to stylistic manifestations, it comes as a small but pleasant irony that grunge (no matter how briefly) brought back into fashion for a whole new generation of rebellious kids the flannel shirts and knitted hats of the pantomime 1970s lesbian feminist. That the girls of this wave of grunge style came back as anarchistic waifs, not tough feminists or dykes, gently reveals how skewed much of the current rejection of 1970s feminism's look is, superficially identifying a style of clothing with politics. As Courtney Love, singer with Hole, says in a July 1993 issue of *i-D*, 'The problem with Riot Grrrl is that a "girl" is seen as pretty, childlike and innocent while a "woman" is a hairy lesbian.'

I want to scrutinize a bit more the caricature lesbian whipping girl, the one who serves as the repository of mainstream hatred and fear of feminism's 'excesses'. Besides the flannel shirt (which in fact has been an androgynous item for many decades) she is often portrayed as an old fashioned bull-dagger butch. She is 'mannish' but not at all stylish and at the same time she is definitely a woman. Therefore she has to be ugly – in other words, butch. Interestingly, the *real* lesbian politics (which as she figures in the media, the diesel dyke butch caricature is *supposed* to represent) often contain angry denunciations of butch/femme relationships – even if delivered by a flannel-shirted adherent. In this interpretation, butch/femme is consigned to reactionary heterosexually influenced role-playing. The 1970s lesbian feminist was likely to be blanketly anti-fashion *and* anti-butch/femme, although as other commentators have remarked, the idealized androgyny of the time made everyone look vaguely butch.

The popular media which use the stereotype to attack the radical politic they want to discredit have no understanding of the complex history of butch/femme, let alone the way it was rejected by 1970s lesbian feminists. Even ostensibly sympathetic articles about lesbianism appear compelled to say what today's lesbian chic is not: 'The stereotyped butch dyke who can't get a man and worse still, can't apply lipstick or use a razor, is a tired old image being pushed to the backburner.' (Bernie Sheehan, 'Lesbian Chic', *Australian Women's Forum*, September 1993).

One of the ways in which the media used to signal their distress about confusing sexual identities, was to repeat *ad infinitum* the question 'Is it a boy or a girl?' Apparently this was supposed to result in general hysteria and a comforting return to 'normality'. It bedevilled earlier 'gender bending' from the 1960s long-haired hippy right up to Boy George in the early 1980s, but nowadays it seems largely to have disappeared. Who gives a fuck? is the general tone of things. However, *who* these indeterminate creatures literally fuck is of interest. Today, through the melded influences of gay, lesbian, feminist and AIDS organizing, an expanded repertoire of named or suggested sex acts can more easily be called into play, making it possible to more openly refer to sexual behaviours rather than being stuck in gender-bending obsessions.

At the same time, there is the possibility that these newly discovered people are simply sexually confusing creatures who challenge the gender expectations of dominant heterosexual culture *and* those of more traditional deviants, both lesbian and gay. Whether male or female, they may appear aggressively feminine, futuristic, or ridiculously masculine. The sex acts they may or may not be capable of desiring or carrying out with each other then become irrelevant when compared to their 'we're here' presence in the pages of various magazines. The repertoire of sex acts and sexual personae made more generally available, are often written about through an excited exploration of transsexuals (or transgendered people), or specific sexual predilections like rubber or sadomasochism.

A December 1992 article by John Godfrey in the *Face* called 'The New Camp' maintains that there is a rise of stars and celebrities whose sexual identity is neither straight nor gay, but camp. 'Because the New Camp is where the old Camp has broken the taste barrier (good not bad), where dressing up is about glamour not gender, and looking good (i.e. the body beautiful) has nothing to do with sexuality.' And in 'Love the one you whip', Lee Tulloch describes fashion's move into fetishism.

'Fetishism is all the rage, as are its subcultures of S&M, B&D, D&S and Fem Dom.' (*Mode*, Feb/Mar 1993). Illustrating the article are examples of stars and models in appropriate poses. There's Cindy Crawford in a *Vogue* fashion shot by Helmut Newton in which she wears a plastic bathing suit, and lies stiffly beside a pool in a position suggestive of bondage and masochism while model Helena Christensen stands above her in designer dominatrix gear pawing at Cindy's spread-out hair with her elegant shoe. (Cindy, it seems, has an ongoing fondness for kinkiness of the lesbian sort.) These forays into sexual diversity, portrayed as riveting and fascinating to a more sedate readership, exist alongside more serious, didactic features on sex in the time of AIDS, which endlessly list different sexual acts and their attendant risks. In these articles the focus is completely on 'naming' and transgression and no one ever mentions that people who live out their lives 'transgressively' may have trouble in the world – trouble with jobs, family or trouble with violence.

A lush and trendy art magazine in Australia (Pippa Leary, *black & white*, Summer 1992/93) carries an article in its first issue called 'Gender Agenda' about transgenderism, in which the author points out:

> In the world of pop music, the androgynous makeup of the Bowies and Annie Lennox has been replaced by the surgical makeover of the Jackson clan and Cher. A quick glance at the fashion photography of *Vogue*, or the Stephen Meisel portraits of Madonna, reveals that ambiguity is the state of play in the sexuality stakes.

Drawing on the buzz names of Foucault and Irigaray, transsexuals in this article are always male–to–female created bodies which the writer claims are now the ideal female model type.

Straight, gay or queer, these articles are primarily about transgressive personae and acts. But equivalent focus on lesbianism as a newly-arrived hot ticket is not hard to find. Back in late 1989, Nicola Shulman in her wonderfully titled *Harpers & Queen* article, 'Bra-Crossed Lovers', was revealing the rise of lesbianism within the nearly hooray-Henry set: 'It is one of the most intriguing phenomena of the late eighties that smart women are turning in droves to lesbianism'. Weighted down with heavy-handed attempts at humour, Shulman manages to convince that lesbianism is in vogue, but that it is a passing style, 'Occupying a place in the nation's consciousness similar to that of, say, roller-disco dancing in 1976'. In fact, it's being taken up by girls who ultimately want a man. To attract said man they need a clean bill of health. Why lesbianism? It's safe – from AIDS!

Shulman's unpleasant article also includes a list of negative lesbian stereotypes which the current crop are not! 'Naturally, you do not wish to deal in cheap parody, so you have straightaway thrown out the idea that these are persons with Eton crops and monocles who drink stout from straight glasses and call each other Jim.' Shulman doesn't get it, doesn't get that in late 1989 it is already perfectly fashionable to have an Eton cop and *not* call each other Jim, or that lesbians could look like either of these images plus many others. And she can't help but compare the unpleasant feminist to the current batch of (temporarily) gay girls. 'Neither do you suppose for a moment they must be feminist guerrillas who trim their hair with the coarse plate of the cheese-grater'. Shulman can have a go at feminists, implying in one short sentence their absurd militancy (guerrillas) coupled with their wilful unattractiveness (hair cut with a cheese-grater).

In the Winter 1993 issue of the Australian *HQ Magazine*, in an article called 'The Gay Divorcee', Julie Clarke wrote: 'It used to go something like this: you fall in love, get married, have kids and settle down. But, nowadays, there's an addendum some women are finding hard to resist: you get divorced and fall for another woman. For them, it's goodbye phallus and sandpaper kisses, hello soft skin and sensational sex.' Clarke posits an idealized lesbian desire for the woman's body in reaction to the brutishness of heterosexual sex. She is obviously writing sympathetically about why previously straight women might find lesbianism attractive and her interviewees extol the joys of lesbianism. But even she has to describe the negative stereotype in order to claim it is not necessarily true. She goes on, 'Sure there are lesbians who believe that the whole world is a phallocentric conspiracy to harm and insult lesbians who are the only intrepid survivors of a vanquished race . . . women. The straight world in turn sees them as humourless "sleeping bags with legs".' By denouncing the stereotype as one, she indicates that some lesbians believe the heterosexual world is out to get them, the ones who in turn are perceived as 'sleeping bags with legs'. The boring, daggy lesbian is the one associated with difficult, challenging politics.

Clarke finishes off with a recent Sydney Mardi Gras Parade scene:

> But when a pack of 50 beautiful bare-breasted women glowered, Harley Davidson roared – and the Dykes on Bikes took off up Oxford Street in Sydney's Darlinghurst one balmy Saturday night in February, the crowd watching the Gay and Lesbian Mardi Gras Parade, mainly het couples, were gob-smacked'. 'Hubba hubba!' exclaimed a woman beside me in the crowd, married, two children, husband an engineer, 'Now I'm tempted!'

The young, beautiful, sexually daring (and baring) dykes on bikes can appeal in a more directly sexual way to the 'normal' heterosexual housewife. The persona of the lesbian overburdened with politics is not seductive for her; lesbianism as part of a newly discovered interest in diversity – of identities and sexual acts *is*.

In a June 1993 copy of the English paper, the *Evening Standard,* Isabell Wolff visits a new lesbian sauna in London, called Dykes Delight. 'Forget the old dungarees image, the latest lesbians are bright, chic and glamorous . . . Everywhere you look, the joys of dykedom are being vigorously and joyfully extolled'. The funny thing is that no one extolled the joys of dykedom more vigorously than the lesbian feminists of the 1970s. In fact, at the time there was a veritable surge of lesbian activity by previously heterosexual women. Lesbianism was the highest form of feminism in which pleasure and politics were joined in perfect harmony. Differences between lesbians were of secondary importance. But however much they sung it from the mountain top, the media didn't choose to hear.

Wolff goes on to opine:

> If prejudices against lesbians still exist, they are probably less frequently expressed since lesbians are, to put it crudely, a lot harder to spot these days. The androgynous, dungareed, cropped-headed dykes with shoulders like the back of a sofa are still around, but in far smaller numbers . . . No longer is lesbianism a byword for dour, physical unattractiveness.

To be fair, the writer does bring in some lesbian voices of scepticism about what all this attention really means, but the overall message is how cool it is to be a dyke, especially now that the boring old lesbians are in retreat. And what did those boring old farts represent besides unattractiveness? Unmistakably, it must be politics. At the end of Wolff's article, 'Jane' – she can't use her real name – claims she does not feel oppressed. 'Jane' then goes on to catalogue the things she can't do openly or in public because she's a lesbian.

> Women are no longer lesbian because they're feminist and man-hating. They are lesbians because that's their preference, and they no longer feel they have to dress in a frumpy way. What we're all saying is 'OK, I'm a lesbian, I'm good looking and I'm going to have lots of fun.'

I'm sad that 'Jane' can't see the absurdity of her statement. She's bought the polarization which the media has grabbed onto and parrots it back to them. She is standing right next to an insight which begs to be seen: she can dress however she wants, still have fun *and* proclaim a fierce feminism. Camille Paglia would love her.

Paglia, who wrote *Sexual Personae – Art and Decadence from Nefertiti to Emily Dickinson* and *Sex, Art and American Culture,* and writes about Madonna as if she personally discovered her, endlessly plays the media's favourite running dog in the campaign against feminism and lesbianism. Like the ex-communist of the cold war period, she claims she knows what she is talking about. Because she couches her critique of feminism and lesbianism in academic and polemic discourses, and because she purports to speak from the position lesbian, her attacks seem more fresh and radical than the tired clichés she actually deploys. Paglia cravenly allows herself to be used as a legitimizer, giving (supposedly) an 'intellectual' veneer to conservative discomfort with the *politics* of feminism and lesbianism. Paglia is the media's current sweetheart, quoted widely whenever anyone wants to have a go at lesbian feminism. The irony is that Camille missed the lesbian–chic boat completely, complaining only a few years ago that there were no hot lesbians to fuck.

Some confusing stuff is definitely going on in the print media, but who gains from it and who gets used or abused or finally fucked over is another question. If lesbians collude mindlessly with the denunciations and ugly stereotyping of an image of the lesbian feminist of the 1970s (always the dungarees, the flannel shirt, the large – or shrewish – body, the plain and politically stern visage) they are not just claiming pleasure and their right to be a different *style* of lesbian – they are also feeding into the larger societal forces which are out to denounce feminism's 'excesses'. This denunciation (which includes nasty jokes) is about a construction of feminism's excesses which are, it is suggested, largely the work of the extremist lesbian. These 'excesses' include much of the radical political agenda of feminism, including its analyses of the social, cultural and economic. By excess, I mean feminism's and lesbian feminism's challenge to femininity, to what it is to be womanly, to fashion, to the uses of language, to notions of the naturalness of motherhood, to male domination, to violence against women. In this discourse lesbianism itself in its *lesbian-feminist* guise is often construed as an excess. Definitely to be avoided; excessive not in the cool, surface-obsessed shock techniques of the late 1980s or early 1990s sexual challenges, but in its endless seriousness. This idea of excess exists within lesbianism itself but there it is often the excess of the butch/femme relationship or of lesbian sadomasochists which comes in for stick – the very images which the popular media call upon and name cool, stylish and sexy.

What we can see is the way in which lesbianism as a practice, lesbianism as a transgressive erotic charge and a signalling of the blurred edge between fashion and a sort of postmodern 'fuck you', *as well as* lesbianism representing the politics of feminism (increasingly attacked as politically correct, rigid, silencing and humourless) all appear much more openly in a variety of media representations. The way in which the lesbianism of the first categories is welcomed by some observers as validating sexual diversity and choice has to be pitted against the continuing, perhaps accelerating identification of the lesbian persona with the ridiculed and reviled radical politics of feminism and lesbian feminism. The two seemingly polarized images of the lesbian I have referred to do not necessarily form a coherent opposition to each other: the fashion shot redolent of lesbianism usually makes no reference to the stridently anti-fashion lesbian politico. The two images of lesbianism exist at the same time, one young and provocatively attractive and fashionable, the second older, dowdy, prescriptive and overtly political. Both images are fantastical; neither image corresponds any more to the multilayered realities of lesbians' lives than other media caricatures of women do.

It's a difficult line to draw – or to walk. On the one hand there is much to critique in the feminisms and lesbian feminisms of the 1970s, but certainly not on mainstream media's terms! Within feminism and lesbian feminism many have expressed an interest in discussions of such things as ambivalence, desire, fantasy; about challenging overdetermined notions of female suffering and victimization as if there were never a space for negotiation or resistance; about exclusionary, racist and ethnocentric practices.

The notion of shifting multiple identities giving texture and meaning to questions of race, class, sex and gender has appealed to many. But – and here is the rub – the way in which all this plays itself out in popular culture is quite different. Diversity, if it is devoid of any serious notion of resistance, is a bit like rainbow 'freedom rings' – pretty and possibly signifying friendliness but nothing much else. Why the hell shouldn't lesbians (or any women) be able to wear clothes which go against what girls are supposed to wear, clothes which are utilitarian and plain? What's wrong with making a political critique of the imperatives of femininity? Why shouldn't feminists strip away the froth in order to reveal the money-grubbing ugliness of the fashion and beauty business? But this sort of politics cannot be taken-on whole by women's magazines – they can't digest it. However contradictory their contents have been for the past twenty years, these magazines are driven by huge industries, not only by cultural imperatives.

And yet . . . the disturbing but wonderful thing about newsstand women's magazines (and other forms of the media) is that I am continuously approaching them with critical ambivalence. I love the thing I am compelled to critique. In the present gallop to embrace popular culture, many lesbian feminists, in a reaction to an overly moralistic and proscriptive condemnation of all things popular (and overwhelmingly heterosexual) by earlier lesbian critics, seem to have lost their way. They wanted to escape the blanket denunciations of popular women's magazines which allowed no room for the possibility of personal pleasure when reading those magazines. But insisting that marginalized or disempowered people can 'read' dominant cultures with affect is one thing. Losing interest in attempts to create alternative challenges to dominant cultures is another. And a loss of interest in anything outside 'culture' is unforgivable.

There is no reason for lesbians to abandon even fierce criticisms, at the same time that they enjoy and consume popular culture. Popular culture as represented in women's magazines has never presented a monolithically smooth face – forget the models for now. At least since the 1970s these magazines have lost any unified frames for themes such as family, marriage, birth control, religion, abortion and, more and more, sexuality. Ironically, some of this was undoubtedly a response to the militancy and direct challenges with which feminism attacked the magazines. Turning the pages of many American, British and Australian magazines is like seeing a discourse stumble, destabilize itself and a page later straighten up and plunge on only to repeat the process.

However, delicious contradictions aside, women's magazines and women's features in newspapers are not the signal of a big new ground shift. To give them that power would be a mistake, even in a time of political uncertainty and the primacy given to representations and language as constitutive processes. There is no reason to give up partaking of women's magazines or some of the fashions they tout because of their weaknesses and conservatism, nor for their sad-assed attempts to co-opt a 'liberated' woman or chic lesbian into their pages. Most of us can come out unscathed after regular and continuing immersion in the glossy or not so glossy pages. And those passing pleasures can be separated from the necessary continuing critiques of the very object which brings pleasure. I refuse to abdicate my right or political need to criticize cultural artefacts which in my daily life I also enjoy. The pleasures I derive from reading and looking at women's magazines form a small part of my life as a lesbian still committed to resistance and change – and that's fun. If I were magically given the choice between reading *Vanity Fair* and immediately achieving some of the radical goals of the sort of lesbian feminism I believe in, I'm not worried about which way I'd go. But the reality of the non-magical world is that change is not immediate, we live our everyday lives, work for and dream of change, all at the same time. Who knows, perhaps lesbians will create new subversive possibilities through *their* appropriation of popular culture's eager but limited fascination with yet another marginalized group's exotic possibilities.

Let's face it, style and fashion are pretty ephemeral wherever they occur – in the pages of women's magazines, hyped up for sales, or on the streets or urban cities, where succeeding age and identity groups lay special claim to the importance and meanings of their look, their style. Lesbian appearance in magazines is often contradictory and deeply ambivalent. The fashion industry constantly searches out novelty (and capitalism new markets). The politics of a generation of women who identify with the naughty but exciting image of lesbians, which surfaces with more frequency in the fashion spreads of various news-stand magazines, will have to sharpen in order to maintain more than a superficial pose of rebellion. They can still wear lipstick and leather if they want. They may still discover that lipstick and leather look hopelessly old-fashioned in ten years' time.

A sharper politics would challenge the co-option of the sexy young kinky girl into fashion at the expense of any coherent politics. It might discover that style is only skin deep and that the questions which 1970s feminists posed deserve attention, possibly new answers, and definitely new tactics, from lesbians in the 1990s. It would not necessarily be a politics to warm the cockles of many older lesbian feminists' hearts. A recognition that the struggles of feminists in the 1970s and 1980s has brought us to a place where their sullen or sexy stares can grace the pages of the fashion mag.

'COP IT SWEET':
LESBIAN CRIME FICTION

Gillian Whitlock

It is Christmas and summer in (Claire McNab's) Australia: 'searing' summer mornings, 'breathless with the stored heat of a series of brassy days'; 'the eucalyptus gums hang their grey-green leaves in the breathless heat'. Close enough, though vaguely asthmatic. Certainly 'tis the season to be pursuing the thrills of reading crime fiction, consuming this body of texts rather than dissecting the corpus. There is plenty ripe for reading: classics of the lesbian crime genre like Wilson's *Murder in the Collective* and *Sisters of the Road*: police procedurals like McNab's Carol Ashton trilogy and Katherine V. Forrest's Kate Delafield quartet; more recent and experimental narratives – Wilson's *Gaudi Afternoon* and Finola Moorhead's *Still Murder* – and the parodic: Mary Wings' *She Came Too Late*. Dyke detectives abound: Ellen Hart's Jane Lawless (sic) is a restaurant owner; Eve Zaremba's Helen Keremos is a Canadian PI readily seduced by the prospect of 'an easy hundred'; Mary Morell's Lucia Ramos is both lesbian and Chicana, doubly marked. Crime fiction is now the most lucrative type of genre writing, and (like it or not) the most prolific and widely circulated form of lesbian writing.[1]

Crime fiction is not only one of the most popular genres for women readers and writers in the past ten years, it is also a genre which lesbians have appropriated. Indeed since the mid 1980s it is probably the main genre in which lesbians have situated themselves, as writers and as readers. Why is this so? A quick glance across the range of recent crime fictions by women highlights the emergence of a number of private investigators who are prime examples of independent, articulate women: Paretsky's V.I. Warshawski, Sue Grafton's Kinsey Millhone, K.V. Forrest's Kate Delafield. Paretsky's creation has been particularly successful, becoming the basis of a film starring Kathleen Turner and a radio serial in Britain. We need to think carefully about what kind of representation of women is facilitated by the genre; here Paretsky's character is paradigmatic: mid-thirties, physically fit, financially and emotionally independent with a strong sense of community and self-sufficiency. The genre promotes a characterization of women which escapes some of the hetero/sexist preferences of the dominant culture. My main concern here will be with lesbian readers and writers of crime fiction.

Consuming crime fiction is proving to be infinitely more pleasurable for readers than for critics. For while on the one hand I have this collection of crime fictions which bring lesbians into popular culture in an unprecedented way, I have on the other hand a muster of critical articles which register anxiety about this form of genre writing. For the past decade or so, many lesbian crime writers and readers find in the rewriting of detective fiction a means of struggling with gender definitions and sexual politics. Lesbian/feminist intellectuals, on the other hand, are wary. As critics they pay scant attention to these fictions, when they do discuss it they are worried, grudging, out of sorts. I want to begin by exhuming this corpus of criticism to consider why those of us who are professional readers, critics and teachers are so hesitant about the dyke detective. I then want to go on to consider what cultural work is being done by lesbian crime fiction, and to suggest that these widely-read novels intervene as agents of change, displacing and replacing negative representations of lesbian women with positive ones appropriated from the dominant culture and transformed in the process.

POPULAR CULTURE AND LESBIAN CRITICISM: THE UPRIGHT READER

In her overview of lesbian fiction from 1969 to 1989, *The Safe Sea of Women,* Bonnie Zimmerman views lesbian fiction as the expression of a collective 'myth of origins'. Her chapters use recent fictions to chart the representative journey of the lesbian hero, from coming-out through falling in love to setting-up housekeeping in Lesbian Nation. This mythography privileges writers such as Monique Wittig, June Arnold and Rita Mae Brown, and celebrates a period which Zimmerman characterizes as 'the collective voice of lesbians'. It is also a narrative of a fall from grace in some respects, for she argues that in the 1990s the lesbian novel is sustained not by community but by commerce. Although the lesbian publishing industry is now more prolific than it has ever been, with an audience which sustains more alternative presses and journals than before as well as a place in the mass market for a lesbian readership, Zimmerman laments the loss of a visionary, communal and mythic voice:

> With the commercial success of lesbian culture, we can buy our books and records and our long holiday weekend at a music festival without giving a second thought to the making and sustaining of an alternative lesbian vision (p. 208).

Like many lesbian critics, Zimmerman is uncomfortable with the commercial success of lesbian popular fiction. Her analysis constructs a binary opposition in which the idea of Lesbian Nation, communal identity and fictions which are selective and mythic have been lost in the present preoccupation with compromise and accommodation. In these terms the emergence of the lesbian detective novel as the quintessential lesbian genre is a sign of malaise. Zimmerman's perspective celebrates the lesbian and feminist subcultures of the 1970s as a golden age. It canonizes, and is organized in terms of, certain forms of writing – the Utopia, the realist novel and autobiography most evidently – and is highly critical of forms of popular culture, like the romance, crime fiction and soaps. The lesbian heritage is carried forward not by the popular fictions of Forrest or McNab or Wings but by the 'complex, resonant and layered' fictions of Winterson, Wilson and Bayer. By examining these preferences closely, we can see that the emergence of a prolific and accessible array of lesbian fictions of all kinds in a mass market is a cause for concern and fret. Commerce threatens authenticity and political correctness.

Zimmerman's argument is produced almost completely within the context of lesbian fictions circulating is the US market. While recognizing the specificity of this context, I would argue that her preferences and priorities are widespread. For example in one of the best and most readable surveys of contemporary feminist fiction, *Sisters and Strangers,* Patricia Duncker considers contemporary lesbian crime fiction in her chapter 'On Genre Fiction'. This categorization is interesting, for it might equally well have been part of a later chapter 'Writing Lesbian'. In fact popular fiction is not considered as 'writing lesbian' by Duncker. In a chapter ranging across a number of fictions which represent 'the search for definition, and the search for a way to articulate and inhabit the word "Lesbian"', forms such as crime fiction and romance do not figure.

To her credit Duncker makes her preferences clear:

> I am not an addict of escapist fantasy and never read myself to sleep with thrillers, predictable science fiction, or romance pulp. I prefer fiction which directly confronts difficulty rather than evades it, and usually sitting upright (p. 195).

Again the values of the academy and the self-characterization of the highly literate are evident: popular forms are 'pulp', 'predictable' and sleep inducing. Readers are 'addicts', lacking discernment and seeking escape into a fantasy world which denies social, moral, ethical, political issues. The vigilant, politically informed reader – both physically and mentally 'upright', aware and engaged – prefers fictions which 'confront difficulty'.

Without wanting to obscure some differences of approach

between Zimmerman and Duncker, I do characterize both as examples of a form of lesbian feminist criticism which has emerged over those two decades which are generally recognized as an epoch in lesbian culture. Between 1970 and 1990 the politics of radical feminism gave lesbian feminists the basis for a vision of strong women-identified communities, the 'Lesbian Nation' as it is frequently referred to in the North American context. As Lillian Faderman recalls in her history of this period, the written word was extraordinarily important in the euphoric and rapid development of the lesbian feminist community.[2] Newspapers, journals, bookshops, publishing enterprises and special courses in women's writing and feminist literary criticism both formed and addressed a committed lesbian-feminist readership, a period which Bonnie Zimmerman recalls in the preface to *The Safe Sea of Women*.

But although most lesbian-feminist critics would, like Zimmerman, both recognize and reject the romanticism of the 'safe sea of women', it nevertheless remains that many of them have a preference for lesbian writing which is oriented to the collective and the mythic. Zimmerman stresses the failure of crime fiction in particular to follow this pattern:

> As a number of critics have recently pointed out, the movement of the lesbian hero toward Lesbian Nation that used to characterize the lesbian feminist novel of development is no longer a foregone conclusion. The detective, for example, may discover a lover as well as a solution to the mystery, but she doesn't necessarily find a lesbian community. Indeed the shift in popularity from SF to the mystery is indicative of the shift from the collective to the individual, since the detective is by convention a loner, while the utopian novel rests upon the assumption of community (p. 220).

There is a gap between the current production of lesbian-feminist writing, in particular increasing numbers of popular genre fictions which cater for this readership produced in the 1970s and 1980s, and the values of lesbian-feminist literary critics whose preferences remain attuned to an academic and cultural lesbian feminism which is sceptical of the mass market. Patricia Duncker addresses this issue specifically:

> The laws of the market-place [have] nothing to do with feminism, nor with quality. Publishers print what sells . . . Ironically a new Lesbian publishing house has taken the point to heart. Silver Moon Books' . . . editorial policy reflects the field research they have done during their years as lesbian and feminist booksellers. They know what sells. Not surprisingly, this is the lowest common denominator – easy cliché genres, romance, thrillers and detective stories. Whether these genres can be so easily transformed into interesting writing by an added lesbian presence remains to be proven (p. 41).

The objections of 'upright readers' to genre fiction are not to be dismissed lightly. These values are determined not by an unthinking élitism or dry academese. The preference for realism and for originality grows from a political commitment to feminist change, to challenging and subverting existing structures rather than reproducing existing forms of racism, sexism and homophobia. Writers and readers who choose a genre strongly marked by a traditional array of necessary motifs, characters, plots, locations and emotions, a 'corset' of conventions as Duncker characterizes them, are both 'supported' *and* 'confined'. The conventional shape of crime fiction carries as cargo heterosexual, masculinist, North American preferences which are hard to unpack.

The question is, at what point do these conventions of crime fiction break down sufficiently to produce what feminist critics might recognize as a political fiction? What has to change?

'SHAPE SHIFTING': IN SEARCH OF THE UPRIGHT TEXT

Some foundations of the edifice of crime fiction have to be undermined for feminist and lesbian writers to produce a politically sound version of the genre in the terms outlined by Zimmerman and Duncker. For example, although crime fiction has always attracted women writers in particular, women and female desire are a focus of hostility in the traditional crime fiction. Furthermore, Stephen Knight points out that the hard-boiled detective character is the unified bourgeois subject par excellence, for the genre developed as a response to the contradictions of the bourgeois society and operates ideologically to contain these contradictions.[3] Crime fiction traditionally locates and personifies social dysfunction in the deviant individual, the resolution of the narrative is a comfortable containment of guilt and violence. Prejudices about class, race, gender and sexuality are endemic to the 'corset' of crime fiction:

> Women don't fit into a trench coat and slouch hat . . . The hard-boiled private eye is a special figure in American mythology. It's a staple of the myth that he should be a cynical loner, a man at odds with society and its values. That's not something women usually relate to. Women aren't cynical loners – that's not how they like to work. It seems to me that if they want to go into the profession seriously, women writers will have to change the myth itself, instead of trying to fit themselves into it.[4]

One writer who is clearly concerned with finding the 'break point' between the conventions of crime writing and a lesbian-feminist mythology is Barbara Wilson. Her first novel, *Murder in the Collective*, is routinely discussed in overviews of the genre. The later *Sisters of the Road* is a more radical subversion; here the separation between the victim and the 'investigator' Pam Nilsen is gradually subverted through the progression of the narrative, with a final violent disruption in which Nilsen herself becomes the victim, comforted by the young prostitute she had set out to protect. As Paulina Palmer suggests, the arrogance and self-sufficiency which are conventionally assigned to the sleuth are replaced by Nilsen's increasing dependence and fallibility. Instead of depicting the sleuth as a unitary figure, Wilson depicts Pam's subjectivity as contradictory and heterogenous.[5]

A later novel, *Gaudi Afternoon*, breaks with the contours of mystery writing more radically. The developments in Wilson's later fiction suggest some of the 'shape shifting' which is necessary for crime and mystery fiction to begin to appropriate the qualities which Duncker associates with lesbian-feminist writing: 'confrontational, contradictory, revealing a witty grasp of the bizarre'. There is significant change in characterization, plot and language between the mystery, *Murder in the Collective*, and the mysterious *Gaudi Afternoon*. Here all ideas of a genuine or authentic sexual identity are put into question, there is a radical critique of all categories of identity. *Gaudi Afternoon* occupies a gay/lesbian perspective which Judith Butler outlines as actively contesting the categories of sex, dissolving the 'natural' or 'original' coherence among sexed bodies, gender identities and sexualities.[6]

The Australian writer Finola Moorhead makes some similar shifts in her crime novel, *Still Murder*. Here too the qualities of what might be described as postmodern fictions are employed to challenge radically the conventions of crime fiction. Although the narrative begins according to convention, with an unidentified corpse and the beginnings of a process of investigation, traditional certainties never take hold. The text itself is not integrated with any single narrator or perspective, there is no omniscient narrator or authoritative detective. In *Gaudi Afternoon* the embedded text – the novel *La Grande y su hija* – draws attention to the fictionality and provisionality of the larger text. So too in *Still Murder* there is no 'whole' text. Rather the novel comprises a series of fragments, provisional texts in different forms (press cuttings, diary, letters, police notebooks, psychiatrist's report, transcript of an address). These refuse to stitch together neatly – only the reader gains access to them all, being presented with a series of vastly different and contradictory discourses. Nor is the reader allowed the comfort of reconciling these differences and contradictions by resorting to notions of 'character'. *Still Murder* foregrounds the discursive construction of text, and the provisionality of character. Here one is confronted with 'subjectivities' – partial and inconclusive constructions of self.

Here the perspective and knowledge of the investigator, Margot Gorman, a Detective Senior Constable in the National Crime Authority, is always defective and incomplete. The institutionalized nature of Margot's investigation is important, for it allows Moorhead to make a critique of the 'boy's network' – the interlocking structures of the police force, the NCA and, ultimately, the military. This novel gradually incorporates various elements of the policing structure and as the narrative unfolds these elements are deeply implicated in the diffusion of guilt and violence. The traditional crime fiction moves to the containment and individualization of guilt and violence; in *Still Murder* this is reversed. So the unidentified corpse found in the park begins a process in which violence and guilt metastasize and reveal the ongoing effects of the Vietnam war in Australian society and culture. The body in the suburban park in Sydney is finally located as part of a chain of violence which began with the rape of a child in Vietnam by an Australian soldier. The individualist and bourgeois implications of the conventional police procedural are found wanting here; violence occurs not in isolated crimes which are solved by logical deduction and investigation, but is part of a systemic, institutionalized and gendered oppression of women by men. Ultimately Margot is forced to recognize the *consistency* of gender, class and race differences, the place of the policing system *within* institutionalized violence.

The detective is also forced to renegotiate her relationship with women in the course of the narrative. At the outset Margot responds to references to phallocentrism ('considered dirty in the police force') in the same way she responds to other things French: dismissively. Her strong working-class orientation and her identification with the NCA causes her to view feminist discourse as academic and irrelevant. Margot's knowledge at the outset is that of 'the cop', yet this is increasingly undermined. One form of reverse discourse occurs in the ravings of the Madwoman, a form which allows Moorhead to introduce chunks of feminist theory and criticism, Shakespeare and the Eurythmics: 'Luce Irigaray considers female homosexuality to be a form of radical rupture in heterosexism and male domination and, at the same time, believes that all sexual practices represented in our culture are effects of an underlying phallocentrism that renders women socially, discursively and representationally subordinate (p. 65). Lesbians are the only outsiders to the culture of the 'Nam brotherhood, only the subculture of lesbian women, with their networks of women's organizations and knowledges, can make an effective response to the violence of the state. Ironically in the very process of recognizing the legitimacy of the lesbian subculture and the limitations of the police culture, Margot is beaten up by women from a Rape Action Group because she is 'the cop who was spying on our rape meeting'. There can be no easy accommodation between cop and lesbian; Moorhead resolutely refuses to entertain notions of a pluralist, liberal order.

Like *Gaudi Afternoon*, *Still Murder* is a complex and thorough re-vision of the genre of crime fiction. The major 'bones' of the generic corset are shaped anew as expectations of plot, characterization and narration are undone. They make the point that there can be an accommodation between crime fiction and lesbian-feminist politics and ideas, between genre writing and lesbian writing. Yet I suspect they do so at great cost. For while this kind of fictional play pleases the 'upright reader', the lesbian-feminist intellectual, part of the contract of genre writing is its engagement with popular culture, its appeal to 'support' a common reader with the corset of convention and expectation. No one ever read herself to sleep with *Still Murder* or *Gaudi Afternoon* – in fact both are relatively unknown, for the price of radical experimentation with form is audience and commercial appeal. We have, I suggest, found the upright text. We have, however, lost most of our readers.

Let's leave the upright reader, and look again at reading 'prone'.

'FUN READS'

I want to come back to that reader we left behind when discussing the 'upright text', the reader who is (in terms of Duncker's opposition) characterized as addicted and escapist and, implicitly, prone. I have to this point been outlining the specific sociohistorical context of a lesbian-feminist criticism in which forms of popular fiction are seen as problematic. To make popular writing visible and something other than an object of derision we need to take a different critical approach, to construct a different idea of text and reader, and a more precise sense of reading practices.

It is misleading to think of discrete audiences for 'high' and 'popular' lesbian writing. Many consumers of crime fiction, like me, also choose to read more experimental and realist fictions too. Nor can we presume that readers who do read only from mainstream, commercial or genre fictions do so without some critical judgment and self-knowledge about precisely what it is such fictions offer. As I have argued elsewhere, there is convincing evidence that consumers of popular cultural forms have strong preferences and 'police' the genre rigorously.[7] The fact is, we still have everything to learn about the audience for feminist detective fiction in general, and lesbian-feminist crime writing in particular. The commentaries I have discussed so far are based upon what Stuart Hall and others have called the 'literary-moral' definition of culture, albeit a definition which has been shaped in particular ways within the subculture of lesbian criticism. This criticism, whilst representing the taste of the lesbian intelligentsia, is not well suited to discerning and respecting different reading patterns, and different subcultures within the lesbian community itself.

Those of us who work with lesbian writing might well learn from lesbian scholarship in other disciplines, where there is a keener sense of different formations of lesbian identification, of specific sociohistorical determinants of what it means to be lesbian. For example the work of Sheila Jeffreys and Lillian Faderman teaches us not only that the term 'lesbian' is a recent invention, but that throughout the twentieth century in particular there have been changing self-definitions of lesbians as well as a number of quite different constructions of the lesbian in literary, artistic, legal, medical, psychiatric and political discourses.[8] Faderman introduces the project of her most recent book, *Odd Girls and Twilight Lovers,* in the following way:

> My goal has been to trace the development of 'the lesbian'. There is, of course, no such entity outside of the absurd constructions of textbook and pulp novel writers of the first half of the twentieth century. I have been interested rather in the metamorphoses and diversity of lesbians as they related individually and/or collectively to changing eras in American life' (p. 7).

There is a pluralist sense of lesbian subcultures at work here: changes through time (various identifications of female same-sex loving as romantic friendship, as sickness, as twilight loves, as part of the Lesbian Nation) and the various sites of lesbian identification in the large cities in particular – the colleges, the bars, the military and so on. From this perspective, lesbian popular culture – not only fictions but also music, cartoons, film, theatre – is part of an ongoing and complex process of lesbian identification.

A grasp of reading as a social event is particularly important for those of us who discuss lesbian writing, for fictions have played a critical role in identifications of, and by, lesbians. There is a profound connection between reading and the social situation of lesbian women. I can think of no better demonstration of this than Alison Hennegan's article 'On Becoming a Lesbian Reader'. Hennegan is one of the few lesbian critics to take up the question of 'how it is and what it is that we 'read' '.[9] She does this in a way which is unashamedly autobiographical and subjective, and in this way conveys the desire for books which would give her pleasure. The autobiographical nature of Hennegan's article also allows her to represent the specific context of her search: in the outer suburbs of London in 1960 – 'any teenager in search of lesbian popular fiction was in trouble . . . "Gay" wasn't there as a term, yet, and for many lesbians "lesbian" was a word arousing terror, self-hatred and contempt' (p. 167). What Hennegan seeks are fictions which are not rigidly organized in terms of heterosexual desire, books 'which would help me recognize, respect and enact my sexuality', and she describes this as a 'need', a critical part of the process of self-identification and recognition (p. 169). Given that there was in 1960 no mass-market lesbian fiction, she finds her own solution: 'I created my own "popular fiction", developed my own much cherished canon. This canon was comprised of little known writers, disobedient readings of fictions by Dickens, Austen, and "my Greeks" – homosexual heroes, philosophers and poets who do not equate psychological maturity, personal fulfilment and social worth with heterosexuality, marriage and parenthood.'

Hennegan's recollection is a powerful statement of how reading is frequently an important part of 'coming out'. It is why in the idealized lesbian bar of K.V. Forrest's novel *Murder at the Nightwood Bar* there is the bar counter and the dance floor, tables set up for games, a jukebox, *Hill Street Blues* on the TV – and a large bookcase: four crowded shelves perhaps ten feet long. Kate Delafield's offsider, Taylor, observes 'I guarantee you . . . this is the only bar in the world with a bookcase' (p. 14). Why? Toward the end of the novel one of the lesbian women gives the answer: 'I found a whole gay *world* through all the stuff I found in feminist bookstores' (p. 174). In *The Beverly Malibu* books become the currency of Delafield's membership of the Nightwood Bar community, a source of warmth and close comfort, and a source of recognition and comradeship amongst the closeted homosexuals of the Los Angeles Police Force.

However, when thinking about the importance of reading and of the written text for lesbians, I also have in mind that radical insight into representation and the making of identities which lesbian studies allow. The 'making' of the lesbian throughout the twentieth century is a fine instance of how provisional, how context dependent, are ideas of identity, authenticity, the 'natural'.

These categories are constantly in the process of being made, of being discursively constructed, in an ongoing social process of contest, struggle and change. The social is unmade and remade, disarticulated and rearticulated as meanings circulate, become vulnerable to appropriation, transformation and reincorporation into new configurations. As Jonathan Dollimore argues, the history of perversion in particular shows how culture is formed, consolidated, destabilized, reformed; here in particular the importance of materialist critiques, which show the contingency of the social and its potential instability, which places meanings in the content of their histories, is clear.[10]

Lesbian writers have deployed diverse strategies to create the lesbian on their own terms. Radclyffe Hall takes on the negative identity of the lesbian and transforms its terms, Rita Mae Brown reverses the dominant/subordinate terms of binary thinking about homosexuality, Barbara Wilson undermines all essentialist notions of gender and sexual identities which, in *Gaudi Afternoon,* become performance rather than expression of identity. In this process of definition and resistance what we read, how we read, which texts become freely available and which remain marginal, are important political issues. Ultimately these are the stakes on the table in debates about the political correctness of lesbian fictions and feminist critiques of popular culture, which need to be seen in a wider context of a struggle over meanings and explanations of lesbian sexuality. To return to Hennegan again, she reminds us that in 1960 'gay' wasn't a word yet, and prevailing connotations of 'lesbian' invited self-hatred. Now, thirty years on, both of these terms circulate in mass-market fictions; however, their meaning is not settled within the lesbian community or in the larger context of the dominant culture. Women now have unprecedented opportunities to create communities and lifestyles; no less than the dominant culture, these subcultures present a rapid and continual flux in values and mores, producing constant metamorphoses in (and debates about) the conception of lesbianism and the nature of lesbian communities and lifestyles.[11]

A scholarship oriented to various lesbian cultures rather than lesbian aesthetics allows us to approach the popular literature which is produced for and consumed by large numbers of lesbian and other readers in a different way. It allows us to ask what this text or this genre means to a given audience – a readership which is historically and temporally situated. This kind of approach to popular culture, in the work of Janice Radway, Angela McRobbie and others, does not present the reader of genre fiction as an addict, lacking in preferences, but as historical subjects with some understanding and control of their own behaviours, even such understanding and behaviour is determined in complex ways by the social formation in which they live.[12] What we badly need now is some sense of how these popular fictions are read outside of the lesbian-feminist intelligentsia, and how lesbian readers either adopt or adapt the various meanings of lesbian sexuality which they encounter, what they take on board as functional in their understanding of their own sexual preferences.

This perspective suggests that our critical practice should be extended. The kind of lesbian-feminist readings of individual crime fictions which have proliferated to date are based upon an aesthetic which accords significance to discrete, individual texts in a way which is foreign to genre fiction. These texts are read in quantity and for repetition to some extent, they should be approached in terms of conventions and types. In fact we need to unpack the term 'crime fiction' and think about the different forms: the 'whodunnit', the country house murder, the hard-boiled detective, the police procedural and so on, for each of these traditions has a different set of codes and conventions – precedents which both writers and readers are highly conscious of. We can approach genre fiction by reading *across* a series of texts in terms of organization by type, perhaps by author function ('Agatha Christie'; 'P.D. James'), or by a character function ('The Pam Nilsen Series'; the Detective Inspector Carol Ashton Mystery'; 'A Kate Delafield Mystery'; 'a V.I. Warshawski bestseller'). I want to conclude this chapter by reading across the Kate Delafield series by

K.V. Forrest, a quartet which specifically raises issues of lesbian politics and identity in the 'corset' of the police procedural. The Delafield Mysteries are published in America by Naiad Press, 'America's Lesbian-Easy-Read' publishers, and in Great Britain by HarperCollins. This series is the most accessible and commercially successful lesbian crime fiction, and a template for other writers (Claire McNab's 'Carol Ashton' series is explicitly related back to Forrest's example). Here we move to texts which have sustained an ongoing contract with a large and international readership, a contract which (as we have seen) is not met by the likes of *Still Murder* and *Gaudi Afternoon*.

Can Kate Delafield come 'out' in the corset of genre writing? How is the lesbian 'made' in the form of the police procedural?

CLOUDS AND BIRTHDAY CAKES

In Omaha, Nebraska, there is a bright yellow building on a main street. It is across from a police station and a parking lot filled with scores of police cars. Having come out as a working-class lesbian in the 1950s, where McCarthyism was still giving its tenor to American life and lesbians were outlaws, I cannot see so many police cars at once without an almost unconscious sharp intake of breath. Police cars always meant trouble in those days, and there is something inside that does not forget. But it was almost the 1990s and I was here with Rhonda . . . [She] brought me to the Max, a huge lesbian and gay bar that is housed in the big yellow building.

She told me that on weekend nights the place is so crowded with homosexual men and women that their sociability often pours out onto the street. 'But what about all those police?' I asked. She did not even seem to understand the import of my question at first. Then she explained, 'But we're happy they're here. There's a strip joint not too far away, and those guys sometimes try to cause trouble. The police

come to help us. It's a real comfort to have them so close.' I
understood for the hundredth time since I began my research
on lesbian life in twentieth-century America that there are no
constants with regard to lesbianism, neither in the meaning of
love between women nor in the social and political life that is
created through it. (*Odd Girls*, p. 305)

This is a lengthy quotation but, as is so often the case, Lillian
Faderman writes with an acute sense of the shifting meanings of
lesbianism, the ongoing metamorphoses in meaning and attitudes
which have occurred throughout the twentieth century. Here she
deftly contrasts herself, a woman who came out in the 1950s, and
Rhonda, a young college graduate who wears lipstick and eye-
shadow and restores cars for a living. Both lesbian, they occupy
quite different worldviews. The icons which gauge their
differences here are important: the gay bar, the police station. For
lesbians in the 1950s the fact that these two institutions might
occupy the same landscape, or reach an accommodation, is
unimaginable. For a young lesbian in the late 1980s, their
relationship is quite different.

The fact that a series of crime fictions in the shape of the police
procedural might become the most popular form of lesbian
writing is, to some, equally unimaginable. Here, too, there is,
metaphorically speaking, a relationship between mutually
exclusive territories. It is much easier to anticipate the setting of
lesbian whodunnits where the investigator is an amateur sleuth, her
'institution' a radical-feminist collective – such as we find in the
Nilsen series. Police enter the Nilsen series hardly at all; when they
do they are the unimaginative and vaguely incompetent boors we
would conventionally expect. The police procedural is a form
where the 'bones' of the generic corset are firmly in place – a
murder is investigated in the rigid terms of police practice, with
the rigours of formal prosecution and institutionalized punishment
in view. There is a clear designation of criminality and attribution
of responsibility for crime. The detective is operating from within

a hierarchically organized police force, which binds him/her into a set of formal relationships and responsibilities as part of a professional code of ethics. All of these conventions are sustained in the Delafield series. The detective, Kate Delafield, is in many respects the conventional authoritative cop of the procedural, with clear ideas of civilization, criminality and social justice.

However, as Faderman suggests, boundaries that seemed inevitable and fixed in the 1950s and 1960s have shifted. The gay bar and the police station no longer stand as markets of institutions which are in eternal and binary opposition as embodiments of freedom and patriarchy, homosexuality and homophobia, authenticity and oppression respectively. Their relationship is more contingent. For me, one of the pleasures of the Delafield series is the way that the police procedural can develop a complex and contradictory set of expectations about lesbian identity, a representation of lesbianism which is finely tuned in historical and social detail. There is a note at the beginning of Mary Morell's lesbian police mystery *Final Session*: 'Fiction is a type of literary work based on imagination rather than reality. This book is an act of fiction . . . Everything and everyone . . . is totally without basis in reality. If they seem to resemble any real person, place or thing, it is sheer coincidence, like a cloud resembling a birthday cake.' The Delafield mysteries are based on a quite different epistemology, where the form of the police procedural *allows* a very detailed analysis of persons, places, things. The idea that generic conventions might facilitate (rather than impede) authorship contradicts deeply held assumptions about writing and creativity. Yet the four Delafield fictions to date suggest that the conventions of the procedural *enable* a complex and very contemporary mapping of the relationships between locations which formerly seemed mutually exclusive and in eternal opposition: the gay bar and the police station.

For example the schematic quality of characterization and plot in the procedural is one of the clearest signs that the fiction has no pretensions to realism, and also a convention which allows a critical exploration of place and identity. The Delafield novels are highly schematic – characters are found in settings which represent their essential characteristics quite faithfully. This is clearly evident in the first Delafield novel, *Amateur City*. Here the detective investigates a murder in a high-rise office block. The space is literally mapped out in the novel, and the placement and furnishing of each office, the dress of each occupant, is indicative of politics, sexuality, ethnicity, gender. Likewise in *The Beverly Malibu*, the third novel, where the crime is committed in a block of apartments. Here too the placement of characters, their dress and surroundings are symptomatic. There is nothing subtle about this – the apartment of the lesbian women has a vague scent of lavender! The detective fails to identify the killer *in situ*, because key items have been removed to blur her true identity. The placement of the second novel, *Murder at the Nightwood Bar*, is no less symptomatic. The Nightwood Bar is a lesbian bar, as I have already suggested it is furnished with various symbols of lesbian identification, and with a carefully selected cross-section of lesbian types: butch, femme, and a distinct US west coast racial and ethnic mix. Through the investigation of a crime, each of these sites is entered by the police, the detectives Taylor and Delafield. Taylor is a straightforward representation of the homophobia, racism and sexism which characterizes the Los Angeles Police Department. It is one of the ironies of the series that Kate Delafield is professionally paired with the homophobic Ed Taylor and privately teamed with a variety of female lovers – Ellen, Aimee, Anne.

It is the identification of Delafield as cop and lesbian, as an inhabitant of the Nightwood Bar and the LAPD, two very different communities, which breaks down any simple binary opposition of these locations. Although markers like Patton, the most radical and separatist lesbian at the Nightwood Bar (a card-carrying dyke', as Delafield might say), and Ed Taylor seem to assert the incompatibility of these sites, Delafield herself marks their interrelationship. The nature of this interrelationship is increasingly complex. In *Amateur City* the separation of public and private life is rigidly maintained by Kate Delafield:

> 'Do I have an L on my forehead? What made you think I'm a
> . . . lesbian?' She could not prevent the slight hesitation;
> reticence and caution had become ingrown self-protective
> behaviour on which her professional survival depended
> (p. 111).

In the second novel the location of the crime at the Nightwood
Bar blurs this distinction, in solving the crime Delafield enters a
space where her private and public worlds become enmeshed.

The difficulties of occupying any identity consistently and
coherently are evident in the characterization of Delafield. The
fictions quite explicitly present behaviours as contingent and not
naturally consistent. For example, the outburst of violence which
has been commented on by critics in *Murder at the Nightwood Bar*
is quite explicitly a source of worry in the text itself, and raised as
a problem of professional and sexual identities: 'A police officer
must always perform with poise' – and while she had used force
out of necessity, her rage as a lesbian woman had also been a major
component (p. 109). The combination of her profession and her
preferences is also explicitly signalled as a seeming contradiction:

> 'Maybe now you can see our whole problem with you as a
> cop. The people you're really protecting are heterosexual
> white middle-class males and their female slaves'.
>
> Kate fought down the surge of fury. Regardless of the
> inflammatory rhetoric, how could she not agree with the
> kernel of truth in what Patton had just said? (p. 92).

These inconsistencies lead to a depiction of identities which are
anything but essential or natural. Across the series of fictions a
number of causes of lesbianism are expressed. Each needs to be read
in terms of an unsettled field of identifications. Various characters
represent lesbian sexuality as an illness to be 'cured' as a disturbance
ripe for psychoanalytic intervention, as a passing phase, as an
immature sexual preference. Ed Taylor has a complicated theory

about the differences between 'perverts' and 'faggots' and 'freaks'. In *Murder by Tradition* a critique of the alleged unnaturalness of homosexuality is a critical part of the resolution of the court case. Delafield also occupies different roles as a lesbian. This is foregrounded when she consults with her dyke mentor, Maggie, about her shift from butch to femme in *Murder by Tradition*. Kate Delafield's assertion that lesbianism is natural, however, is contradicted elsewhere in *Murder at the Nightwood Bar,* such as her earlier refusal to be the authoritative lesbian: 'How the hell should I know, Kate thought in irritation. Am I for chrissakes an expert of all lesbians who ever lived?' As Paulina Palmer cautions, we need to be wary of assuming Kate Delafield speaks for K.V. Forrest. Like Faderman, Forrest is careful to associate lesbian identity with a specific context and speaking position. So Kate's idea of lesbian identity is traced to her age (40-plus) and her consciousness of her sexuality prior to the changes of the late 1960s. Conversely, her lover Aimee Grant's perspective is located in a quite different and much more recent moment in history. There are different generations of lesbian experience across the community. A middle-aged lesbian, Kate's struggle with 'coming out' is contrasted with the gay pride of younger men and women in Los Angeles.

Across the series of Delafield novels lesbian sexuality and culture is an unstable, shifting terrain. *Amateur City* was first published in 1984. The fourth, *Murder by Tradition,* in 1991. In this most recent Delafield mystery, the detective finally severs ties with her offsider and faces the test of integrity foreshadowed in the preceding novel as she faces the prospect of 'outing' in the courtroom. Although these developments could be read individualistically in terms of Delafield's moral development as a character, her growing recognition of 'her community' as a lesbian, the impetus is quite different I think. Each of the Delafield mysteries can be dated quite specifically, and the revolutionary changes in the gay community caused by the emergence of the full dimensions of the AIDS crisis have caused a sea change in the series. Like all police procedurals, Forrest's are absolutely precise in detail of place and time; we are

told several times that this isn't *Murder She Wrote* what might make
for good television drama is damned poor police work! The
Nightwood Bar in 1985 has a collection tin for AIDS Project LA,
in 1990 the full-blown AIDS crisis and the resultant moral panic
has intensified homophobia and, as a response, produced a new set
of coalitions in the gay community. The changes in Delafield's
private and professional life need to be seen in relation to these
rapidly changing priorities of the gay community in the 1990s. In
this most recent novel the detail and legality of police procedures
is represented with unprecedented care and precision. There is no
mystery about 'whodunnit' here, the criminal is found in the first
fifty pages. The suspense is produced by the difficulty of
prosecuting a case of gaybashing as first degree murder. The victim
is a queen and a drug user, the defence alleges 'natural revulsion'
as justification of the crime. It is only a meticulous enactment of
proper procedures at the bloody scene of the crime (a newly
virulent site with the awareness of AIDS) and in the courtroom
which produces the final verdict of guilty.

Across the Delafield series this close attention to detail
characteristic of the police procedural produces a finely-tuned
description of the lesbian subculture on the west coast of the USA.
In *The Beverly Malibu* Paula Grant, a retired scriptwriter, invokes
the technical term 'walla', used in film making to describe the
presence of a scene: 'unscripted, constant background that's
recorded to give a particular scene realism. Like street noise, or
birds or night insects. That's called *walla*' (p. 23). Although the
Delafield novels are not realistic, they do nevertheless capture the
walla of west-coast lesbian ideas, taste, dress, politics in the 1980s
and the early 1990s. The detective is a voyeur par excellence, quite
literally licensed to probe and experience an 'eerie intimacy' with
the subjects of her investigation. As Delafield increasingly develops
her attachment to 'her' community, we come to know 'her' family
of lesbian women in some detail: we know their views about
Phyllis Schlafly and Candice Bergen, their liking for the Pointer
Sisters and *Hill Street Blues*, what parts of Los Angeles they feel 'at

home'. The conventions of the procedural allows all of this *walla* to be included in the interests of authentic detail; along the way it delivers to its audience a chronicle and sanction of the lesbian subculture which the detective frequents.

This reading of the Delafield novels suggests that the kind of discursive play and inconsistency which is foregrounded in experimental writing is not necessarily alien to the forms of genre fiction. We do popular cultural forms a disservice by discounting their complexities or the perceptiveness of their audiences. The 'Lesbian-Easy-Read' might be just that – easy to take up, readily available at the airport bookstore, discarded after one read. Both writer and reader are familiar with the conventions of the genre, tied in a performance of enacting their formulas in both the production and consumption of the text, but if these conventions are regarded as an impediment to a more authentic kind of literary production we disregard the extent to which they can enable a fiction which is discursively complex. I find it hard to lament the entry of lesbian writers into the mass market, and even harder to accept the opposition between 'commerce' and 'integrity' which organizes so many critiques of popular culture.

I am uncomfortably aware that I have now joined the ranks of those who 'slithered' into unreadable academic prose to discuss crime fiction. Patricia Duncker will place me alongside Sally Munt and Paulina Palmer, whose 'academic ingenuity' 'was much more sophisticated than the fiction they discuss'. She suggests 'perhaps they will now both write thrillers themselves' (p. 127).

Hm . . .

'It is Christmas and summer in Australia . . .'

MAKING A DRAMA OUT OF DIFFERENCE: *PORTRAIT OF A MARRIAGE*

Jenny Harding

BBC Television's *Portrait of a Marriage* was lavishly produced in the popular genre of historical costume drama, and transmitted in prime viewing time. Well before it went to air, journalists' temperatures were soaring. Evidently, explicit lesbianism on the BBC could not be ignored, though neither could it be allowed to hog the limelight. Most journalists responded by downplaying the significance of lesbianism and some stressed that the drama told the story of someone torn between two lovers, never mind their sexes. Nigel Nicholson complained to the *Times* of London that the dramatization of his book had concentrated on a brief and crazy escapade in the long and otherwise harmonious marriage of his parents, in which love had triumphed over infatuation (Merck, 1993).

Clearly, *Portrait of a Marriage* was already guaranteed success. It was deeply dangerous, but ultimately safe. Lesbianism threatened family life but was brought to heel through an assertion of duty and responsibility and an insistence on the rightful expression of these values through the institution of marriage. Although historically and culturally remote for many viewers, the marriage portrayed in upheaval could not fail to resonate with contemporary questions voiced in media and political discourses about the meaning of marriage to Britain's diverse populations.

Evidently, there is increasing concern that marriage may no longer function as a core unit in the social organization, cohesion and regulation of British society.[1] In this light, *Portrait of a Marriage* appears to put forward prototype terms and conditions for successful heterosexual marriage, with an emphasis on the mutual respect, indulgence and flexibility (within clearly defined limits) of both partners. However, the dramatization of Vita and Violet's lovemaking, which was passionate and convincing, cannot be explained away in full by the fragility of twentieth-century marriage. The sex scenes deserve more attention, because, in my view, they also attempt to spell out what it means to *be a sex,* and present a precise differentiation of masculinity and femininity.

SEX AND THE DRAMA OF DIFFERENCE

The possibility that *Portrait of a Marriage* may be more about heterosexuality than about homosexuality has been raised by both Elizabeth Wilson (1990) and Mandy Merck (1993). Both authors conclude that the drama provides a way of scrutinizing heterosexuality and the frailty of modern marriage, which is brought into focus through perversity. Wilson asks whether 'gay love' may be 'the lens through which heterosexual society is desperately peering at its own problematic practices' (p. 31). According to Wilson, *Portrait* was broadcast in the context of 'intense cultural ambivalence' as suggested by the 'higher visibility' of homosexuality in the British media at a time of anti-homosexual repression (hot on the heels of Clause 28). Merck adds to this the possibility that the institution of marriage is strengthened by 'the very homosexuality which threatens to destroy it' and the invention of a 'new man' and 'new woman' (p. 116). However, Merck's analysis needs to be developed to show in detail how particular representations of lesbian sex(uality) contribute to the redefinition of sexual difference and, through this, to the reinforcement of heterosexual relations.

Portrait of a Marriage probably did say a lot less about lesbians than about heterosexuals. However, in my view, the drama's representation of 'gay love' was not transparent, as the metaphor of a lens would suggest; rather, lesbian sex was brought into focus and made visible through exactly the same discourse as that which was capable of articulating a crisis in heterosexual marital relations.

In *Portrait*, the versions of lesbian sex presented on screen were not wild cards or disparate moments of sexual diversity, but steady and negative counterparts to revered elements of marriage. Thus, the drama persistently distinguished sexual desire from marriage, infatuation from love. Desire figured largely as homosexual, and love belonged to heterosexual marriage. Desire was treacherous, infantile and selfish, whereas marriage was loyal and secure, safeguarded by a sense of duty and responsibility to others. Set in the framework of this series of opposites, Vita and Violet's affair provided a stage for the continuing rehearsal of sex, as an act, an identity and a social position. The representations of lesbian sex in *Portrait* enabled a redefinition not only of the boundaries of marriage, but also of what it means to be a sex and, more precisely, what it means to be female.

But *how* did particular representations of lesbian sex simultaneously produce different characterizations of 'woman'? And how did this contribute to the reproduction of heterosexual relations? The drama persistently lurched between distinctive moments of gender-bending using the familiar genre of drag. Each lesbian sex scene was preceded by Vita's theatrical 'crossing over', in which her dress, deportment and conduct were dramatically transformed. More precisely, they and she were *masculinized*. When Vita suddenly appeared in jodhpurs, both Harold and Violet commented independently that she looked both mannish and fetching. Their communications of sexual approval appeared to be flavoured by viewing Vita as less feminine and, because of it, a potential seducer. Harold and Violet's comments implied that she had become more obviously sexual because she had become more masculine. Given Harold and Violet's already declared interests in same-sex sex, the brief exchanges around the jodhpurs contributed to a heightened sense of muddled sexuality and discontinuity between sex and gender. Viewers were compelled to wonder whether Harold desired Vita as a woman or a quasi man. Violet, who had always desired Vita, could openly express it now that Vita was less like a woman and more like a man. It was Vita's unfeminine conduct which Violet found especially appealing. Thus, Vita's masculinization crudely signalled a newly discovered perversity. Now, more than before, Vita was capable of having sex with Violet. Viewers were led to believe that her desire for Violet was framed through masculine eyes.

Through this example of drag, the active pursuit of desire and its fulfilment in sex was made entirely the prerogative of masculinity, and lesbianism became visible only through these particular enactments of butch/femme stereotypes. This version of lesbianism, and the narrowly defined version of femininity it implies, was crassly accentuated in a series of very camp scenes. As a prelude to sex, Vita was seen running across fields and leaping over gates in an athletic, uninhibited way, while Violet, dressed much less practically, stumbled and flapped helplessly behind, waiting for a display of gallantry by Vita. Similarly, in anticipation of scenes in which the two women were seen naked in bed, Vita appeared in drag as Violet's working-class soldier husband when the couple contrived to spend a night together in a bed-and-breakfast, and as her flamboyant and dashing tango partner in a bar during their first trip to France.

Drag in *Portrait* was significant because it made sure that lesbianism would be interpreted as a replication of heterosexual relations and that desire would be seen as inevitably heterosexual in its expression. Moreover, heterosexuality was rendered identical with an expression of desire from the position of a masculine subject. The heterosexualization of Vita and Violet's affair reached its conclusion as Vita competed with Denys Trefusis for sexual rights to Violet. Vita insisted that Violet was sexually faithful to her despite marrying Denys. The drama pursued this insistence to the point of explicit violence when, on hearing that Violet had slept with her husband, Vita raped her. In this way, lesbianism was brought into focus and made visible through an emphasis on (hetero)sexual fidelity and property, and the defence of these through violence. Of course, this is not to say that violence between lesbians does not exist. However, Vita and Violet's conduct was most readily understood from a particular heterosexual point of view. This was underlined by a focus on kissing and cuddling at one extreme, and rape, at the other, rather than the different and more obvious ways in which women may find pleasure in sex. In many scenes, passionate kissing petered out to leave a space usually filled by images of heterosexual copulation. Viewers were directed towards thinking of heterosexual pene-tration or drawing a blank – what *do* lesbians do in bed? The outcome was likely to be another representation of heterosexuality as the proper expression of desire. Nothing about *Portrait* contradicted this. The net effect was that Vita and Violet appeared to be copying heterosexuals.

The logic of heterosexuality assumes that male is directly connected to masculine and to man and female to feminine and woman (Butler, 1990). This sequence of association supports the expression of desire in heterosexual reproduction. *Portrait of a Marriage* was very good at sticking to and reinforcing the pairs of opposites – male/female, masculine/feminine, man/woman – which are necessary to the reproduction of heterosexuality. The drama ensured that the connections between male and man, and female and woman, were incontrovertible. The sex of the characters was never in dispute, nor was their social position as man or woman. In addition, 'sex' appeared immutable and fixed, by virtue of 'gender' seeming more plastic and variable (Butler, 1990). Manifestations of homosexuality could be explained as resulting from 'getting into' or 'putting on' the gender contra-indicted by one's sex. Since homosexuality was represented as self-evidently abnormal, the imputed chain of causality linking sex with heterosexual reproduction is further reinforced. If gender was successfully represented as flexible and malleable, it was also thereby rendered more amenable to remedy and regulation, in this case, through the (re)assumption of womanly duties. Thus, between sex scenes, Vita was seen tucking her children up in bed and at dinner with Harold and his parents, and Violet was seen walking down the aisle with Denys.

The probable connections and possible disconnections between sex and gender were openly verbalized in a scene in which Harold confided in his friend, Reggie, that he was made miserable by Vita's passion for Violet and was himself 'no ladies' man'. Reggie replies that Vita was very much 'what they call a man's woman'. As he explained, this meant 'a woman who's tough and honourable. Female rather than feminine'. Since it is possible to be female, while being either feminine or un-feminine, Reggie also implied that femininity was more pliable than sex. His statements further reinforced the idea that masculinity was the proper effect of a male body and femininity the effect of a female body. Variations in the cultural enactment of gender gave rise to 'a man's woman' in contrast to any other sort of woman. Femaleness appeared fixed only because it was assumed to be equal to a pre-given unequivocal anatomical morphology.

The immutability of sex is apparently written on the female body. Hence it was highly significant that viewers were made so aware of Vita's crossing over and that her masculinization was intermittent. It was important too that Vita was shown unambiguously to possess a female anatomy. This was emphasized throughout the drama by filming her body in various states of undress. Scenes showing her naked in bed or sitting around in her underwear, appeared to expose and highlight the essentially female contours of her body. In the first episodes, the logical and fruitful expression of her anatomical sex in heterosexual reproduction are represented in scenes showing her as Harold's wife and Ben and Nigel's mother. When not in drag, Vita appears in 'the most fetishistic female costumes of the drama' wearing glittering dresses, jewel studded hairpieces, extravagant furs and hats (Merck, p. 115). The act of crossing over reveals that masculinity and femininity consist of a particular series of investments in a sexed body, which is always already accepted as irrefutably male or female. The fact that lesbian sex becomes possible when an obviously female body is uncharacteristically presented in masculine attire, implies that lesbianism arises from an irregularity or disjunction in relations between sex as anatomy (body), sense of self (identity) and social category (woman).

Sexual discontinuities were partly echoed in the characterization of Harold as gentle, indulgent and gay. His character was, to some extent, de-masculinized. However, he didn't have to get into a frock. He maintained an air of paternalism throughout the drama. When pushed too far, he put his foot down, asserted his authority and prevented Vita from meeting Violet in France. His homosexuality was represented as much less of a problem than Vita's passion for Violet.

Harold's deviant sexuality was phrased in terms of confession and absolution, disease and treatment, with the implication that it was manageable through words or drugs. Initially, his penchant for sex with men was revealed through his confession that he was being treated for syphilis. Later, in conversation with Reggie, Harold explained that his homosexuality was functional, like shitting and eating, but did not provide a motive for life as did marriage to Vita. Reggie pointed out that sex between men was also therefore as essential as those other functions. Sex between men was thus presented as both a matter of taste and necessity. In contrast, sex between women was not a variant of taste but a voracious appetite potentially raging out of control. Gayness appeared to complement heterosexual marital relations whereas lesbianism threatened to destroy them. Importantly, Harold's insistence that Vita, as his wife and mother of his children, was central to his life reaffirmed the causal logic linking sex (maleness and femaleness) with the expression of sexuality through procreation within marriage. The fact that he was sidetracked by sex with men was less significant than achieving and maintaining this all-important familial status. Family life filled the chasm opened by Harold's announcement of his sexually acquired disease whereupon sexuality in marriage appeared to fizzle out. Harold's conversation with Reggie and Vita and Violet's repeated assertions that infidelities, especially those of the perverse kind, didn't matter and could be better pursued within marriage served to further subordinate deviant sexuality to heterosexual marriage. These statements emphasized the basic important characteristics of a successful and enduring marriage; in this context, love born out of a sense of duty, subscription to the same (ruling-class) values and companionship.

The apparent distinction drawn between same-sex sex involving men and that involving women is significant because it both defines the limits and limitations of perversity and, importantly, says something more about women. It suggests that women are in possession of a sexuality which is wild and boundless and that women themselves are completely without self-restraint. The potential havoc caused by untempered female sexuality is compounded when women get together for sex. The possibility of deliverance from this (fantasy of) female destructiveness is signalled through the interruption and curtailment of lesbianism by the intervention of a masculine subject; in this case, the bridegroom Denys, helped into the role by Harold.

Portrait of a Marriage offers two assurances: firstly, that maleness and femaleness are basically distinct and enduring; and, secondly, that masculinity and femininity are more pliant and prone to deviation but also amenable to remedy and renegotiation. Thus, lesbianism signals the limitations of gender roles within marriage and opens up the possibility of redefining the borders of marriage, masculinity and femininity.

Surely, *Portrait of a Marriage* must be applauded for making lesbians more visible and signalling a greater popular cultural awareness and acceptability of lesbianism and *difference*? It did at least transgress the usual boundaries of sexuality as represented in standard television dramas. Indeed, although lesbianism was made visible through the lens of heterosexuality, the drama was also open to different readings. Lesbians watching *Portrait*, whether they considered the lingering passionate kisses and gentle (non-genital) stroking in the afterglow of having 'done it' erotic or insipid, could variously 'read in' their own fantasies and predilections. Furthermore, an exploration of possible 'lesbian' readings would reveal that women having sex with women, however they dress and whatever they do, is not the same as, nor simply a copy of, heterosexual sex. If Vita and Violet's sex seemed like a copy rather than the real thing, it was because desire between the two women was effectively framed from a particular heterosexual point of view. This is not to say that the rape was any less violent or abhorrent, nor that the images of lesbians were any less negative than I have already suggested. This line of argument inevitably generates other concerns.

The mere fact that BBC producers judge that mass audiences can stomach tastefully filmed sexual deviations does not, of course, mean that these audiences understand or accept them. There is always the possibility that such productions will provoke antagonism towards, or encourage exploitation of, those who are represented as different. The other major difficulty, for BBC producers and lesbian critics alike, lies in a tendency to characterize homo- and heterosexual and sub- and mainstream culture(s) as direct opposites, thereby implying that each is a coherent and distinctive whole. Again, this places limits on sexual diversity by implying that all dykes are basically the same, and so are all straights.

In a recent article entitled 'Doing It: Representations of Lesbian Sex', Kitzinger and Kitzinger (1993) argue that the costs of media representations of lesbian sex hugely outweigh the benefits. They suggest that the invisibility of lesbians and lesbian sex may be preferable to the alternatives which invariably represent women who have sex with women as 'predatory, crazed, psychopathic sadists' and lesbian sexuality as 'dangerous and perverted, inextricably intertwined with violence and despair' (Kitzinger and Kitzinger, p. 10). In addition, representations of lesbian sex are widespread in heterosexual male pornography, and often represented as 'foreplay' or warming up for men: 'lesbianism rarely withstands the arrival of the male on the scene' (p. 11). If a man does not intervene, lesbian sex is a poor substitute, leaving an unfulfilled sexuality and inviting the jibe that all a lesbian needs is a good fuck (by a man). Kitzinger and Kitzinger also point out that, as well as being portrayed through a male gaze, lesbians are often assigned a male point of view. The suggestion that lesbians too can enjoy films produced for heterosexual male consumption necessitates them viewing other women through a male gaze and objectifying them. Kitzinger and Kitzinger reject the idea that lesbians can appropriate these images and remake them for their own pleasure and that this in itself constitutes a radical transformation. They argue that the appropriation of symbols of domination by lesbians reinforces rather than transgresses heterosexual customs and violences. They discuss the production of representations of lesbian sex by lesbians for lesbians and express concern that all 'lesbian-generated images' are also vulnerable to male appropriation and pornographic interpretations. One possible solution, they suggest, 'is simply to refuse to collaborate with the production or distribution of lesbian sex scenes'. They ask:

> If we construct lesbian representations of lesbian sex, how do we know that we have done so as *lesbians*, and from 'a lesbian gaze' as opposed to adopting a male gaze and utilising the conventions of male pornography? Simply claiming that they are 'by women for women' doesn't solve the problem (p. 20).

Kitzinger and Kitzinger reflect on whether lesbians should settle for positive portrayals of female friendships. For example, supportive, intimate and warm relationships between women in *Thelma and Louise*, *Bagdad Cafe* and *Salmonberries*. Just because lesbian sex has been repressed, they argue, it doesn't mean that now it has to be expressed.

I have several problems with Kitzinger and Kitzinger's

argument. Mainly, I am worried by the ideas that firstly, *one* distinctively *lesbian* gaze exists, albeit open to contamination by a male gaze, and secondly, that *lesbian* representations are possible, albeit vulnerable to being ripped off by men. These ideas tend to reproduce the categories 'lesbians', 'lesbian sex' and 'men' as singular and coherent entities, thereby precluding further possible sexual diversities, and the complexity of the (power) relations through which they become visible to differently located viewers. This tendency is reinforced through a discussion of authenticity, motivation and interpretation. Thus, the Kitzingers question whether particular lesbian characters are accurate or distorted representations of lesbians. They want to know which intentions lie behind a particular portrait of lesbianism and how it flavours public perceptions of lesbians. As a consequence, their analysis generates an investment in the idea that a common and general deviant 'experience' exists, is capable of representation, and offers a singular viewing position. This style of analysis ends up discriminating and defending a 'true' sexuality from a false one, and, in the process, represents lesbianism narrowly as opposite and 'other' for a seamless version of heterosexuality. Further, by implying that meanings which attach to things and cultural forms are fixed, as for example a masculine gaze or male appropriation, the possibilities for effecting political shifts to enable new representations are so severely curtailed as to be impossible. A masculine gaze, used in this way, presupposes and reinforces the same discrete dichotomous versions of sex and gender necessary to the perpetuation of heterosexual relations.

An analysis of the representation of lesbians in popular culture must resist assigning a univocal position to a lesbian audience. This goes equally for the representation of any other category of persons. The use of 'we' and 'lesbian' as self-evident and cohesive terms is based on the assumption that they simultaneously refer to an individual sense of self or identity and a collective social position. The political allure of identity, and the collective action it makes possible, may sometimes foreclose an articulation of diverse other political subject positions (Butler, 1990b). Not all women who have sex with other women call themselves lesbians; and, if they do, they are not necessarily lesbians in the same way. Lesbian may be one of the many identities to which an individual lays claim, and not necessarily the first or most common. Being old, Black or unemployed may be a more obvious reference point for some. The BBC representation of Vita and Violet's sexual attraction to each other is a case in point, demonstrating that having sex, however passionately and wholeheartedly, does not necessarily lead to the assumption of an individual or collective lesbian identity. Indeed, the drama showed forcibly that lesbian sex did not provide sufficient grounds for a common worldview. Marriage, on the other hand, embodied a solid and reliable stock of shared values. For this reason, the object of analysis in reviewing *Portrait of a Marriage* must be a peculiar, and singular, version of lesbian sex and *not* lesbian(s) as an identity or social group.

I argued earlier that the dramatization of *Portrait of a Marriage* articulated a separation of sex and gender, and, in the process created a version of homosexuality which was useful in shoring up heterosexual marital relations. The drama reinforced the idea that biological sex is fixed and causally determines sex as a social position. My emphasis on diversity in sexual deviations and refusing lesbian as a single identity also extends to sex. In my view, 'sex' (meaning having a female anatomy) is no more constant and discrete than gender. Instead, it is repeatedly enacted, hence, the unfolding drama of *Portrait* included frequent characterizations of 'woman' as representations of (naked) female bodies and a social position, especially as mother and wife. A recurring focus on the corporeal boundaries of sex, as a foundation of sex as a social status, underlines the basic instability of 'sex'. It indicates that being a woman is as variable and inconsistent as being a lesbian or any other identity. Refusing a view of perversity as a steady and reliable counterpart of various elements of heterosexuality must be the necessary corollary of refusing a globalizing concept of woman.

Representations of lesbian sex, whoever produces them, imply particular characterizations of lesbians and women which are qualified and conditional, setting limits to and regulating their possible meanings. The images of lesbian sex scattered through *Portrait of a Marriage* are deeply embedded in a particular cultural and historical context. They are bound to resonate differently for women who have sex with women in the 1990s, according to the material and political conditions of their lives and the diverse political subject positions to which they may occupy on the basis of race, class and sexuality. In this way, the political importance of discussing images of lesbian sex in *Portrait* and drawing out their possible meanings, to different viewers in different, contexts, is that it makes possible an articulation of different previously excluded subject positions and aspects of perversity. Through discussion of its omissions and limitations, *Portrait of a Marriage* enables an articulation of more elements of sexual diversity and makes it possible to resist the deployment of 'homosexual' as the negative counterpart to, and element in the regulation of, heterosexual relations.

THE GORGEOUS LESBIAN
IN *LA LAW*:
THE PRESENT ABSENCE?

Rosanne Kennedy

That the popular North American television series, *LA Law*, should have a female bisexual character – the gorgeous, sexy C.J. Lamb – is no way surprising. In fact, C.J.'s bisexuality is wholly in keeping with the programme's progressive image. Despite its predominantly white, heterosexual, upwardly mobile orientation, it has distinguished itself by its range of ethnic, sexual and class identities, and by its liberal treatment of controversial issues. The real surprise is that the show has achieved so much credibility, in terms of maintaining a 'lesbian' presence, with so little representation of lesbian sexuality, or even of lesbian issues. Amanda Donohoe, who plays C.J. Lamb, only joined the show in its fifth season, and by the end of the sixth season, she, along with several others, had left the show. Out of the forty or so episodes from those two seasons, she appears as a main character in only eight, and only five of those concern her sexuality. None of those five episodes shows C.J. erotically engaged with another woman. All we see is the disappointingly chaste three-second kiss between C.J. and Abby, the heterosexual wallflower at McKenzie Brackman, and a good deal of titillation and suggestiveness. Indeed, C.J.'s sexiest moments occur in her last two episodes, when she becomes romantically involved with a *man*. On the basis of this track record, how has *LA Law* managed to achieve a cult status among lesbian viewers? And what indeed has *LA Law* achieved? Should we take C.J.'s character as a sign of television's increasing openness and maturity towards, to paraphrase C.J., sexual 'flexibility'? Can C.J., who identifies as neither lesbian nor straight, be regarded as a representation of queer sexuality?

THE BISEXUAL CASE

C.J.'s sexuality is first signified as 'an issue' in the programme's fifth season, in the context of her deepening friendship with Abby. Their friendship reaches a crisis point in the famous 'kiss' episode, when, on parting one evening, C.J. kisses Abby on the lips. Abby, surprised, returns the kiss and scurries away. Timid Abby obsesses over the meaning of this kiss, and later confronts C.J., asking why she kissed her. C.J. returns the question and they declare their sexual cards: straight/flexible – C.J. declining to be categorized. When Abby finally indicates that she's ready to become involved, C.J., playing the sexual pedagogue, tells Abby that she's not an experiment, that she's not available on Abby's terms. Happily for all, they agree to be 'just friends'.

This kiss episode undoubtedly attracted a lesbian spectatorship by signifying C.J. as bisexual, and thereby holding out the promise that future episodes would see her involved with women. Yet the episodes between C.J. and Abby are ultimately disappointing, represent a missed opportunity, and reveal the limits of the programme's politics. In comparison with erotic scenes between the straight characters, the kiss between C.J. and Abby is restrained to the point of being asexual. Apparently, in the heterosexual world of *LA Law* a potentially sexual relationship between C.J. and Abby can only be represented as *an issue*, at the cost of eliminating the sex. What is worse is that this sexual restraint seems to follow naturally from the status of lesbianism as an outsider sexuality rather than from any deliberate strategy on the part of the producers. According to the logic of compulsory heterosexuality, it is only natural that Abby should obsess about what a kiss with

C.J. means, rather than plunge in and think later. Yet, her response is obviously an effect of a number of choices by the programme producers that limit what could occur between the two women. For instance, the kiss takes place in public, where C.J. and Abby can hardly get carried away. More significant, the programme's choice of Abby herself, an unlikely erotic object for C.J., and its liberal commitment to the notion of an essential self-identity, limits the storyline by virtue of what would be in keeping with her character. *LA Law* could have clinched its status as queer rather than liberal by developing the relationship between spunky C.J. and timid Abby – that would have been queer!

Fortuitously, an innocent 'mistake' in a recent issue of *Australian Cleo* (October 1993) reveals the limits of *LA Law's* sexual politics, and suggests how we as viewers might queer the plot. In an article on 'Hollywood's Hottest Lesbians', the author mistakenly identifies a photograph of Donohoe and Cecil Hoffmann, who plays Zoey on *LA Law*, as a photograph of Donohoe and Michelle Green, who plays Abby. While all of *Cleo's* other shots of Hollywood's famous lesbians show them in an erotic entanglement, C.J. and Zoey are shown grinning on front of a camera, C.J.'s head next to Zoey's, in a clownish gesture of friendship. Ironically, the mistakenly identified photograph of Donohoe and Hoffman signifies the level of lesbian content in *LA Law*. Zoey can substitute for Abby precisely because nothing happened between C.J. and Abby; consequently, a photograph of C.J. and *any* woman from *LA Law* would do, because the photo, like the friendship between Abby and C.J., only represents a potential lesbian relationship rather than an actualized one. Indeed, *Cleo's* substitution of Zoey for Abby is an easy mistake to make given the opening credits in series six, in which C.J. and Zoey are shown together in a poolside scene, clad in bikinis, looking at each other and laughing as they do an aerobic dance routine.

THE LESBIAN CUSTODY CASE

The treatment of bisexuality in the Abby episode, as an issue rather than an embodied sexual practice, sets the pattern for other episodes dealing with homosexuality. The next episode involving C.J.'s sexuality occurs in the middle of the sixth season. C.J. has asked her colleague, divorce lawyer Arnie Becker, to represent her friend, Maggie Barnes, in a custody case. C.J. tells Arnie that Maggie's ex-husband has found out that she has been having an affair, since before their divorce two years earlier, with a woman. In response, the husband sues for custody of their two children. At the firm's morning meeting, when Arnie reports that he is representing a client in a lesbian custody case, C.J. acknowledges, to the firm's hushed embarrassment, that she is the client's lover. None of the partners knows quite how to respond, and the moment passes. During the trial, the father is revealed to be an undesirable character – a reformed alcoholic who mistreated his children, and visited them only twice during the first year of separation. His own masculinity on the line, he testifies that his fights with his wife were about sex rather than about his drinking, and that his wife deceived him about her sexual preference. The opposing attorney, James Pavlik, questions Maggie about her lesbian relationships and their effect on her children. A psychologist testifies that a mother's homosexuality can adversely affect her children, but admits that there is no proof that a gay parent produces a gay child. When Pavlik calls C.J. to the stand, she acknowledges that during her relationship with Maggie she had other sexual relationships, and that, like all responsible, sexually active people, she had an AIDS test, which was negative. The question about AIDS seems designed to portray C.J. as sexually 'loose'; however, she gains credibility by answering frankly. Then Maggie's eight-year-old daughter, Jenny, takes the stand, says she misses C.J., and that her father is jealous because Mommy loves C.J. rather than him. In the final scene, C.J. turns up at Maggie's house with a Christmas gift, they exchange loving looks, Maggie invites C.J. in and closes the door. End of story. The message: lesbian sex must stay behind closed doors.

On one level, the lesbian custody episode could be read as queering the mother body, by insisting that mothers are sexual beings whose sexuality will not be limited to reproductive heterosexuality. As in the Abby episode, the programme promotes the liberal message that the issues lesbianism raises, such as whether lesbians can be good mothers, or whether the sexuality of the parent will affect the sexuality of the child, should be discussed. However, two women must not be shown making-out together; graphic visual representation of lesbian sexuality must remain outside the frame of liberal television. In addition, whereas relationships between the programme's heterosexual couples are developed over a number of programmes, C.J.'s relationship with Maggie, supposedly over two years old, has no television history. Chronologically, it doesn't fit in with series five: when C.J. was becoming involved with Abby she never mentioned her relationship with Maggie, which, given her characteristic honesty, seems odd.

THE HETEROSEXUAL CASE

While, in the Abby and Maggie Barnes episodes, the producers can be accused of representing lesbianism only as a political or moral issue rather than a performative practice, the real twist comes in the last two episodes of series six, when C.J. becomes involved with David McCoy. McCoy, an opposing attorney in a trial in which C.J. is involved, is not the first man on the series to show an interest in her. Mikhail, Susan Bloom's husband, makes a pass at C.J., which she refuses. But McCoy is man with a twist: he's blind. Given the symbolic value of blindness as one of the most conventional signifiers of castration, C.J.'s involvement with the blind McCoy cannot be innocent. In terms of the programme's history, it has a logic and an imaginary investment. While McCoy's blindness does not signify him as literally impotent, it does indeed mark him off from the mainstream heterosexual male population. His blindness means he has not participated in a whole series of rituals of masculinity, such as playing contact sports, fighting with other boys, joining the army, viewing pornography; it also means that C.J. is not objectified by the male gaze. For her part, C.J. demonstrates her openness – it does not matter to her that McCoy is blind. In terms of the sexual logic of *LA Law*, it is appropriate for C.J. to go off with a man only if he, too, is in some way an outsider to normative heterosexuality. In sum, two of the three episodes dealing with 'lesbian issues' seem designed to reassure the heterosexual population that they will not be 'contaminated' by bisexuality (both Abby and Maggie's children remain, for the present at least, 'uncontaminated'), while the final episode with McCoy recuperates C.J. for some version of heterosexuality. What we never see, however, is C.J. involved in a committed relationship with a woman.

Given that C.J. is rarely ever shown engaging in explicitly sexual behaviour, how is it that she is signified as the sexiest woman and the queerest character on the show? C.J.'s sexy image is created largely in the opening credits – those short, snappy images of each character in an allegedly typical pose or memorable moment. As her character became more established and popular with audiences, her image was more overtly sexualized. In series five, C.J. appears in the opening credits three times, and each time she is dressed in appropriately professional attire which masks her sexuality. In series six, however, she appears in a suit, but she also appears poolside in a fluorescent-green and black bikini, and sexiest of all, in a short, plunging neckline, off the shoulder, black Lycra dress. In this image, she is literally performing camp, posing her hands and body in a stylized way and looking knowingly at someone off-screen. Indeed, I would maintain that C.J.'s success as a character lies in her appeal to all women, regardless of sexuality. C.J. is simply the sexiest, spunkiest, and most liberated woman on the show. But what really distinguishes her from the other female characters is her cheekiness, wit and sense of fun. If male viewers desire the woman they want to have, and female viewers desire the woman they want to be, C.J. would win, hands down, the woman's vote. I, for one, would much rather be C.J. than Grace Van Owen, who is so busy doing what she thinks is right that she doesn't know what would make her happy, or Ann Kelsey, the picture of happy heterosexuality in a straitjacket. Zoey, like Grace, is uptight and so worn-down by life in the DA's office that she seems to be in a perpetual crisis. In comparison with these women, C.J. is hip, sexy, smart, confident and enjoys life. Consequently, even viewers who do not identify as lesbians may find themselves identifying with C.J. And although C.J.'s bisexuality marks her out as different, it also marks her as less earnest and righteous than the other characters. C.J.'s sexuality is not the reason for her popularity with audiences. Rather, her character appears to the majority of female viewers, regardless of the sexuality, while simultaneously appealing to lesbian viewers by holding out the promise of a lesbian relationship. But the fact that lesbians can get excited about C.J.'s character is more a testament to the absence of lesbianism on television than it is a tribute to *LA Law*'s radicality.

LESBIAN VS QUEER

So, in the final analysis, how should we evaluate C.J.'s character in *LA Law*? And *LA Law*'s scorecard on issues of sexuality? Paradoxically, the episodes which are signified as having overt lesbian content are inherently conservative, because the performance of lesbian sexuality is repeatedly displaced onto a series of political and ethical issues. For instance, Maggie and C.J.'s sexual relationship is simply a backdrop for the political issue of lesbian custody. The same logic of displacement occurs in the episodes dealing with gay issues, such as the AIDS and gay cop episodes. Gay sexuality is turned into a matter of politics or ethics; lesbian and gay practices can be referred to and can even be discussed, but, unlike heterosexuality, they cannot be shown.

Similarly, the Abby episode can hardly be considered a lesbian or bisexual issue; it's about heterosexual panic, the fear of discovering that the boundaries of heterosexuality are permeable. In fact, rather than giving proportional representation to bisexual women, the Abby episode sets out to disprove the lesbian version of the *When Harry Met Sally* proposition that 'a man and a woman can never be just friends, because sex always gets in the way'. It argues that a straight woman and a lesbian can be just friends, thereby affirming bisexuality as a legitimate sexual identity while reassuring straight viewers that there is no need to worry about the contamination of their own heterosexuality. Abby's heterosexuality remains securely intact, and the firm remains uncontaminated by any suspect liaisons. The representation of lesbian and gay sexuality as an 'issue' confirms the 'normality' of heterosexuality; heterosexuality only becomes an issue when it is excessive and transgressive, as in cases of incest and rape. Ordinarily, however, it is the very essence of everyday lived reality. *LA Law* achieves political points for representing gay and lesbian issues without, however, doing anything to revolutionize, or even create a space for, the visual representation of gay, lesbian or queer sexuality on mainstream television. This is, of course, a classic liberal strategy that allows a heterosexual audience to tolerate difference without ever challenging the complacency of its own heterosexuality.

The above analysis does not, however, explain why *LA Law* created such a potentially queer character in C.J., and then limited so dramatically what she could be shown doing. Let me explain what I mean by calling C.J. queer. Queer politics is against identity politics; it rejects the notion of a gay or lesbian identity because identities inadvertently support the binary logic of compulsory heterosexuality; in opposition to a binary logic of homosexuality/ heterosexuality, queer emphasizes that which disturbs the complacency of the opposition itself. Queer shifts the focus from sexual identity to sexual performativity, and claims that queers are everywhere rather than on the margins. Consequently, queer would rather find sex between women in an unexpected place –

in Zoey and C.J.'s friendship – rather than in a relationship between two self-identified lesbians. Queer cannot confront the logic of heterosexuality by being another kind of identity. Queer should disturb all sexual boundaries, and create sexual mayhem, so that any individual may occupy or perform any sexual or gender identity, rather than have a true identity; in this way, queer undermines the very notion of a truth of sexuality. C.J. embodies queer by refusing to be identified as heterosexual, lesbian or bisexual; she refuses to identify herself, to pin herself down, choosing simply to say she is sexually 'flexible'. Abby, embodying heterosexual logic, mis-takes 'flexibility' as bisexuality, and hence tries to pin down C.J.'s sexuality as an identity rather than a performance.

This analysis does not, however, explain why *LA Law*, having created a character who could be read as either queer or bisexual, did not take the relatively safe alternative of developing a lesbian relationship, which would have confirmed *LA Law*'s liberal tolerance, without challenging heterosexuality. The answer, I think, is that C.J.'s character can be read as either queer or bisexual. However, she can only be queer to the extent that she is not overtly sexualized, and she can only be shown engaging in explicit sexual behaviour that is not queer – i.e., when she is shown being heterosexual with McCoy. C.J.'s queerness must be contained; otherwise it would risk queering the show as a whole. So while as a character C.J. resists being pigeon-holed into a sexual identity, she functions, in terms of the logic of the show, as the site of a sexual identity – bisexuality.

Consequently, her queerness is rendered as an identity, parallel to heterosexuality in every way, without challenging hetero-sexuality. By making C.J. the locus of bisexuality, the programme gives fair representation to sexual orientations other than heterosexuality, while at the same time suggesting that both bisexuality and heterosexuality are sexual identities. Hence, none of the straight characters needs to investigate their own sexual identities. C.J.'s sexual otherness is doubly signified through her

Englishness – acceptable as long as it is elsewhere, something that does not contaminate the wholesome heterosexuality of America. In addition, by making C.J. the site of bisexuality, viewers are less likely to queer other characters and situations. We are distracted from imagining a lesbian subtext between C.J. and Zoey by the implied but undeveloped relationship between C.J. and Maggie. The liberal earnestness of *LA Law* means that anything other than heterosexuality can only be represented as the object of compassion, rather than fun. C.J. is queer and cheeky; consequently, she can't be represented having sex, having fun, being camp, because that would be subversive.

LA Law could have had a lesbian relationship only if C.J. were identified as lesbian rather than queer. C.J.'s queerness could not, however, be contained in the kind of boundaried lesbian relationship that would be acceptable to the liberal world of *LA Law*, thereby revealing the limits of *LA Law*'s sexual politics. C.J. can only be queer to the extent that her sexuality takes place off-screen. Thus, her sexuality is an absent presence: it functions as a *raison d'être* for raising issues, but it cannot be represented. The only characters who can be camp, oddly enough, are the very straight Brackman and his ex-wife. When they decide to get back together they engage in silly, romantic, over-the-top behaviour – making sexual puns, ear-licking, acting randy – which is very unlike the earnest sex we usually get on *LA Law*. But that behaviour from Brackman and his wife is acceptable because it does not threaten heterosexual monogamy. However, to substitute C.J. and Zoey for Brackman and his wife in these scenes would be subversive and titillating. Finally, then, we have to say that in terms of the sexual politics of contemporary television, C.J. is a great character, but she represents a lost opportunity.

I would like to thank Judith Ion, Lissa O'Neil, and Emma Partridge for discussing their reactions to *LA Law* with me.

FROM STRING OF KNOTS TO ORANGE BOX: LESBIANISM ON PRIME TIME

Margaret Marshment and Julia Hallam

> History is a string full of knots, the best you can do is admire it, and maybe knot it up a bit more.[1]

> Everyone who tells a story tells it differently, just to remind us that everybody sees it differently.[2]

At a time when postmodernism and polysemy (multiple meanings) are the celebrated modes of cultural production, a realist text which aims to change people's minds about a social issue has a somewhat old-fashioned ring. Jeanette Winterson's first novel, *Oranges are Not the Only Fruit*, was *not* such a text, but the television adaptation of it, shown on BBC television in 1990, was. Winterson said of *Oranges* that it 'challenges the virtues of the home, the power of the church and the supposed normality of heterosexuality', and that in undertaking to transform her novel into a television series 'that would bring viewers in off the streets', she was determined not to 'see it toned down in any way', in the hope that 'TV can have a moral as well as a social function'.[3]

The success of the television version suggests that cultural production aiming to challenge the prejudices of commonsense has everything to gain from working with the forms of popular culture, and that the mechanisms of closure characteristic of popular narrative can facilitate the effective communication of radical ideas.

At first sight, Winterson's novel would seem an unlikely candidate for adaptation as prime-time television drama: some brilliant characterization, but a non-linear plot, interspersed with fables and meditations, that revolves around a young lesbian's betrayal by her fanatically religious mother. *Oranges* is a novel that depends on formal and linguistic acrobatics, rather than narrative and description, for its aesthetic appeal. Its status as a cult novel among women-identified women derived from its funny and sensitive portrayal of a lesbian protagonist. It had won the Whitbread Prize in 1985, and so achieved unusual recognition for a lesbian novel from the British literary establishment. But its theme of lesbian love hardly seemed calculated to endear it to the BBC at a time when the British moral majority's campaigns against homosexuality had recently resulted in legislation prohibiting local government funding for anything deemed to be 'promoting homosexuality'.[4] Yet in January 1990 *Oranges are Not the Only Fruit* was shown on British television to an audience of around six million, received widespread critical acclaim in the press, and was shown again later in the year. Our aim is not to explain this success, but to analyse how the television adaptation was able to achieve it while maintaining the integrity of its lesbian message.

Feminist criticism has often been cautious about the popularization of feminist works, seeing in the need for a larger audience a commensurate need to compromise the feminist message. This may be partly a suspicion of success itself, and partly a suspicion shared by many that the forms and contexts of popular culture are intrinsically hostile to the possibility of radical messages. We would dispute both these claims.

The television adaptation of *Oranges are Not the Only Fruit* successfully employs the strategies of popular narrative forms in order to secure a reading of the text sympathetic to its presentation of lesbian identity as a normative sexuality. This involves the production of a 'closed' text. Because 'closure' has usually been analysed in relation to how it functions to reproduce existing meanings and reinforce the ideological status quo, polysemy which encourages many, sometimes contradictory meanings, has been privileged as the more radical, democratic mode of representation. But it is our contention that to produce polysemic texts as a matter of policy would be a self-defeating enterprise, since closure is itself an important and effective strategy in the creation of oppositional meanings.

Readers of *Oranges are Not the Only Fruit* – a social 'minority' of women-identified women and lesbians – could be expected to respond sympathetically to the novel's focus on women's lives and the affirmation of a lesbian identity for its protagonist. But a mainstream television audience is a different matter. Whatever the gains in terms of social equality and regimes of representation brought about by twenty years of feminist activism, the word 'feminist' does not enjoy positive connotations in the culture at large. What is true of 'feminist' is a hundred times more true of 'lesbian'. (When the two are not, indeed, conflated in popular discourse.) Feminist and gay politics have been accompanied by cultural production with positive representations of lesbians in fiction, the visual arts, poetry and film; but very little of this finds its way into popular media such as television, and certainly not at prime time. The screening of *Oranges* by the BBC (albeit on the less popular channel BBC2) during peak viewing hours, and in winter, therefore constituted a significant feminist/lesbian intervention in the sexual politics of popular culture.

Jeanette Winterson herself produced the script for *Oranges,* working with director Beeban Kidron, producer Philippa Giles, composer Rachel Portman and designer Cecilia Brereton. We can safely assume that this all-female team were aware of the sexual politics of their project, and would have sought to make their production a positive contribution to feminist/lesbian politics.[5] For our purposes here, we shall assume that the text is deliberately constructed to close down the potential polysemy of its subject matter in order to secure from a mainstream audience a reading of lesbian identity against the grain of the dominant ideology's definitions of 'normal' sexuality. Our aim is to identify the mechanisms of closure employed by the text to undermine the presumed homophobia of a mainstream audience, while simultaneously addressing its original women-identified audience. If this was not how production decisions were made, well – it's our way of telling the story.

REALISM AND PLEASURE

For a text to be popular it must be both accessible and enjoyable. Texts aiming to challenge the ideological status quo can do so more effectively if they too are accessible and enjoyable. Those which appear on prime-time television are obviously accessible. Programmes screened during prime-time viewing hours, unlike much late-night programming which is assumed to be geared towards 'minority' tastes, are, almost by definition, assumed to be of general interest. This in itself tends to 'normalize' the subject-matter of such programmes. Additionally, *Oranges* occupied a 'quality' drama slot on BBC2. With its literary pedigree, high production values and provocative subject-matter, it fits comfortably into the traditions of this prestige niche, with the expectation that its concerns should be taken seriously.[6]

Realism is the most familiar mode of narration in our culture. Modernism challenged this dominance in the novel nearly a century ago, but in popular narratives realism continues to be the dominant form. Its implied claim that it simply reflects reality, that it is an empirical project which transparently represents that which is in any case transparent – the 'facts' – appears as particularly strong in the photographic media of film and television which, even as fiction, seem simply to record what is 'there'. It has been argued that in appearing to 'guarantee access to truth', realism hides its own constructedness, is formally incapable of representing reality as contradictory, and is therefore inherently conservative.[7] This is a long-standing and complex debate, and while we do not have the space here to discuss the philosophical aspects of realism's 'adequacy to the real',[8] we do wish to argue, on the basis of our analysis of *Oranges*, that it is certainly able to convey challenges to the dominant ideology.

Oranges is basically a realist text that works within the conventions of mainstream film and television fictions. Its *mise-en-scène* has an attention to detail that makes it appear a convincing reconstruction of a particular community in a particular time and place; it employs continuity editing to maintain spatial and temporal coherence; and creates consistent characters within a cause-and-effect narrative. All this, in supplying the pleasures of familiar aesthetic form, works to 'normalize' its subject matter.

Within this conventionally realist ground, however, the text manipulates references to non-realist genres and modes in order to comment thematically upon the visible action. This is most evident in the opening credit sequences, where older Jess and small Jess are pulled apart in surrealist scenes, set in a fairground and a church, which make symbolic reference to the work's themes of the pain and loss involved in the process of growing up and the nightmare of betrayal. Similarly, a sense of heightened emotion is created at climactic moments in the narrative, such as the use of wide-angle lens, extreme close-up and slow motion to add a sense of menace to the lyricism of the love scene. When small Jess wakes up in a luminously white hospital ward this gives expression to her experience of unreality. The gargoyle-like distortion of her face during the exorcism symbolizes her exclusion from the church. The tableau-like funeral dinner, reminiscent of Peter Greenaway's film style, calls attention to the inhumanly regimented behaviour of the sect members. This last, indeed, forms part of a more general excess in characterization, whereby the elements of caricature and the sharp, sometimes bizarre, comedy of the script have that Dickensian quality of social satire that features also in writers like Naipaul and Rushdie, and that can prepare us for the brutal melodrama of the exorcism. The snapshot-like construction of the narrative (especially in the first episode) embodies the work's concerns with memory and representation. This all gives the film a very distinctive feel, a sense of its difference from 'ordinary television', while being at the same time well within the variations on the conventions of realism as they have been developed, not only in prose fiction and film, but also in the tradition of 'quality' British television drama.[9] They are features which transform the realism of popular forms without fundamentally disrupting its power to give pleasure through the familiarity of its mode of communication.

This power is enhanced when the realism is well executed[10]: high production values not only offer the pleasures of a well-crafted work, but also demonstrate respect for the viewer, a factor that is important for women viewers in works apparently addressed to them and dealing with women's issues. Pleasure is not usually defined as a mechanism of 'closure', but it is clear that viewers will be unlikely to be convinced by a work that they do not, in the broadest sense, enjoy. We would therefore regard the pleasures of *Oranges* as working towards the acceptance of its message.

NARRATIVE

Oranges are Not the Only Fruit tells the story of Jess, a girl brought up by a strict fundamentalist Christian mother in a small industrial town in the north of England. At the age of sixteen she falls in love with Melanie, a girl about her own age. This relationship is brutally destroyed by her mother and other members of the evangelical community: the girls are publicly humiliated and Jess is subjected to a forcible exorcism. Following a second, less traumatic, relationship Jess, refusing to renounce her sexuality, leaves church and home, eventually to go to university. This is the plot which can be extracted from the more thematic organization of the novel, and which provides the narrative structure of the television version. The loose chronology of the novel is thus reordered into the more straightforward and familiar shape of biographical narrative.

However, the structure of *Oranges* does not quite follow a traditional realist pattern of exposition, disturbance, crisis and resolution. It is structured rather like a triptych, with a finely drawn portrait of Jess and her environment hinged on either side of the central plot action, which occurs in episode two. The 'before', which maps out the physical and moral space of Jess's childhood through a series of scenes and events in her seventh year, conforms to the structure of introductions to such biographies in television fiction. It is characterized by the ordinariness of Jess's childhood experience, just as the 'after' is characterized by the ordinariness of adolescent disaffiliation, as Jess develops a sense of her own identity. The narrative crisis is contained within the second episode when the equilibrium of Jess's biographical trajectory from childhood through adolescence to maturity is disrupted by her relationship with Melanie and her conflict with family, church and community. This episode concludes with an uneasy resolution, in which, despite her outer repentance, Jess remains faithful to her love for Melanie. It is left to episode three for the full resolution, with confirmation of Jess's lesbian identity through her relationship with Katy and her subsequent departure from the church. In thus framing the 'crisis' of Jess's biography within a context of more typical events and situations, the extraordinary is contained within the ordinary, and facilitates audience empathy with the protagonist.

GOODIES AND BADDIES

The narrative conflict is constructed around the opposition between Jess's sexuality and the evangelical sect in which she has been raised. This can be seen as a special case of the widespread debates around the morality of homosexuality in Christian discourse and practice. However, the 'specialness' of the case in *Oranges* enables the text to eschew debate in favour of a strategy designed to encourage a mainstream audience to empathize with the lesbian protagonist against the church. This is achieved with the simple and time-honoured device of portraying one side in the conflict positively and sympathetically, and the other side negatively and unsympathetically.

The evangelical sect as portrayed in *Oranges* is so dogmatic and intolerant as to constitute a picture of fanaticism. It does not debate issues. When the relationship between Jess and Melanie is discovered, it is unreservedly condemned as 'a great sin', and explained unambiguously: 'These children are full of demons.' That lesbianism is caused by demons is not a position likely to be shared by many British viewers, so the text supplies no recognizably 'normal' interpretations of Jess's sexuality against which to measure the representation of it from her point of view. Nor is the sect's way of dealing with sexual 'deviance' any more acceptable. Melanie is soon cowed into submission by the public humiliation, while Jess is subjected to an exorcism in which she is forcibly held down by the Pastor and other sect members, tied up, gagged and 'prayed over'. This is a very painful scene, far more violent than its equivalent in the novel. Jess is dressed for school, including knee-length white socks, making her appear more like a child than a sexually active adolescent. The sect members, adrenalin clearly flowing, are shown behaving in a morally repugnant manner: four adults grunting and panting as they terrorize a young girl. This moral ugliness is signified too in the gargoyle-like distortion of Jess's face, and is heightened by the participation of Jess's mother in the violence, suggesting the power of extremist ideologies to corrupt family relationships. In this conflict between lesbianism and religion, the latter is clearly a cruel and violent oppressor, the former its pitiful victim. In other words, here it is Christianity that is 'deviant'.

As an example of the oppression of lesbian women, this scene is very powerful. Few could claim that the world is kinder to those it defines as deviant than the faithful are to Jess. Comparison with the novel, however, reminds us that this is a constructed representation of oppression. Winterson can communicate with a readership of women-identified women through irony and understatement in her novel, because she can assume in them a range of knowledge and sentiment that may sensitize them to her meanings. But the less defined audience of television drama may need more persuasion. So it is not only the differing demands of drama and prose fiction that require such a graphically physical dramatization of the violence done to Jess; it is also a rhetorical strategy, which aims to leave no space for the viewer to respond except with unqualified sympathy for Jess and outrage at the faithful.

In the context of British culture this strategy might seem likely to succeed. The long history of hostility towards minority religions in the British media, from Moonies to Islamic fundamentalists to New Age travellers, would place this representation of an evangelical sect as 'mad and bad' in line with cultural prejudices about religious 'extremism'. The sect portrayed in *Oranges* could not, therefore, expect to find many champions among a British audience. As such, the text's strategy can be seen as one that uses one unpopular minority in order to present another unpopular minority in a favourable light.[11]

NATURAL PASSIONS

The portrayal of the lesbian relationship between Jess and Melanie, is, by contrast, couched precisely within the culture's conventional representations of 'young love'. The viewer is positioned with Jess when she first meets Melanie, the camera assuming her point of view as it travels up Melanie's arm until hit reveals her angelic face surrounded by cascading blonde curls. A classic instance of the 'male gaze' transposed into a lesbian context.[12] This is the only relationship in the work to show evidence of that fusion of companionship, affection and sexual passion that our culture defines as 'love'. There is no heterosexual relationship in the text that is 'normal' in a way that might define Jess's lesbian relationship as 'deviant'. The only heterosexual relationships portrayed are those between her parents and between Melanie and Ian. The latter is too sketchily depicted to serve as more than a signifier of Melanie's betrayal of Jess. Mother's dominance of the impenetrably passive William could not, in our culture, serve as a model of married bliss against which to judge Jess's relationship. On the contrary, it is in contrast with Jess's relationship that the others might be found wanting.

Oranges therefore takes for granted that which the dominant ideology would marginalize; investing the 'deviant' relationship with all the highly valued qualities that 'normal' relationships are supposed to possess, while denying them to those relationships that might technically be defined as 'normal'. It thus establishes within itself an oppositional commonsense that claims a lesbian relationship between two adolescent girls as the moral, and therefore cultural, norm. Within this taken-for-granted ground, there is then space to make distinctions: Jess is more committed than Melanie; Jess is more in love with Melanie than she is with Katy. Lesbian relationships are not special in the sense of being unique or being all the same; they are as different and fraught and fragile as our existing commonsense informs us all adolescent passions are. This makes them 'normal', and, according to the dominant ideology, what is normal is what is natural and what is natural is what is right.

Phillippa Giles, the producer of *Oranges*, has said: 'We decided to make it obvious that the girls were having a sexual relationship, not a wishy-washy thing'.[13] This was not how everyone understood it, however. The reviews in the British press tended to see the relationship between Jess and Melanie, either as a comical comeuppance for Jess's fanatically religious mother, or as 'innocent' romance.[14] There are two scenes in the second episode which, because of their polysemic possibilities, are particularly worthy of closer attention here: we call them 'the seduction' and 'the lovemaking'.

The first occurs shortly after Jess and Melanie have met, in the evangelical church where Jess is a preacher. Melanie is 'saved' in response to Jess's appeal for converts. The hymn 'He touched me' is sung, slowly and seductively, while Melanie responds as if in a trance, gazing all the while into Jess's eyes. By superimposing upon each other the religious conversion and sexual seduction, this collapses the two emotional worlds in which Jess lives – that of her religious faith and that of her erotic love. Jess is clearly in command in both spheres. It is possible to read this either as exploitation of sexuality for religious purposes or as exploitation of religion for sexual advantage, or as demonstrating the fusion of religion and sexual passion in Jess. Yet another reading is to understand the scene as portraying the girls' mutual subversion of a situation which embodies the institutional (male) power of the church. While Pastor and congregation anticipate Melanie's submission to their authority, the two girls establish their own definition of what is happening, at the same time securing the community's celebration of their sexual relationship in the moment of its inception – clearly not what the congregation would want.

The 'lovemaking' scene occurs shortly afterwards. The girls spend the night making love in the house of Jess's friend Elsie, an elderly church member. Their lovemaking is portrayed with a mixture of humour, passion and lyricism, marked by elements of ferocity and even danger. The talk of men as beasts, the slow-motion close-ups of the girls' laughing faces, are threateningly surreal, while the accompanying theme music evokes the nightmarish credit sequences. The scene is intercut with shots of Elsie asleep and Mother reading the Bible in bed. These intercuts may be read as an ironic pointer to the girls' subversion of adult assumptions about the universality of heterosexuality, which, far from preventing girls' sexual liaisons, actively facilitate them. Or it may be that the mother's wakefulness suggests the threat that will materialize when their relationship is discovered. That the release of this tension is not represented as orgasm may, of course, be due to self-censorship, but its effect is to leave the sense of danger hanging, to be resolved in the narrative violence of the exorcism. The scene ends lyrically as, naked, they watch the dawn together. This is when Jess says, 'This can't be unnatural passion, can it?' The answer is obviously 'yes' *and* 'no' – depending on who is defining it.

The explicit sexuality of the scene, much heralded in the press, does not occur in the novel, evidence that the television text was designed to challenge head-on assumptions about the 'innocence' or 'prettiness' of both youth and femininity. There is no fudging here about the kind of sexuality involved in a lesbian relationship; no attempt to present it as somehow 'nicer' than heterosexual sex, or to imply that passion is not, in any case, tense and greedy as well as gushing.

PUTTING WOMEN FIRST

Responses to the text's portrayal of the conflict between religion and sexuality are also controlled through the characterization. The most immediate potential source of pleasure that *Oranges* offers women viewers is the opportunity to identify with a female protagonist. In the novel this is facilitated by means of a first-person narration which ensures that the reader sees all the fictional events from the narrator's point of view. Television fictions can only represent first-person narration by means of voice-over, which occurs briefly, but significantly, at the beginning and end of *Oranges*. Otherwise, point of view is controlled by the narrative centrality of the principal character and by the camera's relationship to her.

Jess is the central character of the drama, as of the novel (except that her name is no longer the same as the author's); it is her story that is told, and she is on screen for most of the drama. Such centrality in itself invites audience identification, and is further encouraged by Jess's character: she is portrayed as intelligent, sensitive and principled, and has the strength to triumph over her ill-treatment.

The visual presentation and performance of Jess's character are important factors in influencing audience response. In the first episode the seven-year-old Jess is played by Emily Aston, whose youth makes her competence endearing, both as an actor fulfilling a demanding acting role, and as a character in coping with her environment. She represents the uncorrupted perception of the child, which punctures the (perhaps unwitting) hypocrisy of adults blinkered by the systems they adhere to. Her innocent logic, derived both from that of the religious sect as mediated by her mother, and in opposition to it, is the source of a great deal of humour, always in sympathy with Jess. Thus, she takes her mother's religious language in a secular sense, assuming the 'unnatural passions' of the women in the sweet shop to be chemicals in the sweets; or shows up the triteness of the schoolteacher's remark that 'winning doesn't matter' by asking, 'Why do you give prizes then?' Small Jess is endearing because she has the vulnerability of a child, which invites adult sympathy; but perhaps more important is her ability to cope, which invites admiration. This mix of sympathy and admiration is one that can be carried into responses to the older Jess when she has to confront her community's hostility to her sexuality.

The most attractive feature of the teenage Jess is a development of her early independence of mind: her principled insistence that her sexuality is not, as the church defines it, a sin. This is most dramatically apparent in the second episode, when she challenges the Pastor's denunciation of her relationship, declaring her love for Melanie, and quoting scripture back at him: 'St. Paul says in Romans, Chapter Fourteen, "I know and am persuaded in the Lord that nothing is unnatural in itself; it is made unnatural by those who think it is unnatural".' This, and Jess's declaration that she will never 'learn to hide what's good', is the most explicit statement in *Oranges* about the morality of lesbian sexuality. It is muddied a little by Jess's subsequent repentance and reintegration into the church: is the clandestine nature of her meeting with Melanie and later relationship with Katy evidence of hypocrisy, confusion or inner strength? It may be that doubts aroused here are overshadowed by the violence of the exorcism, and by the moral comparisons between Jess and Melanie (who does renege on the relationship) and between Jess and Miss Jewsbury (who hides her sexuality as a matter of policy).

UNNATURAL PASSION

A character much expanded from a relatively shadowy figure in the novel, the Pastor, more than any other character, embodies the authority and values with which Jess comes into conflict. It is he who publicly denounces Jess and Melanie, who takes charge of the exorcism of Jess, and with whom there is no final reconciliation. He represents the power of the religious institution and its roots in patriarchy. As her chief opponent, both narratively and ideologically, his characterization is clearly important in determining how Jess and her values can be read.

He occupies that depressingly familiar position of the only male in the group being its leader, a position unlikely to endear him to contemporary female audiences, especially since he so clearly revels in the power and prestige it affords him. Bull-necked, clean-shaven to the point of looking scrubbed of his hair, clothes a trifle too tight, stentorian voice modulated to oily whispers: we are not privy to the Pastor's thoughts, so we must judge him as we see him, and what we see is a striking example of hypocrisy. Not necessarily a conscious hypocrisy, but a sublimation of physical desire into the pleasures of self-righteous power. When he rails against 'unnatural passions', he carries no conviction: Jess is so clearly possessed of a natural passion by comparison with the repressed desire that seems to ooze through his constructed asexuality. When he accuses Jess of having 'taken on a man's appetites', we cannot believe him: the Pastor is the only man around with appetites, and Jess's are clearly nothing like his. What is more obviously visible in his pious rage is patriarchy at bay. The construction of the Pastor as villain of the piece must be said to be totally successful and Kenneth Cranham's performance is almost too convincing. With such an opponent, Jess could only win hands down in a bid for audience sympathy.

WHAT A WOMAN!

Much more complex is Jess's relationship with her mother, undoubtedly the most memorable character in the work. The impact of mother as a character lies in her monstrousness, which is at the same time the source of her appeal. This monstrousness stems from the single-mindedness of her religious conviction, which informs all aspects of her life and relationships. It is impossible not to empathize with Jess's situation as the daughter of such an overpoweringly dogmatic woman. Perhaps all mothers have a monstrous dimension in their children's eyes, merely by virtue of their omnipresence, so that this empathy is one that invites memories of viewers' own childhoods – an invitation reinforced in the first episode by the frequency with which the camera assumes small Jess's low visual angle. Perhaps the mother appears unusually overpowering because her worldview is an oppositional one, rendering visible her 'indoctrination' of the child. So that, for example, while her plan for Jess to be a missionary may seem peculiarly authoritarian, it may be its explicitnesses that distinguishes it from the hopes of most other mothers: for many of us have surely said, as Jess does, 'I'm not what she wants. I'm not what she intended. I've gone a different way'?

However, there is also pleasure for women viewers in the character of the mother. The strength of her conviction is the source of her power; informed by the confidence and determination it gives her, she runs the home and brings up Jess apparently single-handed, commits time and energy to the church, and builds a bathroom. Her mental and physical energy is considerable and compelling. This is powerfully conveyed through the performance of Geraldine McEwan. Known to viewers from other television and stage roles, McEwan is visibly representing a character not her own, which is both pleasurable in itself, and lends distance to a character whose excesses might otherwise evoke a more narrowly hostile response.

In patriarchy, women's power can only be realized through struggle and the expenditure of energy such as the mother is possessed of. This must certainly be an important part of the pleasure she offers women viewers. Notwithstanding doubts they may have about the uses to which she puts her energy, the spectacle of her command of herself and situations is awesome. The logic of her convictions is not that of society's commonsense, so that her behaviour often appears comically inappropriate, if not downright mad. She builds a bathroom, not because she needs one, but because the Lord told her to. She considers Jesus an effective alternative to an airing cupboard for growing hyacinths. She wishes 'the boils of Egypt' and 'the ulcers and the scurvy and the itch of which you cannot be cured' upon the next-door neighbour for being noisy. (Well, they are 'fornicating' on a Sunday!)

It is not comedy at her expense, however; for she is always triumphant: she builds the bathroom, the hyacinths grow without an airing cupboard, the next-door neighbour is both silenced and spotty, and she at least regards these as the proof of her convictions. Many of her adversaries are unlikely to elicit strong audience sympathy: the faithful are stereotypically coded as middle-aged/elderly women lacking intelligence and conviction; the next-door neighbour is an unattractively gormless youth; the schoolteacher is locked into a timid conformity. They do not, therefore, constitute a convincing position from which we might be encouraged either to ridicule or condemn the character of the mother. This is true even of those more likeable characters who befriend Jess, whose function is more to demonstrate shortcomings in the mother than to supply an alternative model.

It is by no means fanciful to compare the character of the mother with popular images of Margaret Thatcher as Prime Minister. As dogmatic and powerful middle-aged women, they both invite the same mix of admiration, incredulity, disapproval and passionate hatred. But the mother, seen in her mothering of Jess, has another dimension – her love for her daughter. 'Be careful with her,' she says, when entrusting her to the temporary care of another woman: 'She's my joy.' And there are moments when her singular vision has a genuinely critical edge, as when she dismisses the importance of a school test with 'It's how you live your life that's the test.'

And Jess is, as the saying goes, 'her mother's daughter'. She inherits her mother's strength of conviction, her principled insistence on pursuing openly what she thinks is right, her passion, her logic and her combativeness. Whether or not, as she says of her mother, Jess also '*likes* to wrestle', Jess does wrestle. In the affirmation of her lesbian identity, she becomes, as Winterson said of herself, an evangelist. As a result, she is her mother's only equal as an adversary in a battle in which neither is defeated. This is the bond between them, the mother's bequest to the daughter.

The theme of betrayal is strong in Winterson's novel:

> There are different sorts of treachery, but betrayal is betrayal wherever you find it. She burnt a lot more than the letters that night in the backyard. I don't think she knew. In her head she was still queen, but not my queen any more.[15]

There is no doubt that the rift between mother and daughter in the television version of *Oranges* is a drastic one. The more central role of the Pastor, however, means that it occurs as part of the conflict between Jess and the church. While the end of the novel portrays the rift between mother and daughter as irretrievable, its non-linear narrative facilitates an emotionally complex reading of the relationship. In the chronologically simpler structure of the drama, to have emphasized this theme of betrayal may have given the conflict between the two women too clear a dominance over the bonds that unite them.

The reconciliation in the concluding scene of the television version is commensurately more established than the feelings of dissatisfaction with which the novel concludes. As in the book, there is no settling of accounts between mother and daughter, but in the television version both script and performance suggest that the mother, in not ignoring that there has been a rift, is implicitly acting to heal it. There is also a sense, conveyed through facial expression and body language, of her distancing herself from the Pastor's hostility towards Jess. The work ends, then, with a pleasurable sense of recognition, as Jess smiles at the spectacle of her mother calling up 'electronic believers all over the north west' on the CB radio she has built herself. She has not kissed her mother, but, seeming to recognize the extent to which she remains indomitably the same, has accepted what reconciliation the mother can offer. This is not quite a resolution, but it is a satisfactory narrative closure that leaves the viewer with a sense of hope encapsulated in the gentle comedy of the scene.

'Fatherhood is a fiction' suggests Stephen Daedalus in *Ulysses*,[16] meaning that, whereas women know which children they have borne, the biological link between father and child can only be assumed, so that fatherhood is a matter of choice, a spiritual rather than a genetic connection. Fatherhood is a fiction for Jess because William plays no active part in her life. But Jess is an adopted child, so for her motherhood too is a fiction, a choice, a spiritual connection. And none the less true and powerful for that.

Oranges is uncompromising in its denial of the role of nature in the mother/daughter relationship. It dismisses it as ruthlessly and effectively as the mother dismisses Jess's biological mother. 'I'm your real mother,' she says, and the text proves her right: the natural mother is never spoken of again. The dynamic of Jess and her mother's relationship is worked through in terms of their filial bond with no attempt to explain their differences as due to the absence of a blood tie between them. This is a strong and liberating message, with its claim that who we are might be the product of circumstance, but it is not written in our genes; it is human choices that shape even our most intimate relations.

WOMEN AND CHILDREN FIRST

Jess's relationships with her mother, lovers and friends take place within a predominantly female community, which is itself a pleasure for women viewers. Both in the church and elsewhere, this community is composed almost entirely of women. It is no feminist Utopia: as well as friendship, support and love, there is jealousy, prejudice and cruelty. The point is not whether women's relationships are idealized, but whether they are prioritized over those of, and with, men.

History has made the inheritance of women invisible. *Oranges* portrays aspects of this history of women. Through Elsie, Jess's elderly friend; through Cissy who gives her a home and a job in the funeral parlour after the break with her mother, and above all though the mother herself, Jess is heir to generations of women's experience. This is expressed particularly through the wealth of stories that the mother tells Jess; stories from the Bible, stories about the conversion of sinners, about her own conversion, about her own past when she 'was slim'. The tradition of women has been a predominantly oral one, its values passed on in the stories mothers tell their children in the course of everyday life. Not the official histories of men, but the intimate histories of women.

The narrative never offers the viewer a masculine point of view, and the camera only does so very rarely – in brief shot-reverse-shot exchanges. With the important exception of the Pastor, male characters and concerns are marginalized in *Oranges*. William, Jess's father, is silent throughout, until he says 'Amen' in the last scene. Graham, against whose attractions Jess is warned, is only a foil for her relationship with Melanie; Ian, Melanie's fiancé is a sign of her betrayal of Jess; both are, in any case, very small roles. Jess and Melanie, in the love scene, laugh at the beastliness of men and dismiss marriage – as Melanie says, 'You have to cook and clean all the time.' They compare their relationship to that of David and Jonathan, who were married, but 'loved each other best'. This dismissal, through narrative and dialogue, achieves the marginalization of men in Jess's consciousness that is explicit in the book:

> As far as I was concerned men were something you had around the place, not particularly interesting, but quite harmless.[17]

All Jess's important relationships are with women and girls. In addition none of the women characters are shown as having an important relationship with a man, so the relationships between women, and most significantly, the lesbian relationships, do not occur in a context that foregrounds the heterosexual institutions of coupledom or the family.

YOU CAN ALWAYS TELL ONE

Homophobic ideology maintains that homosexual people are identifiable by how they look. In the novel, Winterson's narrator explicitly denies that her sexual preference for women means that she is 'aping men'.[18] In the television drama, this denial is embodied in the casting and characterization.

None of the characters who are lesbian, or involved in lesbian relationships, conform visually to butch stereotypes; on the contrary, they may be seen as calculated to challenge them. This is clearly most important in respect of Jess, who, both as child and adolescent, is visually coded as 'normal': whereas in the novel, for example, she says she never wears skirts,[19] in the drama she wears trousers only once – presumably a calculated avoidance of any suggestion of 'butch'. Melanie resembles a pre-Raphaelite heroine, a stereotype of femininity in direct opposition to the butch stereotype, which women-identified viewers might recognize as femme, but which others might see as explaining why anyone, including another girl, would fall in love with her. Katy, with whom Jess's relationship is less intense, is by contrast coded as a sixties teenager, keen on pop music and dressed in the fashion of the time, despite being apparently of (what the British refer to as) 'Asian' origin.

The clear message is that there is no identifiable 'lesbian type'. More than this, because these are the only adolescent girls to appear in the drama, the implication is that lesbianism is not only normal, but normative. The two boys who approach Katy and Jess in the fairground are gently and jokingly dismissed. Graham is of no interest to Jess, despite the suspicions of the faithful. And seen from Jess's point of view, as it is, Melanie's impending marriage to Ian, coded as a scruffy and arrogant youth, is a betrayal, not only of Jess herself, but of sisterhood.

The characterization of Miss Jewsbury, the only adult lesbian in the work, is significant. Younger than the other church members, she is Jess's only active ally when she is denounced for 'unnatural passions'. Here is an example of sisterhood in action, which could be seen as an example of lesbian networking, so one might have expected the relationship between her and Jess to be represented as a close one. Yet when Miss Jewsbury offers friendship at Elsie's funeral, Jess rejects it sharply. Why? Readers of the book might interpret this as due to Jess's sense of betrayal at having been seduced by Miss Jewsbury after the public denunciation. But this seduction does not happen in the drama.

If the reason for their lack of intimacy is therefore somewhat obscure, it nevertheless has significant implications for what the work says about relations between women. If all close friendships in the text are between women, this is not to say that all women are automatically friends. More pointedly, it claims that not all lesbians are automatically friends, let alone lovers. Popular stereotypes about gay people often make precisely that assumption – as if, unlike heterosexuals, homosexuals are sexually attracted to every member of their sexual preference. This, we guess, is why Miss Jewsbury's seduction of Jess is omitted from the dramatization. It would confirm this popular stereotype.

The lack of intimacy between Jess and Miss Jewsbury is also a denial of another homophobic prejudice: that children are in danger of seduction by adult homosexuals. A woman-identified readership may well be able to accept that exploitative relationships exist between women as between men and women, but a general audience would be less likely to read it in that context. Instead, therefore, the mother's attempts to keep Jess away from Miss Jewsbury, are rendered pointless, since she clearly has no influence on Jess and offers her no role model. On the contrary, she is cast as foil to Jess's principled refusal to hide her sexuality. Miss Jewsbury is a closet lesbian, who defines her lesbianism as the 'problem' of 'loving the wrong people'. Visually, this apologetic attitude is coded by her rather spinsterish dowdiness and stiff body language. Narratively, it is made clear that her temerity is not rewarded by acceptance by the faithful, who consider her 'unholy'.

Elsie, on the other hand, is both confidante and friend. Coded as a stereotypically batty, but kind, wise old lady, Elsie is a woman-identified woman. She has been a suffragette, militant enough to have been imprisoned; she colludes in trying to protect Jess and Melanie from the wrath of the faithful, and makes derogatory remarks about men (doctors are 'men of knives'), including, in a gentle way, God himself. She is presumably a widow, although a married past forms no part of her characterization. That she might also identify as a lesbian is a possible inference, but it is sufficient to see her as firmly located within what Rich called the 'lesbian continuum'.[20]

Lesbianism is, therefore, represented as common to all types of women, regardless of appearance, personality, age or ethnic origin. The text claims that lesbians are not identifiable by any particular set of characteristics; that they may or may not relate to each other as lovers, friends or even as fellow-lesbians. The truth of this, does, however, evade the specificity of a shared lesbian identity; it does not represent any sense of a lesbian community, nor any of the choices lesbians may make in relation to appearance, body language or lifestyle. Presumably this evasion was a deliberate one, designed to convey the message that lesbianism and lesbians are 'ordinary'.

RADICAL REALISM

The single most important claim that the text makes in relation to lesbianism is that it is ordinary, a normal way for people to relate to each other; in short, lesbianism is 'naturalized'. By this we do not mean that the text intervenes in the nature/nurture debate; it does not discuss Jess's sexuality or try to explain or justify it – not in terms of hormones, biography or sexual politics. There is, indeed, no mention of the terms 'lesbian' or 'homosexual'. It does not employ the strategy of a liberal text, which would engage in debate with the dominant ideology, taking its commonsense for granted, but seeking to modify or question it, explaining its absences and contradictions, defending alternatives. In relation to lesbianism, the film *Lianna* is an example of such a strategy: the friends of the woman who leaves her husband for a relationship with a woman are shown coming to terms with her sexuality as 'other', accepting her *despite* her lesbianism.

Oranges does not work like this. Instead, it presents Jess's lesbianism as something that, from her point of view – and therefore also from the viewer's – just *is*. What is considered natural in our culture is that which 'just is' – that which is obviously the case, which needs no explaining or arguing for. A work of fiction never feels the need to explain, or argue for, heterosexual relations. Where there is conflict in relation to a heterosexual relationship it is not about why or whether men and women should fall in love with each other. Similarly, *Oranges* does not discuss why Jess is in love with Melanie, or whether she should be: she just is. In this sense, her lesbianism is naturalized just as heterosexuality is naturalized in most other texts.

This is so in spite of the fact that the narrative conflict springs from the sect's hostility to Jess's sexuality. Central to the portrayal of this conflict between fundamentalism and lesbianism is the contrasting representation of each in terms of 'normality'. Both are opposed to what the dominant ideological formations of British culture define as 'normal' sexuality and 'normal' religion. Yet while Jess's lesbianism is portrayed as a moral norm of relationships, the portrayal of the fundamentalist sect calls into question its values and practices, and implicitly judges it against a morality assumed to be more humane and intelligent – which would not persecute homosexuality. The text's problematic is not, therefore, lesbianism, but fundamentalism, which is found wanting by the moral norms embodied in the character of Jess.

This naturalization of lesbianism depends on its representation within the conventions of a realism that is also, and more usually, the medium for the transmission of ideological norms. It is, if you like, an 'illiberal' strategy, constructing the narrative conflict, characters and events in order to encourage a particular reading and exclude (or at least discourage) alternative readings. This is not a question of documentary truth; we can assume that historical reality is always capable of excesses greater than those of fiction; and documentaries can effect closure too. Nor is it a question of bias: all representation involves selectivity and perspective, including non-realist, 'open' texts. As Winterson says, 'I am lying to you, but I am also telling you the truth.'[21]

Nor are the conventions of realism committed to what it is that they represent as the 'real'. In its formal transformations, realism has a long history as the medium of radicalism, of challenges to dominant versions of reality. From Emile Zola to Robert Tressell, from Richard Wright to Alice Walker, from Bessie Head to Chinua Achebe, realism has been the novelistic medium for challenging capitalism, racism, sexism, colonialism. And from *Cathy Come Home* to *Boys from the Blackstuff*, British television drama has employed varieties of realism to challenge the status quo and establish a different worldview, a different morality, as the basis of commonsense.

Oranges works in this tradition to establish a lesbian identity as the basis of its commonsense. In the context of contemporary Britain this is a powerful claim to make.

Far from militating against the possibility of challenging dominant ideological positions, realism remains the dominant medium in our culture through which such challenge can be effective. The avant-garde, in all its forms, can outrage commonsense, can mock it, question it, turn it upside down. What it cannot do is establish a new commonsense. Only realism can do that. This is precisely what the television version of *Oranges* achieves in relation to lesbianism; as realist television drama it is a more radical text, formally and socially, than the non-realist novel from which it was adapted.

A version of this article has appeared in *Jump Cut*, No 39, Spring 1994.

OUT: REFLECTIONS ON BRITISH TELEVISION'S FIRST LESBIAN AND GAY MAGAZINE SERIES

Diane Hamer with Penny Ashbrook

Out on Tuesday was first screened by Channel 4 on Valentine's Day in 1989. Since then, there have been three further series, in three consecutive years, with a fifth to come in 1994. The series was a landmark – it was the first lesbian and gay series to be commissioned by and screened on mainstream commercial television anywhere in the world. Penny Ashbrook was one of the producers of *Out on Tuesday*, which was made almost exclusively by lesbians and gays – a fact which was reflected in the perspective it took up. It was not an objective anthropology of lesbian and gay life, as earlier programmes such as *Gay Life* in the 1970s had been, but offered a highly subjective take on a broad and often surprising range of subjects from a gay perspective – pets, haircuts, country and western music and Hollywood were mixed with a more sober examination of political issues of concern to lesbians and gay men.

Out on Tuesday (later renamed *OUT*) had an enormous impact on lesbian and gay visibility and culture, and on mainstream television itself. The series set a trend and, in Britain at least, the rest of television is now following in its wake. In style (the title sequence of the third series was nominated for the *Prix d'Italia*) and content, *Out on Tuesday* and *OUT* established a precedent which other programmes and programme makers have been keen to follow.

IN OR *OUT* OF THE MAINSTREAM

Out on Tuesday was commissioned by Channel 4 in 1988, only months after the Conservative government's Local Government Bill had been enacted into law. The Act included the now infamous Section 28, which prohibited the 'promotion' of homosexuality by local authorities. It was a popular, though inaccurate, belief that Section 28 would operate to prevent Channel 4 from proceeding with plans for a lesbian and gay series. It did not. Channel 4 did not fall within the terms of the Act, but their going ahead with the series in the shadow of the Section caused tabloid controversy and allegedly made many at Channel 4 nervous.

When it first went on air, *Out on Tuesday* was part of Channel 4's 'minority remit'. It had been commissioned by the independent film and video department, which was seen as dealing with minority interest groups. Its position in the viewing schedule - 11 p.m. on a Tuesday night, confirmed its marginal status.

One of the major concerns at Channel 4 was the likely impact of the programme on advertisers. There was much speculation that they would be scared off by the subject matter of the series and refuse to buy time during its transmission. The late-night slot seemed to offer proof of Channel 4's concern not to alienate its viewers or advertisers. In fact, according to Susan Ardill, one of the series producers, the 11 p.m. slot was liberating for the series, in that it enabled programme makers to be far more explicit about sexual issues than would have been possible earlier in the evening.

What actually happened was that the rating figures for the programme regularly exceeded the one million mark, a figure not much lower than Channel 4's average ratings figures for much of its mainstream programming. The *Media Show*, for example, screened at the prime time of 8 p.m. on a Sunday evening, rarely attracted audiences of that number – its average audience was put at 700,000.

Penny Ashbrook: 'Around this time Channel 4 also showed

Sebastiane by Derek Jarman and advertising agencies wouldn't book slots during its transmission. In fact it got one of the highest viewing figures ever and questions were asked as to why the agencies hadn't booked space. After that it was recognized that lesbian and gay programming was popular programming. Obviously the audience figures showed this and there was a gradual realization that the audience for a lesbian and gay series is a perfect target for advertisers. Double income, no children, no dependents (particularly gay men), make them a prime target for consumer advertising.'

Ironically, far from alienating viewers or advertisers, *Out on Tuesday* and *OUT* established Channel 4's reputation as the station which dared to take the initiative, a channel prepared to take risks. It provoked the greatest viewer response of any programme ever screened on Channel 4. Of the calls logged though many expressed moral outrage or prurient fascination with the subject matter of the series, the majority of viewers were calling to express their appreciation and admiration for the series. Such calls were by no means limited to gay viewers. It is clear from the duty log that the series was also attracting a mainstream heterosexual audience who regarded it as 'cutting edge' television.

The press response was also remarkable. The run-up to transmission was accompanied by a frenzy of tabloid interest. Newspapers searched for salacious stories and sensational angles in order to express their mock outrage and demonstrate Channel 4's folly and low moral standards in bringing such a series to television. But once screened the series attracted rave reviews, often from unexpected sources, like the *Daily Mail*, usually known for its homophobic reporting. According to producer Susan Ardill, the tabloid press were silenced by the richness and complexity of lesbian and gay culture and by the programme's high-quality production standards. If they reacted at all, the press response was extremely positive, demonstrating the irrational and contradictory way the tabloid press approaches sexuality.

P.A.: 'After the first series the world didn't fall apart, the advertisers didn't withdraw their money from Channel 4. There was an audience for a lesbian and gay programme and the figures were very good. I think the series was revolutionary for changing people's attitudes within the medium about what is possible and what is acceptable and these boundaries have been pushed further and further in the years since that first series.'

The second series, screened the following year, was shown at 9 p.m.; a slot which symbolized its move from the margins to the mainstream. Its commissioning editor at Channel 4, Caroline Spry, described it as 'a major card the Channel has to play in keeping an audience into the 1990s'. *Out on Tuesday* was by now part of prime time television.

THE *OUT* AGENDA

A major impact of the programme was to put a whole range of lesbian and gay issues on the televisual map and in the face of the viewing public. P.A.: 'The main thing I noticed was the effect it had on British broadcasting generally. It was striking that after the first couple of series there was much more lesbian and gay coverage across television and the media in general. Several years after *OUT* programmes about sex and sexuality were being made and were, as a matter of course, incorporating a lesbian and gay perspective. That would not have been the case in the past.'

British viewers saw *Sex Talk* and *Love Talk* on Channel 4; *From Wimps to Warriors* on BBC2 and Margi Clarke's *sex* programme on ITV; bisexuality on *Open Space*; lesbian and gay issues on the BBC's *Heart of the Matter* and *Def II*; homosexuality and religion on the BBC's *Everyman*; gay television on Channel 4's *Media Show*; and 'coming out' in the civil service on *Verdict* and *Free for All* (both Channel 4). This list is by no means exhaustive.

Out on Tuesday and *OUT* dealt with issues of sex and sexuality in a mood which was more open and exploratory than had been known before, and undoubtedly affected the making of many of these programmes. Through looking at lesbian and gay sexuality, heterosexuality became the subject of inquiry and was put under the microscope, no longer taken for granted nor its naturalness assumed. Programme after programme continues to take heterosexuality apart and tries to figure out what makes it tick. Also, post-*OUT*, such programmes could no longer forget to include homosexuality as part of their subject matter. The inclusion of lesbian and gay issues and concerns became obligatory not for mere curiosity value but as a genuine area of inquiry. As a topic, homosexuality has become both serious and deeply fashionable.

P.A.: 'One of the worries of having a series was that everyone would feel that lesbian and gay issues had been done and that was it. But it was exciting that the opposite happened; the fact that there was a lesbian and gay series made everyone else sit up and take notice and start to deal with lesbian and gay issues. It had the effect of increasing coverage everywhere rather than ghettoizing it.'

The series also initiated particular transformations around the use of the word 'lesbian' and the representation of lesbianism. P.A.: 'People suddenly were no longer afraid to use the word 'lesbian' on air. This was after fifty years of broadcasting without the word lesbian being spoken. Lesbianism became an issue [and broadcasters] could say the word. I am absolutely certain that the series has contributed to the changing climate, fuelled by many different things, including the number of visible, out lesbians and acceptable media images.'

OUT EFFECTS

Out on Tuesday ensured a continuing lesbian and gay presence in television production as a result of the series producers' employment policy. This policy was continued by the commissioning editor when the programme became *OUT*. Wherever possible, the researchers, directors, producers and production staff who worked on the series were lesbian or gay. P.A.: 'One of the major innovations and achievements of *Out on Tuesday* and *OUT* was to bring new people into television. In every series there have been programmes made by first-time directors and producers. This is one of the series' most positive points; in a very real way it opened up a doorway into television for lesbians and gay men. This was a conscious process.'

Many lesbians and gay men working now on programmes such as *Rough Justice*, *Heart of the Matter*, *The Late Show*, *The South Bank Show*, *First Sex*, *Cutting Edge* and *Dispatches* established their reputations because of, not despite, their involvement with a lesbian and gay programme. The series not only encouraged lesbians and gays to work in television but also to become programme makers. Made in Britain, and subsequently bought by television stations around the world, including Australia, the United States and Holland, the series has also been a force behind an international boom in lesbian and gay film festivals.

P.A.: 'As a programmer of the London Lesbian and Gay Film Festival it was very noticeable that after two series of *Out on Tuesday* had gone to air more lesbian and gay material was being produced in Britain. I was able to put together a programme of lesbian shorts made entirely by British directors, a feat which would have been inconceivable two years before as there was hardly any British lesbian material submitted to the festival before this. Visible series like *Out On Tuesday* help to legitimize issues around sexuality as an acceptable thing to make films and videos about. And it was not that *Out on Tuesday* was imitated – there was a huge variety of material.'

The *OUT* series were indeed landmarks. One can only speculate as to the impact they have had on popular representations of lesbianism. What is obvious is that the series have underscored a more general trend towards embracing homosexuality and lesbianism as fashion statements. Lesbian chic is here and *OUT* continues to take lesbianism into the mainstream at the cutting edge of fashion.

PUSSY GALORE:
LESBIAN IMAGES AND LESBIAN DESIRE
IN THE POPULAR CINEMA

Yvonne Tasker

What is a 'lesbian film'?

This is a question I'll try to answer by looking at lesbian images and more elusive lesbian desire within contemporary mainstream cinema.

Though often heavily coded and 'disguised', lesbian characters and images of lesbian desire (often cast as a disturbing force) have regularly recurred in popular films in the west. Various feminist critics have contemptuously dismissed popular films such as *Lianna*, *Black Widow* and *Desert Hearts*. But women, feminist or not, flocked to see them. Does this simply represent cultural snobbery from the critics? Perhaps not, since such films are simultaneously deemed interesting and yet found wanting in quite complex ways. This double move indicates how the interest and expectations that critics have brought to the popular cinema have repeatedly been disappointed, chiefly because these films do not present 'positive images'. There is a tendency in some feminist criticism to fantasize lesbianism as a pure space, somehow separate from the play of power and hierarchies through which life is lived. Since film (like women) cannot easily match up to this fantasy, the popular cinema is often simply *found wanting*. I'm not suggesting here that the films discussed below are in some way perfect, but arguing instead for the importance of a move away from the straitjacket of a search for positive images that cannot, by definition, be found.

The material presented here is divided into four sections, as follows: lesbians in the popular cinema; hints of perversion in the popular; 'lesbian' films which use mainstream techniques; and lesbian camp and the popular cinema. These different categories aim to take account of the different work and interaction of three key factors, film texts, filmmakers and the audiences for the popular cinema.

LESBIANS IN THE POPULAR CINEMA

The 1980s and early 1990s, while in many respects a period of conservatism, saw an increased visibility for lesbians in British and American popular culture. Moreover the fluidity of sexuality as a category of identity and the perversity of desire are registered in a variety of films. Two recent mainstream films, *The Silence of the Lambs* and *Basic Instinct*, have proved particularly controversial in their portrayal of perverse sexualities.[1] Both films open up interesting sets of questions about lesbian identities and popular cinematic representations. If *Basic Instinct* found itself the object of lobbying by gay activists in the United States, it nonetheless offered a high visible image of polymorphous perversity. The film's ambiguous heroine Catherine Tramell (Sharon Stone), asserts the right to fuck freely. As J. Hoberman put it 'Stone is the ultimate bad girl' who at every opportunity 'flaunts her transgressive power'.[2] She becomes a fascinating figure to the film's policeman hero, Nick, who, in a long-established tradition, sets about a murder investigation and ends up perplexed by the enigma of the *femme fatale*. Here the deadly woman's danger is not only that posed by a serial killer, but that of a figure who does not respect boundaries. Theorists and critics have found such blurring of boundaries a rich area of inquiry. By contrast, activists – who need – have often had to reassert the fixity of boundaries.

The fact that Catherine is (probably) a murderer triggered angry protests about the negative portrayal of a 'lesbian' character. The protests, constituted within the paradigm of positive images, mobilize an important tradition of activism around representation. Yet they also sidestep the difficult questions posed by the status of Catherine's sexuality within the film. If one positions Catherine as a 'lesbian' character, then it becomes possible to read *Basic Instinct* in a variety of ways. It can be read as a reactionary narrative in which the heroine is 'cured', converted to heterosexuality by the sexual charms of Michael Douglas. This is the kind of narrative devolved around the character of Pussy Galore in *Goldfinger*, seemingly in all earnestness in Fleming's novel, though rendered jokingly in the film. Seduced by James Bond, she rejects her lesbian desires. In *Basic Instinct* we see Catherine's girlfriend(s) messily dispatched so that while she remains alive at the film's close, this has been achieved at some cost. While it is possible to read *Basic Instinct* as a narrative of conversion to heterosexuality, it is difficult to reconcile the notional power of a male sexuality with some of the images within the film. Indeed, the comedy of this scenario is rather acutely brought out in the scene in which Douglas's character flaunts his sexual achievement to Catherine's girlfriend. Though he is busy bragging about his sexual prowess, the whole two-shot scene is shot with the aid of mirror and a pot plant to cover Nick's vulnerable nakedness.

The dominating image of Catherine Tramell represents, for some, a fascinating assertion of perversion. She is the heroine who strikingly asserts her existence, her power and her right to take sexual pleasure. Independently wealthy and beautiful, she is also a writer, a creator of images. Catherine's stories are forged from the people she meets and (possibly) kills. She incorporates and transforms identities, acutely looking through the different masks and poses presented by the police. She teases Douglas about his relationship with his male police partner and challenges the law to prove her guilty. Stone's 'repertoire of Lilith wiles and vampire smiles' are ever present in the film, even staring out at us from the promotional poster.[3] There is ultimately little suspense or revelation involved in the final shot which tracks down from the bed that Catherine and Nick share to reveal a hidden ice-pick which fills the screen in a final visual gag.

The Silence of the Lambs, like *Basic Instinct*, attracted a range of reviews and responses. Criticism of *The Silence of the Lambs* centred largely on the portrayal of the film's 'gay' serial killer, Buffalo Bill. Activists protesting against the film pointed to the deployment of signifiers associated with gay male sexuality. Reading the villain as gay is both possible and yet impossible, simultaneously inevitable and absurd. The disturbing sexual dysfunction that characterizes Bill's deviance lies in a wish to change his body. He hides his penis from view, seeking to transform his body into something else. Critics argued that such nuances would be missed by the popular audience who would simply read 'gay man'. Yet, if all sexual dysfunction is understood as 'gay' or 'lesbian', then what categories of sexual identity does a film like *Silence of the Lambs* produce? The 'lesbian' question interestingly comes up around the film's star, Jodie Foster. She is our point of identification in the film, playing a rookie FBI investigator struggling to gain a sense of identity within the male-dominated institution of the FBI. Foster was criticized not for her powerful performance, but for not 'coming out', for refusing to accept in a public way the identity 'lesbian'. Like Catherine's sexuality in *Basic Instinct*, the debates surrounding Foster's role in *The Silence of the Lambs* raises the old question of an essential identity. But as writers like Suzanne Moore have noted, many women found pleasure in these films, with their defiant/deviant heroines.[4] Like Linda Hamilton in *Terminator 2*, Sigourney Weaver in the *Alien* films or Jamie Lee Curtis in *Blue Steel*, these performances play with gendered and sexual identities, rendering them ambiguous and uncertain. These fantasy representations mobilize a range of readings, and the pleasures are many. They are pleasures which can't be easily assessed in terms of the desire for a gay version of heterosexual suburban family life. Neither can we find in such images the reflection of an imagined, stable sexual identity.

Clearly then, thinking about the figure of the lesbian in the popular cinema is not a simple task. As feminist criticism has discovered, representations and the pleasures that they offer cannot be judged through their correspondence to some fantasized essential identity – 'woman'. Exploring the figure of 'the lesbian' is not a particularly productive project when taken in isolation from more general questions of sexuality and representation at any particular moment. A film like *Basic Instinct* was enmeshed in a set of controversies and debates, as well as being situated within a particular generic history. Its pleasures are not easily fixed and are differently available to a range of audiences. It would seem that the popular cinema of the 1980s and 1990s offers a more fluid conception of identity, moving away from attempts to constitute 'homo' and 'hereo' identities as unshakeable categories cast in binary opposition. Not coincidentally, the period in which such ambiguous images have achieved visibility is a time in which a range of radical writings have sought to challenge a binary understanding of sexuality.[5] All of this represents an important set of questions for something called lesbian cultural criticism and film criticism, the beginnings of a body of institutionalized critical work that is emerging with the gradual establishment of lesbian and gay studies.

HINTS OF PERVERSION IN THE POPULAR

Despite the way in which popular cinema, like other mediums of fantasy, operates as a space in which identity is up for grabs, there is nonetheless a particular charge involved in finding that one's surrogate on the screen is a woman. That charge is partly a result of the relative absence of both female and lesbian characters. In recent films like *Thelma and Louise* the representation of female friendship is explored. The hints of perversion are enticing. After all, 'flirty' relationships between 'girls' are such an important part of women's popular culture. *Black Widow* also plays on this aspect of female friendship, more blatantly suggesting a sexualized aspect to such relationships between women. But because the film hints at lesbian desire rather than being explicitly concerned with the portrayal of a lesbian relationship, some felt that the sexually charged scenes between women were merely exploitative, coyly invoking but ultimately refusing the representation of lesbian desire.

Black Widow's narrative of incorporation and identification touches on the themes of the vampire myth, within which lesbian and gay desire has been a recurrent theme. Cinematically though, the film can primarily be situated within the thriller genre, a tradition which it calls on, with references to *film noir*. It is within this genre that the almost supernatural qualities attributed to the dangerous woman have been most insistently played out. *Black Widow* follows the relationship between Alex (Debra Winger), a bored government worker turned investigator, and the mysterious Catherine (Theresa Russell) who marries and murders a series of wealthy men. Catherine (who bears several other names in the film) is a woman whose identity and motivation is uncertain, as she transforms herself from one image (or parody) of desirable womanhood to another. Alex becomes more and more involved in these transformations as the film follows her increasingly obsessive pursuit of Catherine. In an early scene she projects images of Catherine's different personae, taken from photographs and press clippings, onto the wall of her apartment. She caresses the wall on which the images appear before examining her own face in the mirror. She gives up her job/life to follow this mysterious woman. This central relationship between female protagonists reworks not only the themes of *film noir*, in the figure of the dangerous woman under investigation, but those traditions of the thriller which revolve around an eroticized male bonding across two sides of the law.[6] This quite common narrative structure typically features a lawman hero who becomes involved with, or fixed on, a criminal, who increasingly functions as his double. The investigation becomes bound-up in desire, a process which literally involves the shifting and questioning of assumed identities, as different kinds of transgressions are collapsed together. This is exactly the sort of narrative that *Basic Instinct* plays on through the relationship between Nick and Catherine, whose pursuit of each other is entangled in sexual desire. This kind of popular narrative exemplifies the processes by which identifications are forged and blurred within the cinema, generating an uncertainty that is both disturbing and, more importantly, pleasurable.

The fact that *Black Widow* can be situated firmly within this tradition of representation, one that is centred on men, may have something to do with the critical suspicion and uncertainty which has surrounded this film, along with similar cinematic endeavours.[7] Such suspicions stem partly from the kinds of categories which feminist (and other) critics have constructed, particularly through theorizations of gendered genre. While such theories worked in part to open up a study of neglected popular cultural forms associated with women, they have also functioned proscriptively to assert that some forms are more appropriate to men and some to women.[8]

Unfortunately, women's culture often seems to be studied with the ultimate aim of transcending it, hopefully redirecting the viewer to the space of the avant-garde. Against this space the popular must always be perceived as compromised. Yet avant-garde cinema has often revelled in precisely the kind of blurring of boundaries that I've spoken about in the realm of the popular. When I'm speaking about 'hints of perversion' in the popular cinema, this isn't to argue that a film like *Black Widow* isn't a 'proper' lesbian film, one which only hints at its lesbian theme without daring to make it explicit. There is very little that is proper about the movie at all, taking up as it does the messy interplay of identification and desire, the doubling and subversion of identities. The significant transformations that Alex undergoes are situated against the shifting figure that Catherine represents in the film. Alex initially turns herself into a tireless investigator, rejecting her tedious role in the office and adopting a variety of identities to get close to Catherine. Her embrace of the cinematic codes of masculinity and femininity produces her as a complex figure, rather than a compromised one, in a film which explores the limits and pleasures of these categories. The whole notion of positive images of 'proper lesbians' in 'proper lesbian movies' presupposes a developmental model in which a grown-up sexual identity – gay or straight – is achieved, definable and stable. The popular cinema works to challenge and explore the pleasures available outside such clear political categories of identity.

'LESBIAN' FILMS USING MAINSTREAM TECHNIQUES

During the 1980s several successful mainstream films which explicitly revolve around lesbian relationships and lesbian desire have been in circulation in the west. Surely if any form of the popular cinema could be termed 'lesbian' it would be this. *Desert Hearts*, a film that has been both hugely popular and roundly criticized for its use of a mainstream narrative form, is obviously a key point of reference. The story of a developing romance between two women, the film picks up on the themes and images associated with the women's film, that of a rhetoric of self-discovery. *Desert Hearts* throws up definitions of a lesbian cinema and the 'lesbian subject' of that cinema.[9] In an essay on women's cinema in the 1980s, Teresa De Lauretis praises Sheila McLaughlin's *She Must Be Seeing Things* as a film which 'locates itself historically and politically in the contemporary North American lesbian community with its conflicting discourses, posing the question of desire and its representation from within the context of actual practices of both lesbianism and cinema'. This praise is then contrasted to 'the romance or fairy-tale formulas adopted by films like *Lianna*, *Desert Hearts* or *I've Heard the Mermaids Singing*'.[10] While I have no intention of criticizing McLaughlin's fascinating film, it is nonetheless important to note that two very different kinds of cinema are being contrasted here. *Desert Hearts* is situated within popular traditions, rather than those of the underground art movie. It mobilizes the established forms of the romance and women's fiction to tell a *lesbian* romance. For director Donna Deitch the lesbian nature of the romance is both crucial and unimportant to the story being told.[11] The film explores the relationships between a range of women in a fantasized context that dramatizes the restrictions and tensions though which desire is played out. Within the context of the 1980s, *Desert Hearts* could not help but be a political film, a controversial object. If Deitch knows this, she nonetheless attempts to tell the story, based on Jane Rule's novel, within the codes of popular cinematic pleasure.

Surely there can be room for such a film within the schema of a lesbian cinema? Not for a critic like De Lauretis, for whom the term 'lesbian' becomes associated with a radical space of 'guerrilla cinema', a cinema that is knowing about regimes of looking, aware of and manipulating the voyeuristic power that is at work in the cinematic image. Perhaps more worrying than De Lauretis' dismissal of popular lesbian films, is her simultaneous invocation and neglect of the diversity of lesbian identities. Admitting conflict and diversity within that category she nonetheless produces a proscriptive formula for what the cinema should be, and a unitary lesbian subject. Like feminist criticism, is a lesbian criticism being evolved that does not speak to the experience of lesbian audiences, dictating to rather than listening to voices that have already been marginalized? Suzanne Moore's review of *Desert Hearts* similarly argued that by 'setting the story in the 1950s, and by removing the central character, Vivian, from any social background, the film comfortably avoids dealing with the particular challenge of non-heterosexuality'.[12] There is nothing inherently radical in being lesbian or gay, no essence which locates 'us' outside the play of power. Fantasizing, as De Lauretis does, a lesbian look that is 'neither masculine, a usurpation of male heterosexual desire, nor a feminine, narcissistic identification with the other woman' renders these terms somehow unproblematic. Identification does not preclude desire, as *Black Widow* demonstrates. These identities are diverse and struggled over, not simple monolithic categories. Equally, there is no necessary relationship between a modernist aesthetic and a 'lesbian' film. The dismissal of a film like *Desert Hearts* has the unhappy consequence of negating not only the pleasures of the text, but the very real struggles involved in producing such a film within a cautious film industry.[13]

An involvement in the forms and pleasures of popular culture has been and continues to be an important aspect of diverse lesbian identities. Popular culture forms part of the texture of social lives. Films like *Desert Hearts*, while not directed at the assumed coherence of 'the lesbian audience', work to produce those popular pleasures within a lesbian film.

LESBIAN CAMP

Camp functions as a set of styles and practices appropriated from popular culture and reformed within the context of gay male culture.[14] The notion of camp also offers some interesting ideas when attempting to define a lesbian cinema, based not on some fantasized viewing position but on the interplay of popular cinema and lesbian lives. This isn't necessarily to argue that any film is a lesbian film once it is watched by a lesbian audience. Instead I'm pointing to a tradition of spectatorship which has taken pleasure in and appropriated popular films such as *Calamity Jane* or, more recently, *Thelma and Louise*. Teresa De Lauretis' criticism of *Desert Hearts* also talks of the dispensable woman in the film's schema, the equivalent of the 'whore', a woman rejected by Cay in favour of educated Vivian. De Lauretis asserts:

> *Desert Hearts* does not distance this image and role or reframe them in a lesbian camp tradition or in the lesbian history of the forties and fifties, as it might have done, but only invokes a general fifties mood typical of many films of the eighties.[15]

This is perhaps to say that the film is not 'feminist'. Yet it is the very links between such a film and other popular films of the period that is interesting, pointing to the connections between the supposedly discrete cultures of 'lesbian' and 'mainstream' representation. *Desert Hearts* also makes explicit its reference to a tradition of lesbian camp, which has evolved out of a set of appropriations of popular forms. It is within this tradition that a television show like *The Golden Girls*, with its arch 'all girls together' humour, can be read as a lesbian text. *Desert Hearts* does invoke popular cultur.l reference points. To suggest that a film which opens with Patsy Cline singing 'Leavin' on Your Mind' isn't located in lesbian culture seems rather bizarre. De Lauretis may be correct in saying that the film doesn't historicize a lesbian experience of the 1950s, but the film is very much a part of the contemporary lesbian culture that produced it, betraying an affection for the excessive songs, styles and poses of country and western music. *Thelma and Louise* also draws on the cowboy/cowgirl image, a theme which emphasizes the particular white Southern culture within which the protagonists are located. Clearly, *Thelma and Louise* can't be described as a 'lesbian film' in the same way as *Desert Hearts*. Yet in its focus on the developing central relationship between *Thelma and Louise*, its juxtaposition of C&W music and styles with, for example, Marianne Faithfull's 'The Ballad of Lucy Jordan', *Thelma and Louise* draws on a similar iconography. Both films draw on the kind of popular music, style and imagery that has been appropriated by lesbian audiences in other contexts. In this sense *Thelma and Louise* is itself available to be appropriated as a lesbian film.

The transformation of Vivian's character in *Desert Hearts* is traced partly through the clothes that she wears, shifting from her city suit to glitzy cowgirl clothes. It is no coincidence here that the clothes worn by all the characters in the film map out different gendered identities, playing with the crossover between male and female dress. The multiplicity of lesbian identities involve engagements with different forms of popular culture, of which the cinema is only a part. A recognition of this history of appropriation and pleasure is important. Judith Butler finds that the 'notion of an original or primary gender identity is often parodied within the cultural practices of drag, cross-dressing and the sexual stylisation of butch/femme identities.[16] She rejects a feminist critique of such practices, which finds its point of reference in an opposition between original and imitation. Perhaps such recent work offers the beginnings of a critical paradigm within which to think about the diverse perversions represented on the screen.

FOSTERING THE ILLUSION: STEPPING OUT WITH JODIE

Clare Whatling

As lesbians[1] we are all experts at the art of inserting ourselves into the texts of mainstream films, the narratives of which are rarely anything but heterosexual. Such a process is overt in the work of photographer Deborah Bright who literally inserts herself into film stills, cheekily placing herself between Spencer Tracy and Katharine Hepburn, popping up alongside a recumbent Vanessa Redgrave or stealing the limelight from George Segal as she catches the roving eye of a bored Glenda Jackson.[2] As she argues, 'The lesbian subject wanders from still to still, movie to movie, disrupting the narrative and altering it to suit her purposes, just as I did when I first watched those films.'[3] Bright's work simply performs a witty reenactment of what, in the darkened cinema or on the domestic sofa we all do. Every time we watch a film we insert ourselves into the film text through identification with one or another character on screen.

Much feminist film criticism, however, is out of step with such viewing strategies and traditionally has limited the possibilities of identification for women. In the work of Mulvey, Kaplan, Doane and others the female viewer is confined to the masochistic position of the seen, existing only as an object to the sadistic or fetishising male voyeur.[4] Only by her investment in a 'transvestite' masculinity can a woman take up the position of subject/voyeur.

Few attempts have yet been made to theorize other possible viewing strategies for women, still fewer for lesbians.

However, as the example of Bright's work demonstrates, usurpation of the male in his pursuit of the heroine as erotic object has always been a familiar strategy for the lesbian viewer. Such a strategy allows the lesbian viewer identificatory access while retaining the erotic signification of same-sex desire. Nor is lesbian identification confined to this stance, since the hero is himself open to a narcissistic appropriation by the lesbian viewer. Take James Dean for instance, a figure who, already having been appropriated as a gay male idol, has also now become a lesbian hermaphrodite.[5]

Film heroines also present their own identificatory possibilities; their strengths presenting an attractive role-model for the lesbian viewer to embrace if she so wishes. In her guise we can experience not only the desire to be like the heroine – a vigorous, sassy whipcracking Doris Day – but also the desire to be wanted like her, with all the force of a heterosexual economy of passion which this implies. Thus, as a viewer, one is clearly not limited to a singular identification at any one time. As Bright's work shows, the individual viewer is free to make virtually what she wants of any film, turning a text with no obvious lesbian credentials into something we can call our own. Such a process inevitably involves a certain amount of semantic violence on the text which are, on occasions, appropriated to a lesbian erotic by force.

In this essay I want to identify a new kind of viewing strategy available to us as lesbians. I want to explore how a handful of films, with no obvious lesbian reference points, have been appropriated for a lesbian economy of desire as a result of extra-textual information available about its star or stars. This extra-textual material frequently circulates, in the tabloid press and by word of mouth, as rumour and gossip, and concerns the sexuality of particular Hollywood stars. I suggest that knowing a particular actress is, or is rumoured to be, a lesbian enables an appropriation of those films in which those actors star, regardless of the possibilities the films themselves offer.

This exercise also raises collateral questions about the outing of Hollywood celebrities, and what I see as its correlative, the argument for positive images of lesbians and gay men in the mainstream media. My focus throughout will be on the North American actress Jodie Foster, a star whose recent outing demonstrates both the benefits and the pitfalls of the contemporary insistence on openness at all costs.

Hollywood has always offered us images of ourselves. These images have taken various forms. One is that of the pathologized homosexual character, whose presence signifies malign forces of evil or madness. More recently they are covert images in films that remain on the surface heterosexual, but which offer a suggestive, albeit tantalizingly brief, glimpse of what we might call lesbian desire. In the case of such films it is not an act of semantic violence that is required so much as an effort of translation. *Julia, The Bostonians* and the recent *Fried Green Tomatoes at the Whistle Stop Cafe* are just a few of the films which allow this kind of access. The response of the viewer who recognizes the allusions and picks up on the textual hints is to forge the links in a text which will transform covert lesbian components into a coherent lesbian narrative. These are texts which to a greater or lesser degree make a concerted effort not to offend or alienate the heterosexually identified viewer. An audience can go away none the wiser, deviant love having been sublimated into the noble resignation of desire into friendship. To some, this is a mark of their failure. A recent review of *Fried Green Tomatoes*, for example, criticizes the film for what it sees as the closetry of its lesbian message.[6] But such films can also serve as seductive icons to the knowing observer, who reinstates lesbian desire in the face of platonic same-sex representations. One of the chief delights of these films is that they allow free scope for, indeed even depend upon, the play of the viewer's imagination, teasing her to make the connections and fill in the silences. There is a very particular pleasure in piecing together the lingering looks, smiles and moments of fingertips barely touching which form the covert lesbian subtext of such films.

And then, of course, there's *Basic Instinct*. It is a film which in many ways is in line with a long Hollywood tradition of deploying homosexual characters as signifiers of criminality. Here, the lesbians are all killers. In this sense, despite the hype, *Basic Instinct* offers little that is new. However, as the film which kindled the contemporary debate around positive images it deserves some comment. Because what is different about *Basic Instinct* is how glamorous its lesbian characters are. It is of course a film that plays outrageously (in order to outrage) on its lesbian content, proving that Hollywood is only too happy to use lesbianism as subject-matter so long as it pays. In fact, the film's 'lesbian' characters are actually bisexual but this does not preclude it from a lesbian appropriation. Indeed, its popularity with lesbians is well documented. It is a popularity no doubt fuelled by the antics of its leading actress, Sharon Stone, who in interviews has played cheekily on the possibility of her own bisexuality.[7] All this may be disingenuous – it is certainly good for publicity – but it is also a distinct change from the disclaimers that usually accompany films with a lesbian content. Think back to the media debate around *Desert Hearts* for example, and especially to its star, Patricia Charbonneau, who made every attempt to distance herself from the character she portrays in the film.[8] An instance of extra-textual discourses imposing on the film itself, the de-lesbianizing of the female star who features in those films with overt lesbian content often effects a de-lesbianizing of those films whose lesbian credentials are otherwise impeccable.

Occasionally, however, it is precisely those extra-textual discourses which provide the impetus to read certain films as lesbian. This, I suggest, signifies another kind of film text available to us as lesbians. This is the text which is almost certainly not about lesbianism, but which may be lesbianized by the viewer as a result of information about its star or stars which circulates outside the film itself. It is different to those films which are appropriated by the lesbian viewer solely via her own desire, because here her desire is accompanied by an external impetus. Such processes are evident in *The Accused* whose stars, Jodie Foster and Kelly McGillis, become objects of lesbian interest as a result of the grapevine gossip about their supposed on-set relationship. The rumours circulated around bars and at dinner parties. Their sources and 'proofs' were the tabloid press, hearsay and, above all, the willingness of the viewer to believe. My argument is that once received within the context of 'backroom' lesbian speculation and intrigue, a film like *The Accused* is open to a positive appropriation by the lesbian viewer.

When venturing into the realm of filmic rumour, it is worth drawing up a few distinctions between the various categories of historical subject. Historically, there have always been lesbian and gay actors whose orientation has been available knowledge to those 'in the know'. Garbo, Bankhead, Waters, Dietrich, Crawford, Valentino and Dean, each remained hetero-iconic to the mainstream, while whisperings, innuendo and filmic allusion added fuel to the myth of their various homo-identifications. Unlike this first category of stars, my second category never played on their reputation for sexual ambivalence but rather played against it. They include actors like Rock Hudson or Montgomery Clift whose heterosexual identities remained watertight as the result of a concerted press campaign to promote their heterosexuality, however circumscribed or shaky its foundations. Hudson's marriage of convenience to Phyllis Gates at a moment when, it has been suggested, he feared exposure as homosexual presents one instance of such a promotion.[9] A third and, for our needs, final category of rumour is that which surrounds what we might call the 'desired' homosexual. This category refers to those figures, Mae West, Bette Davis, Doris Day, Vanessa Redgrave, Sigourney Weaver, whom we virtually *will* to be lesbians since their filmic status, as strong, tomboyish, articulate heroines is so easily recuperable into a lesbian fantasy erotic. Prior to her outing Jodie Foster would probably have been numbered amongst this category. Her outing and the gossip which accompanies it places her in category two. In not exactly admitting the rumours but not actually denying them either, she is perhaps pushed towards category one. Whatever, as Hollywood's favourite child, Foster's outing goes right to the heart of the Hollywood star system. As such, her sexual status has over the last year been subject to considerable speculation.

The Accused is a film about the prosecution of the perpetrators of a vicious gang rape.[10] It is also a film about the developing relationship of trust between two women, a lawyer and her client. It is a relationship that negotiates the difficulties of class and educational divides as well as legal and ideological differences between the two women. A relationship whose dynamics are in many ways conventional, as it is portrayed on the screen, the relationship is not a lesbian one. What I am arguing, however, is that by virtue only of the extra-textual information and gossip we are offered, one is able to access desire which is appropriable to a lesbian erotic. I suggest that this extra-textual information can alter the focus, not of the film, but of a single scene or set of scenes. In the closing scenes of the film, for example, knowing what we do about the two stars concerned, we come upon the rarest of chances to witness a potential manifestation of same-sex desire on camera. Sarah Tobias (played by Jodie Foster) and Kathryn Murphy (Kelly McGillis) are left alone together. While they wait, Sarah reads Kathryn's horoscope, a trope which has recurred throughout the film. They are seen, at the table, looking at their futures together, futures very different but momentarily sealed in the signature which Sarah confers as gift and thanks for Kathryn's help. The exchange of looks that frames the shot constitutes an intimate moment between two women, nothing more, nothing less. However, in it a bond is confirmed. It is a bond cemented in the successful consummation of the case where the look is again exchanged, the camera intercutting from one face to the other, from Sarah to Kathryn then back again. Following upon this is the time-lapsed coming together of traditional romantic meetings, which culminates in a barely glimpsed hand clinch.

Of course asserting that a lesbian subtext underscores the

women's exchange of looks is not the most obvious or likely reading of the scene. All I suggest is that the lesbian viewer may fantasize the transposition of the look between the two women from the 'safe' context of the actual film narrative, into something more akin to their own desire. What we invoke by the force of our desire to believe the gossip about Foster and McGillis, is the tantalizing possibility that they, the actresses, *are not pretending*. I could be accused of fetishizing this moment, of giving it more weight than it deserves. I agree. The whole point of this reading is the way in which my desire as a lesbian viewer gives it special significance. But what moment do we not fetishize in a medium which relies on the power of the fetish, rendered even more accessible to us since the advent of the stop/pause button on the VCR?

The inclusion of Jodie Foster in the recent campaign in the United States to 'out' public figures can only add fuel to a lesbian interpretation of her work in the light of her own alleged lesbianism. This is all very fine for us, though possibly less pleasant for Foster in the light of the homophobia of the film industry, media and 'fans out in Nebraska'.[11] Her refusal to admit continues to disappoint, though her status as lesbian icon seems stable. Indeed, a recent *Pink Paper* personal, 'Thirty-something seeks k.d. lang or Jodie Foster lookalike, to drink wine, watch sunset and fall in love', would seem to confirm Foster's place within a conventional lesbian erotic.[12] Her press campaign, however, continues to be virulent in its denials of the imputation of lesbianism, concentrating in recent interviews on her image as a 'regular' girl,[13] somewhat akin to the promotional reheterosexualization of Jason Donovan. As if in response to the speculation, Jon Amiel, director of her latest film, *Sommersby*, promised to 'steam up' her image after her role as the relatively asexual Clarice Starling in *The Silence of the Lambs*. Amiel predicted that the love scenes between Foster and her co-star, Richard Gere would be 'hotter than hell'.[14] Indeed they are, and all credit here to the acting ability of the actors involved. However, in the light of the recent outing of Foster (and the rumours about Gere) it is hard not to read this compulsory reheterosexualization as the product of a deep cultural anxiety. The contradictory messages suggest that stars may be as much victims of their press agents, fearful of falling offers should heterosexual identification not be properly established. The anxiety which accompanies any imputation of homosexuality ensures that a star's sexuality stays firmly fixed within the heterosexual economy even to the point of perjury.[15] The effect is to present a narrative fiction of a coherent heterosexual desire which contrasts ironically with the ever potential ambiguity of the filmic space.

Foster is of course also relevant to the concerns of this essay in the way that her outing has become central to the positive images debate. Those who advocate 'outing' claim two benefits. Firstly, outing is about 'providing the gay community with role models'.[16] Secondly, it is meant to inform the star of their responsibility to the lesbian and gay community. Whether it performs either of these roles is of course subject to virulent debate. It does, however, explain why Foster was castigated for her role in *Silence of the Lambs*, which was interpreted by some gay activists as 'toxic homophobia'.[17] But this denunciation says more about the society in which the film is received, where Jame Gumb becomes a gay character by external assent rather than by any homophobic impetus from the director or stars themselves.[18] Foster's actual role as the independent Clarice Starling, 'saviour of women in peril',[19] seems on the other hand irreproachable. The description is Foster's own and makes (or so we can fantasize!) a covert appeal to her lesbian audience. Certainly it is a role which tends to promote rather than inhibit identification for the lesbian viewer, since it shows a woman who is out on her own, unhampered by ties to men or family. As Diane Hamer notes in conversation about the film:

> Foster's role in *The Silence of the Lambs* [is] interesting because of the way she [is] not sexualized in the context of any man but is the protagonist who [drives] the narrative forward

through the powers of her investigations. It [is] an exciting role and Clarice Starling a thrilling character because she is so unfeminine.[20]

As I see it, however, Clarice is not so much unfeminine – her sexual attractiveness is made obvious to us from the very beginning of the film – as standing in an uneasy relation to her own femininity. This unease, as Lecter observes from his first encounter with Clarice, has as much to do with class as it does with gender. Indeed, it is in the intersection of the two that her discomfort lies. Here Lecter dissects Clarice's background with ruthless precision:

> You know what you look like Starling with your good bag and your cheap shoes? You look like a rube. A well-scrubbed hustling rube with a little taste. Good nutrition's given you some bone, but you're not one generation from poor white trash are you Agent Starling? . . . You know how quickly the boys found you, all those tedious, sticky fumblings in the back seats of cars while you could only dream of getting out, getting anywhere, getting all the way to the FBI.[21]

Lector's perspicacity is confirmed in Starling's reply, 'You see a lot Doctor Lecter.' Clarice is pursued by a number of men throughout the film, from the slimy Dr Chilton to, by implication, Lecter himself, and of course, in the denouement, by the killer, Jame Gumb. All of these men are posed as a threat either to her life or to her career, though in the course of the film she manages to elude them all. Her only meaningful relationship, apart from her professional encounters with Crawford and her battle of wits with Lecter, is with her friend and colleague, Ardelia Mapp. In the film the two women are shown working together at crucial stages of the investigation, Mapp taking over the domestic support role usually reserved for the sympathetic boyfriend or husband. The film seems unconcerned by this, playing up where necessary the scenes between the friends, though it is never suggested that their relationship is anything but innocent. The lack of an obvious romantic interest is a site of anxiety in the book, by Thomas Harris, on which the film was based. Harris attempts to right this by ensuring that each exchange between Starling and Mapp manifest a compulsory heterosexuality at its most banal and by forging an unconvincing alliance between Starling and the entomologist, Pilcher. The patent unlikelihood of this event only serves to encourage disbelief – it is not, for instance, pursued in the film. None of this makes Starling a lesbian of course. But it does make her a character who is never comfortably recuperable to a heterosexual paradigm.

Interestingly, Foster's first film as director, *Little Man Tate,* continues rather than dissipates this unease, skirting any hint of sexuality in a film where the (virtually compulsory) romantic interest is missing and the only romantic lines are spoken to a seven-year-old boy. It has been suggested that the story of Fred Tate is semi-autobiographical. Certainly the transposition of Foster into a boy child ('an unconscious reference to her lesbianism?')[22] is interesting, but really no more than speculative. Still, the limitations of the role Foster takes on as Tate's mother do perhaps point to her difficulty in finding a satisfactory sexual niche in Hollywood in the light of her outing.[23]

The question of responsibility seems to me to be a red herring. Gabriel Rotello, editor of the now defunct *Outweek*, argues that public figures 'have to recognize that they are members of an oppressed minority and that membership carries with it intrinsic responsibilities'.[24] What such responsibilities entail for someone like Foster is, firstly, to come out, and then to use her position to construct positive roles for lesbians in film. How she is to achieve this in the face of 'unbelievably homophobic'[25] Hollywood remains unclear. Few stars get to name themselves through as elegant a vehicle as Percy Adlon's recent *Salmonberries* which allowed k.d. lang to finally and eloquently come out.[26]

But there is a more fundamental problem with the notion of 'positive images', which is that as a coherent and collective political discourse it remains a myth. Why else is it that we love to hate certain representations and defend others to the death against our own community? When a pressure group like the Gay and Lesbian Alliance Against Defamation cry out that, 'you don't see yourself upon on the screen',[27] they fail to theorize the subjective nature under which recognition is obtained. For one thing, it refuses to allow for the plethora of subjectivities that look to see themselves reflected in a multiplicity of situations, however incongruous or at odds with an established politics. What it also fails to recognize is the *pleasure* we obtain from so-called negative images of ourselves, what are to some, 'the baddies'. This gestures towards a twofold inquiry; first, it begs the question, just who are the baddies? The answer of course is, it depends who's watching. Secondly, I wonder, what narrative pleasure do we miss out on if we attempt to exclude these baddies? Do we not recoup some pleasure from the fact that they are the ones we *love* to *hate?* Take the example of the headmistress in *Maidens in Uniform*. She is a draconian type (in many readings a trope for the rise of Fascism in Germany in the 1930s) without whom much of the film's narrative tension would be lost. As she stands as a stylistic opposite to the two feminine (though in Von Bernburg's case, austerely so) heroines, the mannish principal is arguably recuperable into her own lesbian erotic. Like the contemporary *Swoon*, a film which, in its portrayal of gay killers, plays on the line between identification and resistance,[28] such a reading renders a simplistic distinction between good and bad increasingly unsustainable.

My belief is that if we insist on Foster's responsibility to the community in a prescriptive way we do her an injustice. Her responsibility as an actress is surely to play characters that entertain and convince. If, to a lesbian audience, this means only playing the 'good' ones then I am not interested. Just as outing fixed sexuality into the 'absolutely' lesbian or gay or heterosexual, rather than questioning the separation of sexual identity into binary oppositions, so 'positive images' finally fixes representation around certain images of ourselves over others. As such, it is a strategy doomed to failure.

Outing is testimony to the increased visibility and vocality of the contemporary lesbian and gay scene. However, as outing, and its correlative, 'positive images', result in simplistic equations and political proscriptions (not to mention free publicity for run-of-the-mill Hollywood blockbusters) it has proven to be counter-productive. As a political discourse it shows little awareness of the complexity or the vagaries of reception. No matter how many times Tom Selleck is designated 'absolutely queer', housewives will still fancy him, just as little girls continue to scream for the very out and very vocal Jimmy Somerville. In this sense it is clear that desire has more to do with the one who is desiring than it does with the object of desire. By such terms it does not really matter whether Jodie Foster is a lesbian or not since as desiring subjects we can still admire her and her films, co-opting them to a lesbian agenda. That she *may* be a lesbian merely adds a little extra frisson to our desire and to our interpretation of her films.

No film text belongs to one constituency. It seems as foolish to argue that any text is intrinsically lesbian as to argue that any text is exclusively heterosexual, for this would deny the multiple possibilities of interpretation and revision that we as lesbians rely upon in our reception of mainstream films. Of course as lesbians we will never agree on just which representations confirm our image of ourselves as good. As B. Ruby Rich adjures, confronting the ideology of positive images head on, 'claim the heroes, claim the villains, and don't mistake any of it for realness'.[29] The chief danger I see in the outing/positive images debate is the temptation to confine lesbian representation to a singular mode of identification. The bid-to-name of the positive images strategy thereby becomes a profoundly isolationist one in a viewing world where we still have the chance to call everything our own.

With thanks to Rachel Driver and Fiona McNeill

LOOKING LESBIAN:
AMAZONS AND ALIENS IN
SCIENCE FICTION CINEMA

Paula Graham

FEMINISM AND THE LESBIAN SPECTATOR

Though feminist film theory is now a well-established academic discipline, very little work has been done on lesbians and popular film. Much of the work done by feminists concerns psychoanalytic readings of heterosexual femininity and male spectatorship. Lesbian critics meanwhile struggle to insert the lesbian subject into a psychoanalytic framework which excludes the possibility even of full, adult *female* subjectivity. This paper is an attempt to theorize the position of the lesbian spectator within mainstream film, taking the *Aliens* trilogy as its starting point.

Recently, feminist theorists have argued that gender positioning is less stable than has been assumed in the past. Critics such as Silverman, Studiar,[1] and Clover,[2] influenced by Deleuze's analysis of masochism, do not see masculine subjectivity as necessarily fixed in phallic identification. This approach has expanded possibilities for imagining a lesbian subjective space.

Teresa De Lauretis' work has employed psychoanalytic techniques to develop lesbian film criticism.[3] Juxtaposing films such as *Desert Hearts* with the more experimental *She Must Be Seeing Things* she sees in the latter a dissemination of lesbian subjectivity through multiple subject positions, both on and off-screen, in a way which challenges the subject–object structure of heterosexuality itself. However, her analysis expresses a scepticism towards the possibilities for 'realist' popular cinema to offer alternatives to heterosexual structures of identification.

Although a welcome addition to the corpus of feminist film criticism, De Lauretis' approach focuses more or less exclusively on lesbian filmmaking. What is still missing is any analysis of lesbian identifications in popular cinema, which also need to be thought through; unless important forms of lesbian resistances, as well as pleasures, are to be 'written off'. I have chosen the *Alien* trilogy because so many lesbians enjoy and identify with the 'Amazon' protagonists. It is also particularly interesting that, in these narratives, the warrior-woman opposes a 'feminine' monstrosity – which would seem to pose a paradox for the female (and particularly the lesbian?) spectator!

FEMINISM, MILITANCY, MOTHERHOOD AND MONSTROSITY IN SCIENCE FICTION

'Amazons' and cross-dressing 'warrior-maids' are dear to most lesbian hearts, giving us both a sense of history and of possibility. However, it is precisely at historical moments at which gender categories have been 'opened out' under pressure of social change and political contestation that mainstream literary Amazons pop up in western cultures. The Amazon has a doubled-edged sword – she can be a sign of resistance but she can also be the father's brainchild.

Lesbian identification in the *Alien* trilogy seems firmly with the 'Amazon' while academic feminist criticism has attended more to the subversive potential of the 'monstrous mother'. Williams suggests that women tend to identify with 'the monstrous-female'.[4] Lesbians often also identify with fantasy witches or vampires – but are equally often angered by images of 'monstrous' femininity. Perhaps it might throw light on lesbian subjectivity if we look more closely at what happens when *both* poles of lesbian subcultural identification (Amazon and feminine-monstrosity) are present in the same narrative.

These films bring an Amazon into conflict with a monstrous 'mother' (animal or mineral) protecting a 'genus'. Williams concludes that there is a subversive representation of a potent, non-phallic sexuality in the monstrous-female.[5] Jardine and Creed argue that anxiety around the instability of the postmodern subject is displaced onto 'the feminine' as the uncanny through a process dubbed 'gynesis'.[6] The subversive potential of horror lies in unsettling the normalizing constructs of gender through significations of 'feminine' power. For this reason, it is at the level of the uncanny that 'the feminine' is interpreted as subversive.

Images of non-biological generation in science fiction are products of its most central preoccupation: the perpetual renegotiation of what it means to be 'human'. Images of monstrous motherhood, parthenogenesis and artificial birth, are related to fears of disturbance in the 'natural' order – and the very *demarcation* of nature and culture. Contemporary western 'man' has been challenged not only by changes in the world order but also by feminism, homosexuality and the 'interface' between the human and the technological (implied by the technologies of artificial intelligence, cybernetics and virtual reality).[7]

The question of the 'lawfulness' of the 'natural' order has characteristically been dealt with through the theme of monstrous birth. This theme is often worked out through representation of the feared collapse of the boundaries of the biological and the technological (as in *Frankenstein*) thus vitiating gender categories as the essence of 'the human'. Technology is usually considered a male bastion, and represented as emphatically phallic tool of human progress. However, science fiction has consistently concerned itself with the question of the legitimacy of 'science' itself ('masculine' technological control of 'feminine' nature) – of 'man-that-is-born-of-woman'.

Representations of the imagined social role of women in a future world usually refer more or less directly to

In *Alien*, the first of the trilogy, a corporation cargo ship Nostrodamus with a small crew consisting of Captain Dallas, Lt Ripley (played by Sigourney Weaver), Science Officer Ash, and crew Kane, Lambert, Parker and Brett, is ordered to divert and investigate an alien ship. Kane is infected by a parasitical alien organism. Ripley tries to quarantine Kane but is overruled by Ash – an android ordered by the Corporation to bring back the alien for any exploitable defence application and to treat the human crew as expendable. The alien 'fertilizes' Kane's chest cavity by penetrating the mouth and throat. A 'baby' alien erupts from Kane's chest, escapes, grows fast and embarks on relentless predation of the crew. *Alien* mixes and destabilizes genre and narrative conventions, deploying anti-narrative devices associated with more experimental film to generate an atmosphere of uncertainty and paranoid suspense. Through visual techniques, the scopic relay is disrupted and mastery of the image is denied both to protagonists and to the cinematic spectator. In the opening sequences, there is no central focus of identification (Ripley emerges gradually as protagonist). Ripley's female body further undercuts the mastery of phallic subjectivity as protagonist.

In the representation of the 'everyday-life' – the real – on the cargo ship, familiar struggles unfold. Issues of class, gender and race are addressed. Just after Ash has pushed the spidery alien onto Ripley (any girl will remember this from the playground), Ash, Dallas and Ripley discuss returning the dead alien to earth. Dallas and Ash's heads are foregrounded, Ripley's head is smaller in the background. As Ash ridicules Ripley's concerns (as feminine 'irrational' fears), he faces out from the screen looking towards Dallas (and the male spectator) in a familiar male-exclusionary manoeuvre (any girl will remember this from the office).

The final scene of *Alien*, in which Ripley is displayed as sexual spectacle in her underwear before overcoming the alien, has been criticized by feminists because it objectifies the female body as site of sexual violence. Clearly, this sexualization of Ripley's body functions as a disavowal of the lesbian implications of her 'phallic subjectivity'. Lesbians may, however, respond quite differently to this scene – in which Ripley is simultaneously female object of desire and active protagonist.

Without her masculine clothing, Ripley appears feminized as a vulnerable sexual object. The lesbian spectator generally resists identification with the feminine object and may slide into the phallic position in the classical scopic relay. As there is already strong lesbian identification with Ripley, when the lesbian (female) spectator looks pleasurably (as phallic voyeur) at Ripley's bi-sexualized body, subjectivity takes on the self-and-also-other structure of lesbianism described by De Lauretis.

This evokes a familiar lesbian strategy for resisting objectification and then coping with the 'impossibility' of reciprocal female subjectivity: 'phallicized' female sexual subject desires self-as-other female reciprocally. This resistance/desire dynamic is characteristic of inter-subjective lesbian sexuality. The lesbian resists passive objectification by adopting 'phallic' agency, yet desires a woman as sexual object. This paradox structures conflicts around lesbian sexual identity.

The passivity of Ripley's objectification is also quickly undercut narratively, and the polarity of sexual subject/object is further destabilized. The alien is initially constructed as (male) rapist/slasher here. 'He' is concealed in the shuttle observing her where she thinks she is safe, has removed her clothes, and relaxed her control. The spectator is, then, initially in a position of voyeuristic control.

The alien hand grabs at Ripley and she backs into the stored spacesuits, her heavy breathing signifying fear/arousal. The camera is angled low and the effect here is to empower Ripley as an eroticized presence, and convey active female sexuality to the lesbian spectator. Ripley's barely covered breasts and genitals dominate the image and serve to invoke lesbian desire. The alien hand slides sensuously over the metal and tubing of the ship; the inner set of teeth (which slashes out and kills in previous scenes) protrudes slowly, drooling KY jelly. Ripley rhymes its actions, repeatedly smoothing the spacesuit she has crept into with her palms and dripping sweat as she pants for breath.

There is recognition of self as also other, and an implication of mutual wariness. A shot-reverse-shot sequence conveys an *exchange* of looks between Ripley and the alien conveying a sense of recognition and *competition* for survival rather than voyeuristic sadism on the part of protagonist or monster. Its 'otherness' feminizes the alien and allows mutuality between the woman and the monstrous-other, undercutting the phallic control of the image by androgonizing *both* positions and implying reciprocal wariness (and fear-arousal). Ripley forces the alien out of its cranny with jets of gas. Better adapted to the environment (in a space suit on home territory), she thrusts the alien through the airlock. When it tries to re-enter like a persistent spider up a drainpipe, she uses the ejaculatory thrust of a grappling iron and the ship's jet propulsion to thrust it off.

At the same time, the scene is 'feminized'. The suggestion of spider/insect as metaphor for alienness is strong here as Ripley confronts feminine-phobic fear (with a faint reminiscence of eyeballing a huge spider in the bath!). Ripley's struggle to resist and transform panic into controlled action is signified by singing and chanting like a child. Fear, aggression and arousal combine in an intense adrenalin-high. The noises she makes become increasingly 'ejaculatory' as her fear mounts. The look on her face after expelling the alien is one of post-orgasmic bliss, before climbing into her virginal bed, returned to asexuality.

As Greenberg points out, the alien is '*mysteriously ungraspable, viciously implacable, improbably beautiful*, and *lewd*' [emphasis his].[8] The alien/other has phallic characteristics, but is generally coded female, both in its reproductive functions, its fatal, implacable beauty and its amoral survival instincts. In the traditions of SF, it is associated with the mad scientist Ash, and the evil corporation, signified by 'mother' (the implacable, amoral central computer).

On the level of realism, Ripley is 'positive' – strong, capable, intelligent and feminist. However, at the symbolic level, the *mise-*

en-scène conveys misogynistic disgust for 'female plumbing', and the narrative implacably expels the uncanny 'other'.

ALIENS: 'HAVE YOU EVEN BEEN MISTAKEN FOR A MAN?'

In *Aliens*, the second film in the trilogy, the alien planet now has a human colony which the alien has set about converting from colonizer to colonial host. Ripley is sent with a team of commandos to tackle the alien but, again, the Corporation has a sub-plot. It is a standard (mixed) genre piece which has a very different narrative form from its predecessor. The pleasures of its young male audience depend on reliable repetition of a known formula. It picks up many of the visual techniques used in the first film, but to quite different effect. The techniques of visual frustration signal occasions for assertive-phallic action. Phallic mastery is challenged only to be reasserted after a suitable period of predictable suspense.

At its realist level, there is some superficial critical engagement with feminism, 'machismo', militarism and the duplicity and exploitativeness of the corporation. However, this is expressed through the standard form and (male) attitudes of a 'kick-ass' action movie. *Aliens*, the second film, plays out a sort of 'Oedipal drama' of dismemberment and reconstitution of self through Ripley as 'final girl'. Ripley has to face and overcome the nightmares of mutilation with which the film opens and can only do so by ensuring that the alien threat (who 'feminizes' by 'impregnation' and mutilation) is completely destroyed.

Clover argues that the 'final girl' as protagonist allows the playing out of such Oedipal fears because the male spectator can effectively deny or distance himself from identification with the (female) body being threatened with terrifying mutilation.[9] However, it is usual in adventure films for numerous *male* bodies to be mutilated, or at least thoroughly beaten up, on the protagonist's road to 'manhood'. This is evident in action-genre films as diverse as *Bloodsport* and *Robocop*, which inherit the Oedipal obsessions of Westerns. The *Alien* trilogy shows the penetration-impregnation, bursting, burning, mutilation, dismemberment and phallic impalation of the male body. If the male spectator were that squeamish about the male body, he would have to steer clear of the average 'kick-ass' flick. It would seem that, actually, it is the overt *eroticization of the violence* which requires a female victim/survivor. Greenberg's comments on the final confrontation between Ripley and the alien in *Alien* are illuminating here:

> Simultaneously suffering with her, and voyeur to her victimisation, the viewer (especially the male viewer) experiences a powerful comingling of raw sexual excitement and mortal terror; an effect often sought but rarely achieved so well in suspense cinema.[10]

Neale argues that the male gaze in the Western and action genres is not purely constituted in the relay suggested by Mulvey, but also contains an element of voyeuristic looking at the male body. The male body, stripped for action, becomes object of (the desiring) male look as well as site of suture for the male spectator. The homosexual eroticism occasioned by this feminization of the male body is assuaged through violent action on the part of the protagonist, restoring a sense of sadistic control for the male spectator. Neale comments on suppressed homoeroticism in such genres:

> The repression of any explicit avowal of eroticism in the act of looking at the male seems structurally linked to a narrative content marked by sado-masochistic phantasies and scenes. Hence both forms of voyeuristic looking, intra- and extra-diagetic, are especially evident in those moments of contest and combat . . . at which a narrative outcome is determined through a fight or gun-battle, at which male struggle becomes pure spectacle . . . taken to the point of fetishistic parody . . .

the look begins to oscillate between voyeurism and fetishism as the narrative starts to freeze and spectacle takes over.[11]

When the female body is substituted for the male body in such narratives, the element of homoeroticism in the male look *at* the male protagonist is displaced onto the female body and thus rendered acceptable for the male spectator.[12] However, what then becomes evident in the resultant masculinization of the female body is an element of lesbian-eroticism for the female spectator. This, no doubt, goes some way to explaining the appeal of such films to lesbian audiences.

In contrast to the relatively complex exploration of 'otherness' in *Alien*, *Aliens* marginalizes, narratively resolves or fetishistically conceals difference. Marginal identities are stereotyped and tokenized in a bunch of 'squaddies', tensions defused through joking: Vasquez is stereotypically 'butch' and holds her own amongst the men:

'Hey, Vasquez – have you ever been mistaken for a man?'
'No, have you?'

'PC' is knowingly sent up. The android objects to the term 'robot', preferring 'synthetic human' and the alien is referred to as a 'xenomorph' ('you mean a bug-hunt,' jeer the marines). Homosocial bonding, exclusion and ridicule of Ripley by the male-military hierarchy, are broadly sketched – but differences are cancelled by death or submerged in male bonding through mutual reliance in militarized action. Even Ripley and the android-other *authenticate* their masculinity in terms of the narrative. Ripley's 'missing' phallus is more than generously supplied – she wins out through firepower and phallic hardware rather than cautious, 'feminine' reflection and self-control as in *Alien*. There is sheer phallic pleasure in wielding all that wham-bam megavolt hardware and blasting those ugly critters to smithereens.

In the adventure/kick-ass genre, the masculinized female protagonist simultaneously avoids the problem of homoeroticism for the male spectator and disavows castration anxiety in the erotic spectacle of the female. However, for the male spectator, the spectre of female sexual aggression is raised and must be controlled or disavowed.

Through her relationships with the child Newt and with Hicks, Ripley is narratively returned to the heterosexual family structure (absent in *Alien*). Motherhood is a central theme of *Aliens* and functions as an 'excuse' for female transgressive behaviour, as disavowal of lesbianism, and as *locus standi* of all female aggression. The Amazonian Ripley reluctantly dons the girdle of male aggression to protect the family and to correct injustice, corruption and excessive violence in the patriarchal order – the traditional 'civilizing' influence of heterosexual femininity. As though this 'mission' were not justification enough, her orgy of violence at the climax of the film is more immediately inspired by the 'instinct' to protect 'her young'.

In *Aliens*, the feminine coding of the alien is amplified and the sub-textual misogyny of *Alien* is more explicit. The 'Amazon' meets the 'monstrous-feminine' in gladiatorial spectacle. Ripley's 'immaculate' motherhood is repeatedly juxtaposed to the slimy, drooling, biological, female-plumbing of alien motherhood (the female-reproductive body). Alien eggs are being laid by a sort of queen-bee alien deep in the bowels of the space-station. In rescuing Newt – her 'young' – Ripley encounters the queen-bee and destroys her 'young'. The monstrous alien-mother pursues Newt. Ripley puts on a phallicizing hydraulic robot-body-shell, appearing almost like the alien body with angular, metallic planes and hydraulic muscle, suggesting reptilian armour. At the same time, the image is extremely phallic. Ripley's feminine vulnerability has become immensely satisfying armoured power.

Ripley challenges the alien to hand-to-hand combat saying: 'Come on, you bitch!' Lesbian 'recognition' in the alien-feminine may well set up a resistance at this point. However pleasurable Ripley's transgressive, orgiastic violence may be, the misogynistic construction of female reproductive processes – the female body –

as monstrosity becomes disturbing. If a male protagonist had used the term 'bitch' before exerting sadistic mastery over parthenogenetic-female-biology-as-monstrosity we might be somewhat concerned as feminists. Could it be that the male spectator is disavowing his misogynistic aggression towards 'uppity' feminine militance (and the threat of submission to the 'monstrous regiment' of feminism). By the substitution of the (fetishized) Amazon for the sadistic-controlling male protagonist, he can disavow his vengeful fantasies as well as his sexual anxieties. As Springer remarks (with reference to Theweleit's comments on Fascist misogynistic identifications[13] the 'machine body becomes the ideal tool for ego maintenance'.[14]

While *Alien* permits a much greater degree of ambiguity to subsist, *Aliens*, with its comic-book narrative, reasserts phallic dominance through sadistic violence, and narratively hetero-sexualizes the female protagonist. But what happens when the 'machine body' is female, the threat feminine, and the spectator lesbian? Does the lesbian spectator risk internalizing and then disavowing anti-feminist misogyny in the pleasurable rush of transgressive violence? Is this violence transgressive of the dominant order because it is carried out by women?

ALIEN 3: THE DESTINATION OF IMPOSSIBLE SIGNS[15]

Alien 3 picks up some of the formal style and themes of *Alien*, pulls together and closes the narratives of the previous two *Alien* films, forming a trilogy (rather than a set of serial sequels). This last film returns to the self-reflexive exploration of 'alienness' and horror characteristics of *Alien*.

Alien 3 returns to the visual techniques of claustrophobic alien-ation and narrative disruption used in *Alien*. Like *Alien*, the film begins with a superimposed 'computer readout' giving the information that this is a 'YY chromosome' high-security correctional facility. This is a reference to a currently fashionable medical myth of genetic criminality that certain chromosomal variations produce psychotic, criminal or 'sexually deviant' syndromes. The 'YY' chromosome is associated with violence and criminal 'deviance'. Homosexuality is also believed to be a genetically based 'condition'. This opening statement, therefore, makes it clear that we are not dealing with prisoners who may have committed crimes for social reasons, but with the *deviant body*. These *men* are 'the other' – those whom society excludes in order to constitute itself as a stable order. Despite their marginalized position, they have forged an alternative 'order' presided over by a black man, Dylan, whose style of eyewear and 'preaching' strongly recalls Malcolm X. The prisoners thus combine marginalized sexual and racial identities with a marginal political 'voice'.

The prison movie genre has always been a vehicle for liberal social critiques in which the prison works as a trope for a dehumanizing institutionalized society. Prison-movie codes and plot conventions are used here (and overt references, including visual reference to *Tattooed Tears*). The commodification (objectification) of the male prisoners is further signified by tattooed bar-codes. Again, at the level of the real, pro-feminism is articulated by reference to restriction and humiliation of women as Ripley deals with the prison hierarchy. Just as the prison governor is calling Ripley a 'foolish woman', the alien snatches him up from behind (there was practically a cheer in the Wednesday matinee at the Camden Parkway!). Framing, editing and camera position problematize the hierarchy of looking.

There are also viscerally pleasurable moments. Ripley refuses to be segregated from the sexually violent men 'for her own safety'. Dylan (a former rapist) intervenes in a violent gang-rape attempt. Identification and bonding is initiated between the two 'others' as Dylan sets about 'spiritually re-educating the brothers' with a baseball bat and Ripley floors one of her assailants with a powerful blow of the fist – viscerally satisfying to the female spectator. The relationship between Ripley and Dylan resembles the mutually respecting homoerotics of the male 'buddy' bond rather than heterosexual attraction.

Ripley – this time bringing the alien *with* her rather than finding it in situ – has herself taken on a kind of marginal identity. Her 'pretended family' from *Aliens* is killed off during the opening credits. When she makes a pass at Clements and he comments on her 'directness', she replies: 'I've been out there a long time'. Her shaven hairstyle is interpreted as 'Sinéad O'Connor' chic by some reviewers, but this would seem a misreading. Ripley is shown in a misted-over mirror while the camera runs salaciously upward over her torso to her misty face. As she wipes the mist from the mirror, her shaven head is clearly meant to be a shocking juxtaposition to her feminine body. Mirror-shots are a stock in trade of horror and the spectator also half expects to see the alien reflected behind (next to) her. This is not a fashion statement.

The prison order is intensely homosocial – not only because there are no women present, but because the men are too 'sociopathic' to relate to women except as objects of violence. It is constantly reiterated that sexuality will upset the male bonding upon which the prison's social order depends. Not only must the homoeroticism of the male order be controlled, but it also may not be interrupted by desire for 'the other'. Ripley has clearly slept with Clements, but this is not shown. Clements is objectified/ commodified (he is marked with a feminizing bar-code) and Ripley initiates. Ripley's implied heterosexuality is thus equivocal to say the least. Her phallic-feminine sexuality is an 'impossible sign' (gender-indeterminate) and cannot be shown. Its narrative implications are controlled by killing the feminized Clements.

At the scene of Clements' death, Ripley is menaced by the alien, recalling the final scene of *Alien*. Mysteriously, the alien does not kill her, but scuttles off. The development of Ripley's 'relationship' with the alien retrospectively pulls together with previous two films' incoherent treatment of this 'relationship' to a coherent development. The mutual recognition implied in the first film becomes, in the second, a confrontation between the two 'mothers' fighting for survival of their 'genus'. In *Alien 3*, Ripley internalizes the alien, she has *become* the alien.

As Ripley discovers that she is 'carrying' the foetal alien 'mother' within her own body, she determines to sacrifice herself to prevent the birth of the implacable 'mother' who will end (reabsorb) the human race. She sets off to find the alien, whom she hopes will dispatch her. She jokes with '85' that she 'knows where to find it − it's in the basement'. 85 points out that the whole prison is a basement and Ripley retorts that it was 'a metaphor'. Searching around with an inadequate torch beam (denial of visual mastery constructing suspense), she (and the spectator) misread a slimy pipe for part of the alien's body. Striking the pipe, it cracks open and a revolting mess of squirming cockroaches spreads on the floor, opening out the metaphorical construction of horror through terrestrial reference (human-parastitic lice, cockroaches). Ripley calls to the alien: 'Don't be scared, I'm one of the family now' − indeed she is now part of the parasitic alien life-cycle (reabsorbed by the mother). As she returns to Dylan's cell, to ask *him* to kill her, she is generically coded as the alien rearing up behind him.

In *Alien 3* there is no spectacular confrontation between the protagonist and the alien as the distinction has been cancelled. The strategy is collective and Ripley grapples unarmed with an alien from 'the basement' which has lost its uncanny threat for her − which she can no longer exclude.

In *Alien 3*, not only are Ripley's body and dress masculinized but her appearance has taken on codings that lesbians will associate with lesbianism. She takes initiative and is in command, sexually and socially. Although temporarily weakened (feminized) by the crash, her body is de-eroticized in that she has ugly bruises and a bloodshot eye. At the same time, she has internalized a 'monstrous femininity'. This is an extremely powerful image.

Ripley has effectively become 'parthenogenetically' herm-aphrodite rather than chaste androgyne − the unrepresentable, floating in the 'out there'. The power of her image is becoming uncontrollable and unlocatable in either gender. She can neither be situated as phallic protagonist nor as 'feminine other' – her destination can only be death. She has become the ultimate horror – not only the woman who acts, who 'looks back', but who actually does not *need* (recognize) men. Ripley has become an image of the uncontrollable *female* for the male spectator. The monstrous feminine regime, no longer 'out there' but within the lesbianized *body*.

CONSTRUCTING THE LESBIAN SUBJECT AND POSITIONING THE LESBIAN SPECTATOR

It seems that lesbian identification tends to focus on the representation of the masculinized-active female *body*. Lesbians express both desire for and identification with the bodies of Weaver (and Hamilton in *Terminator 2*). As Neale argues, there are two 'moments' in male looking at the cinematic representation of the male body: voyeuristic and identificatory. Lesbian looking at the 'phallic' female protagonist could thus enable both a lesbian identification with and desire for the masculinized female body. As both female protagonist and spectator occupy 'phallic' positions in the relay, this desire is 'homosexualized' in films such as *Aliens* and *Terminator 2*. Where female identification is disseminated across the 'phallic-protagonist' and 'feminine-object' positions, a more specifically lesbian identification is possible, along lines suggested by de Lauretis.

The male spectator inserts himself into conventional film narrative through the process of 'suture'. The representation of the (male) protagonist's *body* becomes 'a relay to the body of the spectator within the already formulated institution of classical narrative films and their system of "suture"'.[16] The representational *body* of the male protagonist in conventional film narratives must, then, interfere with any satisfactory process of suture for the female spectator.

Theories of lesbian identification in film have offered either the possibility of 'transvestite' identification with the male position (in a relay which must be interrupted by the spectator's sense of discontinuity between her body and that of the protagonist); the complex process of feminine masquerade behind the representation of excessive femininity; or pre-Oedipal identifications. None of these would seem to offer the lesbian a satisfying 'suture' effect. 'Transvestite' identification gives an 'estrangement' effect combined with some of the male spectator's erotic pleasures for the lesbian spectator. 'Feminine excess' offers all kinds of 'camp' pleasures to the lesbian spectator, but cannot offer the element of powerful agency *located in the pleasures of bodily action* which is an important element of effective agency denied to women.

'Suture' in a relay through the masculinized female body, in films such as the *Aliens* trilogy and *Terminator 2*, gives more satisfactory access to the dream-like pleasures of big-budget Hollywood for the female spectator – including an illusion of phallic omnipotence. A strong illusion of physical *presence* in the narrative opens up visceral and erotic pleasures to lesbians, uninterrupted enjoyment of which is usually reserved for the male spectator.

To a lesser degree in *Alien* and *Alien 3* than *Aliens*, lesbian identifications seem based in a process of cinematic 'suture'. The figure of the masculinized female body acts as a relay through which the lesbian spectator may constitute an effective fictional agency. The lacking female is effectively endowed by her armouring and her sadistic-controlling violence. The lesbian spectator is thus able to enter a satisfying and reassuring 'dream' of stability and potency normally offered only to the male spectator.

However, this does not necessarily mean that the lesbian subject steps into a heterosexual male identification. The lesbian spectator is also receptive to the element of 'homoeroticism' (in the extra-diagetic, objectifying, moment of the look) as she looks at the phallicized-female body of the protagonist on the screen.

The site of 'the feminine' here is occupied by the body of 'the monstrous' (or disembodied as the regime of the evil mother-machines, or the evil corporation), and so identification with 'the feminine' is interrupted for the woman. The representation of the female body through which the female spectator identifies with the feminine position is missing. The *site* of 'the feminine' (monster or machine) easily becomes the *object* of sadistic-punitive looking for the woman, relayed through the female protagonist. It is by this process of negating *femininity* (not necessarily coincidental with female *persons*) that the woman may be aligned with the narrative's misogynistic perspective. This schema undergoes significant modifications in the different films discussed, but I believe it holds as a basic structure across all of them.

Is lesbians' identification thus a 'misrecognition' on the part of lesbians, through which we participate in the re-subordination of 'feminine-aggression' to 'phallic' control? Do Ripley and Connor in *Terminator 2* only signify a lesbian appropriation of the phallic insecurities of contemporary white, middle-class men? If the non-heterosexual female subject consists in a dissemination of subjectivity across destabilized gender positions, is lesbian identification with these protagonists simply the adoption of a heterosexual-male subject position reproducing a heterosexual binary?

These representations certainly try to effect a separation between 'good' feminist aspirations to become a token presence in a minimally revised male 'reality'; and 'bad' feminist aspirations to 'impose' a 'fanatical' feminine regime. But are lesbian pleasures thus entirely vitiated as self-defeating, or even self-hating? Are *Alien* and *Alien 3* better films than *Aliens* because Ripley's phallic protagonism is more 'feminized'? Should lesbians identify instead with the 'subversive potential' of the monstrous feminine?

It does not seem that '*the*' lesbian spectator is always aligned with the male position, nor necessarily disseminated between gendered positions, nor contained in the space of the feminine. In films such as *Alien* and *Alien 3*, lesbian subjective identification may shift from alignment with a male subject-position to dissemination between such a position and the space of the feminine – signified by the monstrous (or the monstrous-technological). This might be seen as having the most subversive potential for the lesbian spectator. In films such as *Aliens*, lesbian looking may be much more 'locked in' to a relay *through* the protagonist *onto* the space of the feminine. But this cannot be seen as solely a negative effect, empowering lesbians, as it does, with a pleasurable illusion of powerful agency and same-sex eroticism.

If you ask a lesbian why she enjoyed a film with pleasurable lesbian-erotic undertones but anti-feminist content, she will almost always reply with the classic form of fetishistic disavowal: 'Well, I know, but . . .' Perhaps this gives a clue. Male fetishistic pleasure in disavowing castration anxiety involves the simultaneous experience of fear of castration. If this fear were entirely overcome (or forgotten), the basis of the fetishistic pleasure would disappear. Fetishistic pleasure depends on the objective embodiment of the fear which is to be allayed. For the male spectator, the *body* of the female protagonist embodies castration anxiety; and her phallicision (for example as protagonist) allays it. At the same time, the homosexual anxiety associated with male looking at the eroticized male body is allayed by substituting the female body. In order for the image to 'work' for the male spectator, he must 'believe' several contradictory things at once.

As Williams points out, 'part of our pleasure in cinema derives from the contradiction between our belief in the perceptual truth of the image and our simultaneous knowledge that it is only imaginary – the discrepancy between the perceived illusion of the presence created by the image and the actual absence of the object replaced by the image.[17] The gaps, discontinuities, and contradictions in the constructed cinematic 'reality' are never entirely submerged by the processes of 'suture'.

Oppositional reading practices must, in order to exist as such, be maintained in tension against dominant discursive practices. However neatly the lesbian subject may be stitched into the dominant discourse, lesbian subjectivity can never be wholly absorbed into heterosexual power relations, which depend on its exclusion. The suppression of lesbian possibilities opened up in the dominant text (as it tries to control female resistance within acceptable limits) produces a new subjective space for lesbian resistance.

But lesbian 'sub-texts' are not necessarily intrinsic. The possible implications of 'phallic' identification have been suppressed in these narratives – partly by presenting the female warrior as asexual. This asexuality is characteristic of the heroines of all the films under discussion (heterosexual orientations are mainly implied rather than enacted). The active sexualization of the Amazon would raise lesbian implications whilst her passive sexualization would interrupt her credibility as protagonist. It requires a certain subcultural competence to recognize suppressed lesbian eroticism and to 'read in' lesbian identifications.

Lesbian identity and lesbian reading are active processes and not 'found' in static narrative or psychic structures. It may be that there *is* no single lesbian spectatorial position, or definitive structure of lesbian subjectivity, offered by the text and readable in isolation from other 'textualities'. The lesbian reader is a point of 'intertextual' transmission. Deploying a subcultural matrix, she is able to resist the heterosexualization of feminist appropriations of 'phallic' power by the dominant order, and to access the pleasures of a suppressed lesbian eroticism. The subcultural 'language-games' of lesbianism are fabricated from such resistant readings of texts, and refabricated as opposing conceptualizations work themselves out.

There may be many reasons why lesbians would identify with the female protagonist in films which, at best, recuperate feminism to a revised male order or, at worst, are blatantly gender-conservative. One reason may be subcultural codings. Certain stars, or physical types, etc, may become subculturally 'coded' as lesbian. Lesbian 'traditions' of cross-dressing and 'passing' for men (especially soldiers), and associations of the Amazon with lesbianism may also be a factor.

Since the lesbian spectator of films such as the *Aliens* trilogy can hardly help but be aware of the lesbian-erotic elements of looking at the fetishized body of the female protagonist, textual suppression of lesbianism is not going to be effective. Overt demonization, as in *Red Sonja*, is also something we have a long, shared subcultural experience of resisting and reappropriating. This is not to say that there is a timeless lesbian psychological structure or 'lesbian sensibility' at work here. The lesbian mobilizes her critical readings by reference to the discursive spaces of lesbianism through which she constructs an identity.

Some feminisms dismiss forms of sexual or erotic pleasures designated 'male' and therefore oppressive. Lesbian feminism has a history of downgrading desire. 'Pro-sex' lesbian commentary, on the other hand, often seems reluctant to analyse feminist resistances, in favour of prioritizing lesbian 'desire'. Heterosexual feminist analysis of horror focuses either on the subversive potential of 'monstrous' feminine excess, or on the male spectator, (or on the sexualization of the female protagonist which is read as nullifying her impact as 'positive image'). Thus *either* lesbian pleasure *or* feminist resistance is being discussed, as though the two bore no relation to each other.

It seems to me, however, that resistance is a condition of lesbian pleasure in the image of the female warrior. Lesbians resist sexual objectification (as the primary western form of exclusion and disempowerment of women) in order to act powerfully. One resistant strategy (amongst many) is to take up a 'phallic' subject position. Having done this, a woman is excluded from the heterosexual order of desire. She cannot desire a woman because that would imply lesbianism; she cannot desire a man as object (from her phallic subjective position) because that would still imply homosexuality; and she cannot be desired (objectified) without abandoning her 'phallic' position. In order to desire a woman, she must objectify a woman – who, as a lesbian, will resist objectification. To stabilize this paradoxical tension, subjectivity may be disseminated across the subject and object positions.

When the lesbian spectator looks at the body of the female

warrior, the female warrior is sexually objectified, but also identified with as 'phallic' (*desiring*) subject – opening up a lesbian subjective space. The male spectator enjoys a displaced homosexual pleasure. Paradoxically, therefore, it is the heterosexual feminist identification which colludes with the suppression of the element of (homosexual) desire in looking at the Amazon. This may be why heterosexual feminist analysis focuses, instead, on the male spectator and the 'monstrous feminine'.

This is not to argue for a definitive structure of lesbian identification, but to offer a conceptualization of how lesbian spectatorship might work in specific narratives. Nor is it to say that all mainstream representations of 'strong' women, are necessarily recuperable for lesbian identifications and pleasures. Such judgements depend on (historical) context. Which representations of female protagonism (or female bonding) are seen as subculturally recyclable or as irredeemably heterosexist – and by whom – remains a matter for continuing discursive struggle.

BASIC INSTINCT:
DAMNING DYKES

Angela Galvin

A catalogue of overtly and implicitly gay characters in Hollywood films highlights the pathologizing social and medical models into which mainstream culture places homosexuality. Enter Catherine Tramell in *Basic Instinct*. Her portrayal by Sharon Stone has been described as:

> One of the greatest performances by a woman in screen history. (Camille Paglia, in Sessums 1993).

> A complex, compelling, Nietzschean Uberfraulein who owns everything about her own power. (Naomi Wolf, in Sessums 1993).

> Nothing to do with the women I know, gay or straight. (Amanda Donohoe, in Yates 1993).

PSYCHO DRAMA

During the late 1970s and early to mid 1980s, the film industry had reflected changing social attitudes with the production of a few films which attempted to portray gay characters in a way which was more meaningful to the gay audience. Of this wave of films with positive or at least identifiable characterizations, *Desert Hearts* was possibly the most commercially successful (arguably because its portrayal of a sexual relationship between two 'attractive' women satisfies a male, or perhaps a general heterosexual, spectatorial fantasy). Even so, the film's release in 1986 coincided with a reported upsurge in gay-bashing across the United States (Russo 1987).

By the time *Basic Instinct* went into production the lesbian and gay subculture was particularly threatened by a backlash against the small but significant steps towards equality which had been achieved during the previous two decades. Lesbian and gay activism had also increased during that period, spurred largely by the lack of governmental initiatives to combat the AIDS crisis. It is surprising then that director Paul Verhoeven was taken aback by the violent reaction to his plans to produce an Hitchcockian homage whose central character was a psychopathic lesbian (*Guardian,* 18 March 1992).

GLAAD TO BE GAY

In the USA, a lesbian and gay coalition protested against the film, both in production and on its release. The Gay and Lesbian Alliance Against Defamation (GLAAD) has a campaigning history and was joined in protest against *Basic Instinct* by the more radical Queer Nation. Both groups comprise lesbians and gay men, but their differing tactics emphasize that even where there is some unity across genders there can be political divisions within the gay 'community'. Whereas GLAAD's main emphasis was on persuasion, Queer Nation opted for disruption. Queer National activists disrupted the shoot in San Francisco by blowing whistles and capitalizing on the Gulf War by displaying 'Honk if you support our boys' signs on the adjacent freeway. The alliance also picketed cinemas where the film was being shown in San Francisco, Los Angeles, Seattle, Chicago and New York. GLAAD distributed lavender leaflets with the message:

We think the movie could do us harm by reinforcing ignorance about homosexuality and by providing an excuse for assaults on an escalating number of lesbians and gay men.

Queer Nation wore T-shirts with the identity of the killer on the front and 'Ice-pick wielding fag-dyke', on the back (*Guardian* 18 and 23 March 1992). Yet these different approaches were in response to the same problem – a film in which the three lesbian characters are depicted as killers.

Basic Instinct is, to a lesser or greater extent, homophobic, misogynist and badly scripted. One might ask whether the film has been a box office success despite or because of this combination of elements? To the mainstream cinema audience, *Basic Instinct*'s intertextual status may have been more important. The film is not simply a thriller, but also a tribute to Hitchcock (*Vertigo*), directed by Paul Verhoeven (*Total Recall*), scripted by Joe Eszterhas (*Jagged Edge*), starring Michael Douglas (*Fatal Attraction*) and Sharon Stone (*Total Recall*).

For a lesbian audience, *Basic Instinct* can be viewed intertextually, with reference not simply to the films listed above but as part of a continuum of film texts carrying negative portrayals of a gay existence. *Basic Instinct* has undeniably absorbed signs and meanings from films which preceded it, reflecting society's hostility to homosexuality. Roxy and Beth Garner join a long list of lesbian characters murdered in the course of mainstream cinema – from Alice Roberts in Pabst's *Pandora's Box* (1929) onwards. Similarly, Catherine Tramell is not the first murderous lesbian, (see, for example, Glora Holden in Hillyer's *Dracula's Daughter*, 1936). The list could go on. The representation of lesbians in a Hollywood film is not a novelty *per se*. Catherine Tramell's novelty lies in her being a Hollywood lesbian who is rich, gorgeous and sought-after by men and women alike.

Arguably, the lack of positive portrayals of women in general and lesbians in particular has resulted in lesbians devising ways of seeing and gaining pleasure from ostensibly negative characterizations. Lesbians have developed a kind of tunnel-vision which focuses on the positive elements of a character (Catherine Tramell is very physically attractive) and ignores the negative (Catherine Tramell kills people). Like other narratives, *Basic Instinct* obviously holds different values and different meanings for different spectators – there are possibilities for both positive and negative pleasure arising from selective lesbian vision which, in turn, arises from the desire to access empathy and identification despite negative plots and characters. (The most extreme example of this in my own experience being a women's screening of *The Loudest Whisper* (Wyler 1962) which was drawn to an abrupt end before Shirley Maclaine's character could kill herself.

Quite apart from the intervention of an autocratic projectionist, there is a potentially infinite diversity of meaning based on each spectator's subjectively constituted world. There are some lesbians, for example, who advocate that the image of a psychotic, murderous bisexual is one which should be endorsed and accepted within the lesbian subculture. Perhaps they agree with Paul Verhoeven in his insistence that the lesbians are the most positive characters in the film (given that the male protagonist, Nick, is in therapy for shooting tourists, this may well be the case).

It is certainly interesting to note that, in general, men (straight and gay) have been far more disapproving of the film than women. One possible explanation for this is suggested by Paul Canning ('Psycho dykes and killer gays' in *Australian Women's Forum*, September-October 1992). With reference to the knicker-free scene in the interrogation room, he quotes Cherry Smyth in *City Limits:*

'I found that scene really hot. She's saying "I'm going to get you with my pussy." That's great. It made me laugh . . . But a man beside me didn't laugh at all – perhaps he was straight. (Or perhaps he was a politically correct male trying to figure out what exactly his reaction should be).'

Thus *Basic Instinct*, though a simple narrative, reflects the complexity of audiences watching films as gendered spectators.

The potential for women and men to read the film in different ways is illustrated by the fact that, whereas men have been more reserved in their judgement, both heterosexual and lesbian women have taken some limited pleasure from *Basic Instinct*. In this sense, the obvious intention to appeal to the male audience through Catherine Tramell's various states of undress has been subverted by the female audience's complex system of identification, empathy and selectivity. Women can derive pleasure from not only Catherine's conventional beauty but also her unconventional behaviour – from smoking to wearing no knickers to driving aggressively to sleeping with women to killing men – depending on one's scale of values.

A BRIEF HISTORY OF CRIME

The film's central character is not Catherine Tramell but the detective, Nick Curran, assigned to solve the violent murder of a former rock star. But the narrative is less concerned with investigating the crime than it is with investigating the emasculation of nineties man as revealed through the psyche of Nick, his psychotherapist (Beth Garner) and Catherine. This triangular relationship is as much a case-study in the preoccupations of pop psychology as it is a psychological thriller. In these terms, the choice of the therapist–patient relationship as pivotal to the narrative is an interesting one. It acts to disclose a series of neuroses and psychoses which undermine the terms of difference between Nick and the two women, and between the two women and each other.

In the course of his therapy, Nick provides the audience with a brief overview of the psychoanalytic concepts which are self-consciously present throughout the plot:

Number One, I don't remember how often I used to jerk off, but it was a lot;
Number Two I wasn't pissed off with my dad, even when I

was old enough to know what him and mom were doing in
the bedroom;
    Number Three, I don't look down the toilet before I flush it;
    Number Four, I haven't wet my bed in a long time;
    Number Five, why don't you two go fuck yourselves.

Of this five–point summary of the history of psychotherapy –
masturbation, the primal scene, the anal phase, psychosexual
development and phallocentricity – Nick's reference to the primal
scene (number two, strangely) is perhaps the most salient. Lacan
posits the primal scene as the site of either too much pleasure
(resulting in personae like Nick and Catherine) or too little (the
asexual Gus – who may have a crush on Nick – and Beth, who
can't 'make it'). The narrative unfolds to reveal a hypothesis based
on the premise that those who attribute the primal scene with too
much pleasure live dangerously, those who don't become obsessed
by those who do and then they die.

   In psychotherapeutic terms, the relationship between the
therapist and the patient is produced and maintained by a set of
rules which generate a characteristic situation and interaction. The
interviews between Beth and Nick serve to show that whatever
rules there may have been have surely been broken. Their
relationship has been sexual and, by the look she gives him as he
leaves her office after their first on-screen encounter, we know that
she would like this to continue. Apart from establishing the (once)
sexual nature of their relationship, this first interview also acts to
establish Nick as an addictive, even obsessive, personality; it is not
so much the fact that he has forgone sex, cigarettes, alcohol and
cocaine that interests us as the fact that he had been doing all four.
We cannot be surprised when he succumbs again to three of his
addictions in quick succession, or that by succumbing to sex (with
Catherine) he finds himself with an obsession more addictive and
dangerous than all of the others.

   The position of both Beth and Nick in relation to Catherine is
posited as the most interesting aspect of the relationship between

the two women. In particular, their relationship reveals the script's self-conscious play with the notion of transference between therapist and patient. Nick's initially repressed wish for Catherine motivates him to continue analysis with Beth – she is not Catherine but she might lead him to her.

The narrative suggests that Nick has been coerced into therapy as a condition of rehabilitation within the police force. He displays little or no self-motivation to visit Beth for therapy. The motivation materializes when he sees Beth as a means of finding answers to the questions he poses as a detective – he doesn't want to find himself but he does want to 'find' Catherine.

The suggestion of interchangeability between the two women is reinforced within the plot. When the Stamford professor offers the detectives his psychological profile of the former rock star's killer, it is Beth who interprets the psychological jargon for her male colleagues ('It takes one to know one.') When Nick later confronts her about having modelled herself on Catherine by dyeing her hair blonde, Beth replies that she used to be a redhead too – thus confirming her transferable 'any woman' status.

Beth offers to listen to Nick, she supports him through his conflicts with authority both past (the tourist–shooting incident) and present (the 'did he shoot his boss?' inquiry). But her availability is a source of tension which she cannot resolve because Nick's desire is for Catherine rather than her. Beth's accessibility highlights Catherine's, initial, unavailability. Nick's relationship with Beth becomes dominated by his sexual obsession with and desire for Catherine. His role as a detective, investigating Catherine's involvement in murder and the subsequent implication of Beth's criminal involvement, is a search for 'truth' which mirrors that of the psychoanalytic/therapeutic process.

Catherine figures within this therapeutic scenario as a repressed wish. Nick cannot consciously express his desire for her because this would expose him to ridicule or censure – she is suspected of murdering her last lover, he is supposed to be seeking incriminating evidence against her. Similarly, Beth cannot express her former intimacy and current desire for Catherine because of Catherine's position as a criminal suspect and the ridicule to which her 'gayness' would expose her. (She ironically suggests to Nick that she declares to the other detectives 'Hey guys, I'm gay and I've slept with your suspect.') There is the further complication of her place in Nick's desires having been usurped by Catherine.

Nick's desire for Catherine is partly motivated by her ability to pull the wool over the other detectives' eyes and her ability (which he shares) to deceive the lie detector. Catherine's attraction to Nick is similarly based on her awareness that he too is a killer and that he has fooled the lie detector in order to get, partially, off the hook. Clearly, the thrill of desire for someone who might at any moment kill you is limited to the anticipation of the event rather than its afterglow. Whereas Beth could meet Nick's more conventional (though still violent) sexual demands, Catherine represents the desire for complete loss in the form of death.

YOU LIKE WATCHING, DON'T YOU?

The relationship between Nick and Beth as patient and analyst and Catherine as the object of their mutual desire displays three forms of transgressive behaviour: Beth's desire for Nick, Beth's desire for Catherine and Catherine's desire for Beth. The potential for Nick's desire for either of them (particularly Catherine, as the one most clearly placed as lesbian) being transgressive is negated by the narrative placing her as an object of the male gaze within the text. She is contained, her difference controlled, by the repetition of the looks of male characters (Gus and Nick, the five men in the interview room and so on) and by the voyeuristic point of view which consistently places her as the object of an illicit look – particularly on the occasions where Nick and the audience see her undressing, but also via the video screen as she takes the lie–detector test and in the mirror as she has sex. The voyeuristic device is also used in the rape of Beth by Nick which takes place in front of uncurtained windows, overlooked by a dance class.

The audience's position as voyeurs of these scenes is emphasized in the script with references to how 'you' like watching her – using the ice-pick (Catherine to Nick) and having sex (Nick to Roxy). Although the comments are directed from one character to another, taken in tandem with the point-of-view they imply a collusion on the part of the spectator. This complicit voyeurism degrades both the audience and Catherine's character. Stone herself has stated that in order to film the first scene in which she undresses while Nick watches, she needed all of the women involved on the set to sit in the room with her to support her (with 'female energy', Sessums 1993). Whereas Camille Paglia claims the famous interrogation room scene as a portrayal of men 'enslaved by their own sexuality' (Sessums 1993), the women with whom I first watched the film saw the scene as a presentation of female vulnerability. Although almost ironic in its over-the-topness, its reference to prison/torture scenes through lighting, colour and point-of-view, foregrounds vulnerability and powerlessness more than it subverts sexual power relations. The scene precisely references scenarios of both vulnerability and power, but it is naive in the extreme to suggest that the power is firmly placed with the female character. Can the question of sexual choice, freedom and power really be resolved by abandoning one's nether garments? Catherine may portray a 'fully sexual woman' but her sexuality is for the (voyeuristic) pleasure of others.

IT TAKES ONE TO KNOW ONE

Catherine's declared sexual interest in other women does permit the female spectator to be the subject of the look without assuming masculinity. But can lesbian pleasure be extricated from the constraints of gendered perspectives? Jackie Stacey (1987) queries whether women necessarily take up a feminine, and men a masculine, spectator position. Yet, in relation to *Basic Instinct*, 'gendered' theories grounded in women gaining pleasure through masochism and narcissism have a clear territorial advantage. These are theories which themselves reflect Verhoeven's (and Hitchcock's) preoccupation with pop psychology. In relation to *Basic Instinct*, Bellour's contention that 'Woman's desire only appears on screen to be punished and controlled by assimilation to the desire of the male character,' is persuasive. The elements of punishment and control, most evident in relation to Beth and Roxy, would certainly contribute to a theory of masochistic pleasure:

> Beth tolerates violence, rape, abuse and ultimately death at the hands of Nick. He rapes her because he has been sexually aroused by Catherine. Despite her own obsession, Beth never exchanges looks with Catherine within the narrative. Nick kills her because to believe what she says about Catherine would interfere with his false reality, manifested by his obsession. When he goes to shoot her the audience is made aware of the crime for which she is being punished; he doesn't ask whether she has killed his partner (Gus) but 'You still like girls, Beth?'

> Roxy experiences emotional abuse (from Nick and Catherine) and dies at the hands of Nick after a car chase during which he thinks she is Catherine. He calls out 'You wanna play? Come on,' as he embarks on the chase like a form of foreplay. But unlike Catherine, who avoids accidents despite having an aggressive (masculine) driving style, Roxy doesn't have the power or control to beat Nick at this game. His reaction on reaching her crashed car and finding Roxy rather than Catherine's (unblemished) corpse is a confusion of pleasure and disappointment.

Although *Basic Instinct* is replete with unfeminine 'authorial markers' and lacks reference to everyday life as the majority of spectators know it, other aspects of the narrative facilitate female pleasure as learnt from soap opera and other cultural forms designated as 'feminine'. (see Curti 1988). In particular, the lack of distancing and the physical fascination with Catherine as the embodiment of the key traits of North American soap queens: unimaginable wealth, independence, nice car, expensive clothes, lovely house. Strangely though, for a film which features a lesbian as a central character, the pleasurable criterion of female intimacy and friendship is conspicuous by its absence. The only on-screen female–female intimacy between Catherine and Roxy forms an extension of Catherine's relationship with Nick – her and Roxy's display of breast-fondling at the beach house, dancing together at the night-club and, implicitly, Roxy watching Catherine and Nick have sex. Catherine is labelled lesbian but is portrayed in almost exclusively heterosexual activity. Her lesbianism is voiced by other characters (notably Roxy) or in laughably theatrical set-pieces. Her relationships with other women seem to be a part of her academic interest in psychology, with the effect of distancing her – her friends are really 'cases'. Catherine's intimacy/friendship with other women is sinister and threatening because the narrative's thrust is that any of the female characters could not only be a lesbian but also a killer. The off-screen intimacy between her and Beth reinforces this message with the gradual revelation that the two had been lovers and that Beth could be the murderer. Indeed, it is the knowledge of this sexual nature of the Beth/Catherine relationship which motivates Nick's complicity in Beth's destruction.

Nick's need for Beth is portrayed as one of convenience – for sex and for his career. Whilst she consistently explains her actions (handing his confidential file to Nilson, visiting his flat, interviewing him) as acts motivated by her love for him, the audience is fed the suggestion that 'He started banging her to get off the hook with internal affairs,' and left to draw its own conclusions. However, the secret of her sexuality becomes a focus for the threats to Nick's career and manhood. The Stamford professor's psychological profile of the killer tells the audience all they need to know about Catherine and Nick. Textual references to 'it takes one to know one' only confirm the argument that Nick can find the killer because he knows what it's like to kill and, as his addictive personality confirms, he is prey to psychosis.

HERS IS BIGGER

Nick's character personifies the threatened and haunted male of the 1990s. Masculine identity has been destabilized by economic, social and cultural change; for this threatened, haunted destabilized male, sexual roles, behaviour and power relationships have been further undermined by the fear of HIV. Yet, after having sex with Catherine, the use of a condom is simply a matter for a joke with Gus. Sex with Catherine is, by its very nature, unsafe. The threat of an ice–pick is more immediate to Nick that the risk of HIV but for the spectator the ice–pick is symbolic of the threat of women in general and HIV in particular. Other films of the thriller genre employ images of "the toothed vagina" – the vagina that castrates' or the talking vagina (see Creed 1989) for the purpose of portraying female sexuality as a monstrous threat to the male. Catherine's sexuality is also invested with a life of its own. As Nick briefs Gus about the murder and his view of Catherine's role in it, Gus replies 'That's her pussy talking, not your brain.'

While female spectators may vicariously enjoy Catherine's wealth, possessions and independence, to men the very symbols of her wealth, ergo her independence, are seen as a threatening and indeed castrating. Gus and Nick comment on two Picassos owned by Catherine and her murdered lover. They note with a mixture of admiration and defensiveness 'Hers is bigger.' Similarly, Catherine's traditionally 'male' attitude to sex without love (you still get the pleasure) shocks those same male detectives who condone Nick's sexual relationship with Beth. This castration anxiety is present throughout the narrative but emerges most strongly around Catherine's lesbianism. In the bathroom scene, after he has had sex with Catherine for the first time, Nick talks to Catherine's girlfriend 'man to man' and masculinizes her name to 'Rocky' in a demonstration of his assumed possession of the phallus and her apparent lack. His tone is both smug and mocking – he's got one, she hasn't, and he won't let her forget it.

In relation to Catherine herself, however, the story is different.

Her material possessions and her sexuality outweigh her lack of phallus and consequently act both symbolically and literally to undermine the male characters. Nick is driven by his fear of Catherine and his desire for her. Already dissolute and murderous, he is able to justify his own behaviour by objectifying someone who is yet more dissolute and murderous than himself. The film charts Nick's neurotic decline as his obsession with Catherine increases, despite or even because of his knowledge that the cost of this obsession could be his own death by ice-pick.

CONCLUSION

Basic Instinct's intention is to thrill – targeting the known audience for the thriller genre and capitalizing on a sexually explicit subtext. The storyline is familiar (particularly to those who have seen *Jagged Edge*, also scripted by Eszterhas). Plot variation hinges on the character of Catherine Tramell and her manifest threat to manly pride. The narrative, such as it is, hinges on a collection of psychological theories strung loosely together with scant regard for accuracy. In this sense there are strong parallels with Hitchcock's *Vertigo*, 'basically only a psychological murder mystery' (*Variety*, 14 May 1958) which hinges on the hero's acrophobia, and Hillyer's *Dracula's Daughter* (1936), during which the murderous lesbian vampire is unmasked by a psychologist.

The history of lesbians in mainstream film has been a history of moustachioed murderesses and suicides (see Russo 1987). In this context, lesbian identification and pleasure in film has necessarily been fragmented. The novelty of *Basic Instinct* may well lie in our heroine's absence of facial hair.

In response to Michael Douglas' statement concerning *Basic Instinct* 'Gee, you can't show blacks, gays, Italians or women as villains, only straight white men' (*Face*, December 1991), I would suggest that while the filmmaker or audience may not want every film to be a gay celebration, it is fair for a lesbian audience to expect at least some reference to its own reality. But Verhoeven's reality is one in which few propositions could be more threatening to a heterosexual male than death at the hands of a lesbian.

There *are* pleasures to be gained from *Basic Instinct*. Indeed, Catherine Tramell has become a focus of pleasure for some women. However, finding the gorgeous Ms Stone physically attractive should not obscure the fact that her character is clearly placed as an object of male fantasy ahead of lesbian or heterosexual female identification. The debate around the film, prior to as well as after its release, reveals that the filmmakers' motivation was the box-office draw of current fears and prejudices about women's and gay sexuality. Eszterhas and Verhoeven simply took the lowest common denominator of fear and dressed it up as truth.

Catherine Tramell's 'crypto-lesbianism' (Hoberman) begs the question, 'When is a lesbian not a lesbian?' To which some might reply 'When she's having sex with a man.' Catherine's lesbianism is an aspect of her sexuality used as a simple and lazy device to illustrate her otherness, her threat and her psychosis. Just as her lesbianism signifies mental ill-health, her mental ill-health (and that of Nick) is inferred to be an understandable response to a sick society, of which she is both symptom and victim. As such, her character joins the catalogue of cases where lesbianism has been equated with sickness and criminality. Lacan asserts that the narrative is a diagram of everything we cannot have. The narrative of *Basic Instinct*, like the history of Hollywood filmmaking, would appear to confirm the view that what lesbian spectators cannot have is a positive endorsement of lesbian existence.

NOTES

CROSSOVER DREAMS: LESBIANISM AND POPULAR MUSIC SINCE THE 1970S

1 Herbert Gans, *Popular Culture and High Culture*. See also Angela McRobbie's comments on the importance of looking at 'identity-in-culture', in 'Post-Marxism and Cultural Studies: A post-script,' in *Cultural Studies*, Lawrence Grossberg, Cary Nelson and Paula Treichler (eds), London, Routledge, 1992.
2 In Gans, p. 95. Stuart Hall's 'Cultural Identity and Cinematic Representation', in *Framework*, No. 36, is also relevant to this discussion.
3 Jon Savage, 'Tainted Love: The Influence of Male Homosexuality and Sexual Divergence on Pop Music and Culture Since the War', in Alan Tomlinson (ed.), *Consumption, Identity and Style*.
4 Michel Foucault, *The History of Sexuality, Vol. 1*, New York, Random House, 1978.
5 See also Bonnie Zimmerman's study of lesbian feminist fiction, *The Safe Sea of Women*.
6 On the 'massification' of authentic cultures, see Walter Benjamin, *Illuminations*.
7 On the history of women's music and its relationship to American radical feminism, see Alice Echols, *Daring to Be Bad*. For a history of women in music which places women's music in a larger historical perspective, see Gillian Gaar, *She's a Rebel: The History of Women in Rock and Roll*.
8 Holly Near, interviewed by Gillian Gaar in *She's a Rebel*, p. 154.
9 In Simon Frith, *Music for Pleasure*.
10 Arlene Stein, 'Androgyny Goes Pop', in Stein (ed.), *Sisters, Sexperts, Queers: Beyond the Lesbian Nation*, p. 101.

11 Arlene Stein, 'Sisters and Queers: the Decentering of Lesbian Feminism', *Socialist Review*, January–March 1992.

12 For example, Olivia Records turned down overtures from Melissa Etheridge before she was signed to a major label. Redwood Records, the label that Holly Near founded, tried to sign Tracy Chapman when she was still in school in Boston, but could not compete with Elektra.

13 This was the reverse of an earlier embrace of androgyny by male pop stars like David Bowie, influenced by gay drag's tradition of artifice and costume.

14 Susan Wilson, 'Talkin' 'bout a revolution for women in pop?' *Boston Sunday Globe*, 20 November, 1988.

15 Lisa Lewis, *Gender Politics and MTV: Voicing the Difference*.

16 On the Madonna phenomenon, and its relationship to lesbian/gay subcultures, see Cathy Schwichtenberg (ed), *The Madonna Connection*.

17 Arlene Stein, 'Androgyny Goes Pop', p.103.

18 In a rare acknowledgement of the lesbian roots of the late 1980s folk boom, Michelle Shocked, upon accepting the award for Folk Album of the Year at the 1989 New Music Awards in New York (nominated along with Phranc, Tracy Chapman, and the Indigo Girls) quipped 'This category should have been called "Best Lesbian Vocalist".' But she later complained to an interviewer about being lumped together with all the other emerging women performers, while others avoided the subject entirely, refusing to be interviewed by lesbian/gay or feminist publications.

19 'Folksinger', by Phranc, from *I Enjoy Being a Girl*, Island Records, 1989.

20 Ginny Z. Berson, 'Who owes what to whom? Building and maintaining lesbian culture', in *Windy City Times*, 22 June, 1989.

21 Interview with author, 1991.

22 Audre Lorde, 'Age, Race, Class and Sex: Women Redefining Difference', in *Sister Outsider*.

23 Lawrence Grossberg, 'MTV: Swinging on the (Postmodern) Star', in Ian Angus and Sut Jhally (eds), *Cultural Politics in Contemporary America*.

24 Arlene Stein, 'Androgyny Goes Pop', p.108.

25 Barbara Bradby, 'Lesbians and Popular Music: Does It Matter Who is Singing?' in Gabriele Griffin (ed), *Outwrite: Lesbianism and Popular Culture*.

26 Holly Kruse, 'Subcultural Identity in Alternative Music Culture', in *Popular Music*, vol. 12, No. 1, January 1993.

27 Biddy Martin, 'Sexual Practice and Changing Lesbian Identities', in *Destabilizing Theory: Contemporary Feminist Debates* (Stanford, 1992).

A QUEER LOVE AFFAIR? MADONNA AND LESBIAN AND GAY CULTURE

1 Westview Press have recently published an academic study of Madonna, edited by Cathy Schwichtenberg and entitled *The Madonna Connection*. And Cleis Press released *Madonnarama* in 1993.
2 Suzanne Moore's comments were made during her contribution to 'Madonna's *Sex*', a discussion at the ICA in London held on 30 March 1993.
3 For a fuller discussion of Madonna's relationship to feminism see Schwichtenberg's *The Madonna Connection*, especially her own article 'Madonna's postmodern feminism: bringing the margins to the centre', pp. 129–45.
4 This resulted in an image of a heroine literally, as well as metaphorically, staggering under the weight of contradictory signs; an image beautifully captured in the still for the film's poster in which Weaver is depicted clutching an enormous gun in one hand and the child in the other. Attempting to convey the message – yes, she's tough but she's also tender – it ended up as parody.
5 Toni Nealie, 'Gay abandon' in the *Guardian*, 18 April 1992.
6 Although, considering the obtuseness of heterosexual audiences, it is doubtful how much of her gayness was readable.
7 Some of Grace's work is featured in Boffin and Fraser's book, *Stolen Glances*.

SHE THINKS I STILL CARE: LESBIANS AND COUNTRY MUSIC

1 Angela Phillips and Jill Rakusen (eds), *Our Bodies Ourselves*, London, Penguin, 1978.
2 Faderman, Lillian, *Odd Girls and Twilight Lovers*.

NETTING THE PRESS: PLAYING WITH MARTINA

1 Martina Navratilova (with George Vecsey), *Martina*, New York, Fawcett Crest, 1985.

'COP IT SWEET': LESBIAN CRIME FICTION

1 See Katherine V. Forrest, *Amateur City* (Tallahassee, FA, Naiad, 1984; London, Pandora, 1987), *Murder at the Nightwood Bar* (Tallahassee, FA, Naiad, 1987; London, Pandora, 1987); *The Beverly Malibu* (Tallahassee, FA, Naiad, 1989; London, Pandora, 1990), *Murder by Tradition* (Tallahassee, FA, Naiad, 1991; London, Grafton, 1993); Ellen Hart, *Hallowed Murder* (Seattle: The Seal Press, 1989); Claire McNab, *Lessons in Murder* (Sydney, Allen & Unwin, 1990; London, Silver Moon Books, 1990), *Fatal Reunion* (Sydney, Allen & Unwin, 1990), *Death Down Under* (Sydney, Allen & Unwin, 1992; London, Silver Moon Books, 1991); Finola Moorhead, *Still Murder* (Ringwood, Victoria, Penguin Books, 1991); Mary Morell, *Final Session* (San Francisco, Spinsters Book Co., 1991); Barbara Wilson, *Murder in the Collective* (Seattle: The Seal Press, 1984; London, The Women's Press, 1984); *Sisters of the Road* (Seattle, The Seal Press, 1986; London, The Women's Press, 1987); *Gaudi Afternoon* (Seattle, The Seal Press, 1990; London, Virago, 1991); Mary Wings, *She Came Too Late* (London, The Women's Press, 1986), *She Came in a Flash* (London, The Women's Press, 1988); Eve Zaremba, *Work for a Million* (Toronto, Amanita, 1986; London, Virago, 1990).

2 Lillian Faderman, *Odd Girls and Twilight Lovers: A History of Lesbian Life in Twentieth Century America*.

3 Stephen Knight, *Form and Ideology in Crime Fiction* (London: Macmillan, 1980). See too Anne Cranny Francis, *Feminist Fiction: Feminist Uses of Generic Fiction*.

4 Marilyn Stasio, quoted by Cranny Francis, *Feminist Fiction*, p. 143.

5 Paulina Palmer, 'The Lesbian Feminist Thriller and Detective Novel' in Elaine Hobby and Chris White, (eds), *What Lesbians Do in Books*. p.19. See too Sally Munt, 'The Investigators: Lesbian Crime Fiction' in Susannah Radstone, (ed), *Sweet Dreams: Sexuality, Gender and Popular Fiction*, pp. 91–119.

6 Judith Butler, *Gender Trouble: Feminism and the Subversion of Identity*.

7 'One or Two Women?' *Meanjin* 48, ii (1989), pp. 269–276.

8 I have in mind Jeffreys *The Spinster and Her Enemies: Feminism and Sexuality 1880-1930*, Faderman's *Surpassing The Love of Men* and the more recent *Odd Girls*.

9 Alison Hennegan, 'On Becoming a Lesbian Reader' in Susannah Radstone (ed), *Sweet Dreams: Sexuality, Gender and Popular Fiction*, pp. 165–190.

10 Jonathan Dollimore, *Sexual Dissidence: Augustine to Wilde, Freud to Foucault*, p. 87.

11 Faderman, *Odd Girls*, p. 307.
12 Janice A. Radway, *Reading the Romance*, p. 6.

MAKING A DRAMA OUT OF DIFFERENCE: *PORTRAIT OF A MARRIAGE*

1 As Mandy Merck points out, the autumn 1990 UK transmission of *Portrait of a Marriage* coincided roughly with railings against increases in divorce and single motherhood at the Conservative Party Conference. Again, at the 1993 Conservative Party Conference, single motherhood was in part blamed for social disintegration and lawlessness (p. 114).

FROM A STRING OF KNOTS TO ORANGE BOX: LESBIANISM ON PRIME TIME

1 Winterson, J. 1985 (1991), p. 166.
2 Winterson, J. 1985 (1991), p. 91.
3 Winterson, J. *Oranges are Not the Only Fruit*; *The Script*, London, Pandora, 1990, p. vii & p. xvii.
4 The Local Government Act, 1989, included the notorious Clause 28, which forbade local councils in Britain from funding organizations and/or projects whose aim was deemed to be 'promoting homosexuality'. This was preceded by widespread protest from the gay community, and followed by a climate of fear concerning any activity which might possibly be covered by the Act, which did not include broadcasting.
5 *Moving Pictures*, BBC2, March 1993.
6 'Quality' drama has, since the 1960s, been the single television form to attract serious critical attention. Characteristically a single play by a known author, in a series such as *Armchair Theatre* or *Play for Today*, it usually dealt 'realistically' with serious and provocative subject matter. In recent years it has more typically been a serial adaptation of a work of 'literary' stature, characterized by 'high production values'. See, for example, the discussion by Brunsdon, 'Problems with Quality', *Screen*, vol. 31, No.1, Spring 1990.
7 McCabe, C. p. 310. 'Days of Hope: A response to Colin McArthur', in T. Bennett, S. Boyd-Bowman and C. Mercer, J. Woollacott (eds) *Popular Television & Film*, London, BFI, 1981.
8 See Tallis, R. *In Defence of Realism*, London, Edward Arnold, 1989, especially chapters 2 and 4.
9 In terms of British television, Alan Bleasdale's series, *Boys from the*

Blackstuff is perhaps nearest to *Oranges* in its incorporation of non-realist elements within a realist base. Fay Weldon's *The Life and Loves of a She Devil* (not, however, scripted by her) departs further from its realist base, while Dennis Potter's *The Singing Detective* was more clearly identifiable as a postmodern text.

10 Tallis, p. 172, suggests that realism is only properly defined as such when it is well executed.

11 A point also made by Hinds, 1992, p. 164.

12 L. Mulvey, 'Visual Pleasure and Narrative Cinema', *Screen*, vol. 16, No. 3, Autumn 1975.

13 Quoted in Hinds, 1992, p. 165.

14 Hinds, 1992, pp. 165-67.

15 Winterson, 1985 (1991), p. 110.

16 'Fatherhood, in the sense of conscious begetting, is unknown to man. It is a mystical estate, an apostolic succession, from only begetter to only begotten . . . *Amor matris*, subjective and objective genitive, may be the only true thing in life. Paternity may be a legal fiction. Who is the father of any son that any son should love him or he any son?' Joyce, J., *Ulysses*, London, Penguin, 1971, p. 207.

17 Winterson, (1985), 1991, p. 126.

18 Ibid., p. 125.

19 Ibid., p. 126.

20 A. Rich, 'Compulsory Heterosexuality and Lesbian Existence', in A. Snitow *et al.*, 1983.

21 Winterson, 1990, p. viii.

TV Credits

Oranges are Not the Only Fruit, BBC2, January 1990
Producer: Philippa Giles. *Director*: Beeban Kidron. *Script*: Jeanette Winterson. *Designer*: Cecilia Brereton. *Music*: Rachel Portman. *Constume Designer*: Les Lansdown.
Cast: Geraldine McEwan (*Mother*), Charlotte Coleman (*Jess*), Emily Aston (*Small Jess*), Margery Withers (*Elsie*), Kenneth Cranham (*Pastor*), Celia Imrie (*Miss Jewsbury*), Cathryn Bradshaw (*Melanie*), Barbara Hicks (*Cissy*), Tania Rodrigues (*Katy*), Elizabeth Spriggs (*May*), Freda Dow (*Mrs Green*), Pam Ferris (*Mrs Arkwright*), Peter Gordon (*William*).

PUSSY GALORE: LESBIAN IMAGES AND LESBIAN DESIRE IN THE POPULAR CINEMA

1 Perversity seems the most appropriate term here, since the cinema does not function through categories as clearly specifiable as 'gay' or 'straight'.

2 J. Hoberman, 'Fantastic projections', *Sight and Sound*, May 1992, p. 4.
3 Ibid.
4 S. Moore, *Guardian*, 7 May 1992, p. 34.
5 I'm thinking particularly of Judith Butler's *Gender Trouble*, though
   several recent collections have dealt with these themes in fascinating
   ways (see Bibliography).
6 This common narrative is one more variant of the buddy movie, a
   form in which Hollywood seems to delight.
7 My main reference points here are the two essays by Teresa De
   Lauretis discussed in more detail later in this section. However, I'm
   also drawing on responses to papers I have given on the films
   discussed, in which audiences oscillate between pleasure in the
   image and an angry rejection of what is perceived as mainstream
   cinema cynically exploiting themes such as lesbian desire and female
   friendship. A more complex analysis, in which the drive of the
   narrative (seen as an erasure of lesbianism) is played-off against the
   powerful images invoked by *Black Widow*, is to be found in Valerie
   Traub's essay on the film in J. Epstein and K. Straub (eds) *Body
   Guards: The Cultural Politics of Gender Ambiguity*. Traub also
   acknowledges the cult status of the film, speaking not only about
   the text, but what it has come to mean to audiences.
8 I'm thinking here of formulations of 'gendered genre' which I
   discuss in detail in 'Having It All' in C. Lury, S. Franklin and J.
   Stacey (eds), *Off-Centre: Feminism and Cultural Studies*.
9 Teresa De Lauretis, 'Guerrillas in the Midst', pp.6–25. See also
   'Film and the Visible' in Bad Object Choices (eds), *How Do I Look?
   Queer Film and Video*, p. 225–64.
10 Teresa De Lauretis, 1990, pp. 24–25.
11 J. Root, 'Interview with Donna Deitch', *Monthly Film Bulletin*,
    September 1986, pp. 228–9.
12 S. Moore, 'Finding Themselves', *New Socialist*, September 1986,
    p. 42.
13 See Deitch's comments on raising the money for *Desert Hearts* in
    'Interview with Donna Deitch', Root, and in an interview in
    Women's Review, September 1986, pp. 20–21.
14 Amongst all the writings on the role of camp in male gay culture,
    Andy Medhurst's 'Pitching Camp', *City Limits*, 10–17 May 1990, is
    one of the shortest and sweetest. For Medhurst, 'camp just isn't
    accessible to intellectual analysis, because it bases itself on the
    ephemeral and the experiential'.
15 Teresa De Lauretis, 1991, p. 256.
16 J. Butler, *Gender Trouble*, p. 137.

FOSTERING THE ILLUSION: STEPPING OUT WITH JODIE

1 The definition of the term 'lesbian' will remain provisional, but for the purposes of this essay it implies a subject who enters the cinema with a self-named (motivated by sex, politics, sociality, or any combination of the above) identity as lesbian. Such a lesbian self-naming, as it remains strategic, situated and multiple, is meant to elide any essentialism implied in the term.

2 As Bright makes clear, celebration stems partly from the fact that, 'The cinematic traits these stars shared in their films from the 1940s to the mid-1960s included supple, athletic bodies in tailored suits, strong facial features, dominant rather than subordinate body language, displays of superior intelligence and wit, and (by definition) roles that challenged conventional feminine stereotypes' (Deborah Bright, 'Dream Girls', Tessa Boffin and Jean Fraser (eds), *Stolen Glances*.

3 Boffin and Fraser, *Stolen Glances*, p. 154. This strategy is similar to Levi-Strauss' concept of *bricolage*, which Richard Dyer invokes for the screen in *Gays and Film*, p.1.

4 L. Mulvey, 'Visual Pleasure and Narrative Cinema', *Screen*, 16/3, 1975; E. Ann Kaplan, 'Is the Gaze Male?' in Ann Snitow (ed), *Desire*; Mary Ann Doane, *The Desire to Desire*.

5 'I know you've seen the type: no tits, no cock, oozing with a kind of vulnerable "masculinity" and sheathed in a '50s style black leather motorcycle jacket. Or to put it slightly differently, it's James Dean with a clit.' Sue Golding, 'James Dean: The Almost Perfect Lesbian Hermaphrodite', in Boffin and Fraser, pp. 197–8.

6 See *Pink Paper*, April 1992.

7 See, *Daily Mirror*, 5 July, 1992.

8 She gave interviews and appeared in the popular press photographed with her husband and child. Of course her anxiety is no doubt a reflection of Hollywood homophobia and the danger of being typecast. Still, the question must be posed, in what political context does her distancing in itself become lesbophobic?

9 See Richard Meyer, 'Rock Hudson's Body', in Diana Fuss (ed), *Inside/Out*, p. 272.

10 On its release the film was criticized for its depiction of the rape scene which it was argued played into the hands of the sadistically motivated voyeur. While I would agree with this argument, the ethics of filming a rape is not my focus in this essay.

11 *Independent on Sunday*, 16 June 1991, p. 13.

12 *Pink Paper*, 14 June 1992.

13 See *Hello*, February 1992.

14 Quoted in *Sunday Express*, 23 August 1992.
15 A double deception in the case of Rock Hudson, whose marriage to Phyllis Gates was masterminded by his homosexual agent, Henry Willson. See Meyer, 'Rock Hudson's Body', p. 272.
16 *Independent on Sunday*, 16 June 1991, p. 12.
17 B. Ruby Rich, 'A queer sensation', *Village Voice*, 24 March, 1992, p. 44.
18 Although I do agree with Tom Kalin's pronouncement (*OUT*, 1 July 1992) that the film would benefit from a more lucid analysis of sex and gender, in particular, to point out that the two are not inextricably linked.
19 As Foster herself puts it in an interview. (*The Late Show:* Silence of the Lambs *special*).
20 Diane Hamer, personal correspondence.
21 *The Silence of the Lambs*, 1991 Orion Pictures Limited.
22 Hamer, personal correspondence.
23 For an alternative reading and also an historical contextualization of Foster's work, see B. Ruby Rich, 'Nobody's Handmaid', *Sight and Sound*, December 1991.
24 Gabriel Rotello, quoted in *Independent on Sunday*, 16 June 1991, p. 13.
25 Ibid.
26 An act she confirmed in *Capital Gay*, June 1992.
27 Jehan Agrama, quoted on *OUT*, 1 July 1992.
28 'We are appalled at the callousness of their crime, yet charmed by Leopold's passion for Loeb'. *Weekend Guardian*, August 15–16, 1992, p. 19.
29 Rich, 'A queer sensation', p. 44.

LOOKING LESBIAN: AMAZONS AND ALIENS IN SCIENCE FICTION CINEMA

1 Gaylyn Studlar, 'Masochism, Masquerade, and the Erotic Metamorphoses of Marlene Dietrich', *Fabrications: Costume and the Female Body*.
2 Carol J. Clover, *Men, Women and Chain Saws: Gender in the Modern Horror Film*.
3 Teresa De Lauretis, 'Film and the Visible', in Bad Object Choices (eds), *How Do I Look? Queer Film and Video*.
4 Linda Williams, 'When the Woman Looks', in Doane, Mary, *et. al.* (eds), *Re-Vision: Essays in Feminist Film Criticism*.
5 Ibid.
6 Alice Jardine, *Gynesis: Configurations of Women and Modernity*,

Cornell University Press, 1985; Creed, ibid.

7 Claudia Springer, 'The Pleasures of the Interface', *Screen*, 32:3, 1991.

8 Harvey R. Greenberg, 'Reimagining the Gargoyle: Psychoanalytic Notes on *Alien, Close Encounters: Film Feminism and Science Fiction*, (ed.) Penley *et al*. Minnesota UP, 1991.

9 Carol J. Clover, *Men, Women and Chain Saws: Gender in the Modern Horror Film*.

10 Greenberg, ibid.

11 Stephen Neale, 'Masculinity as Spectacle: Reflections on Men and Mainstream Cinema', *Screen*, 24:6, 1983.

12 Helen Solterer, 'Figures of Female Militancy in Mediaeval France', *Signs*, 16:3, 1991.

13 Klaus Theweleit, *Male Fantasies* I & II, Minnesota UP, 1987, 1989.

14 Claudia Springer, 'The Pleasure of the Interface'.

15 See Claire Johnstone, 'Femininity and the Masquerade: *Anne of the Indies*', *Jacques Tourneur*, BFI, 1975.

16 Linda Williams, 'Film Body: An Implantation of Perversions', *Cine-Tracts*, 3:4, 1981.

17 Ibid.

BASIC INSTINCT: DAMNING DYKES

1 Bellour, R. 'Hitchcock the Enunciator' in *Camera Obscura* 2, Fall 1977.

2 Creed, B. 'Horror and the Monstrous Feminine: An Imaginary Abjection', in J. Donald (ed) *Fantasy and the Cinema*, London, BFI, 1989.

3 Curti, L. 'Genre and Gender' in *Cultural Studies*, vol. 2, No. 2, May 1988.

4 Hoberman, J. 'Fantastic Projections' in *Sight and Sound*, May 1992.

5 Medved, M. '*Hollywood vs America*', New York, HarperCollins, 1992.

6 Russo, V. '*The Celluloid Closet*', N.Y, Harper and Row, 1987.

7 Sessums, K. 'Stone Goddess', in *Vanity Fair*, April 1993.

8 Stacey, J. 'Desperately Seeking Difference', in *Screen*, 28/1, 1987

9 Yates, P. 'The Good Bad Girl' in *Sunday Mirror Magazine*, February. 1993.

BIBLIOGRAPHY

Angus, Ian and Jhally, Sut (eds), *Cultural Politics in Contemporary America*, London, Routledge, 1989.

Ash, Juliet and Wilson, Elizabeth, *Chic Thrills: A Fashion Reader*, London, Pandora, 1991.

Bad Object Choices (eds), *How Do I Look? Queer Film and Video*, Seattle, Bay Press, 1991.

Bannon, Ann, *The Beebo Brinker Series*, Florida, Naiad Press, 1987.

Bellour, R. 'Hitchcock and Enunciator' in *Camera Obscura* 2, Fall 1977.

Bennett, T, Boyd-Bowman, S., Mercer, C. and Woollacott, J. (eds), *Popular Television and Film*, London, BFI, 1981.

Benjamin, W. *Illuminations*, New York, Harcourt Brace and World, 1968.

Blue, Adrianne, *Grace Under Pressure*, London, Sidgwick & Jackson, 1987.

Boffin, Tessa and Fraser, Jean (eds), *Stolen Glances: Lesbians Take Photographs*, London, Pandora Press, 1991.

Bright, Susie, *Susie Sexpert's Lesbian Sex World*, Pittsburgh & San Fransico, Cleis Press, 1990.

Butler, Judith, *Gender Trouble: Feminism and the Subversion of Identity*, London, Routledge, 1990a.

Butler, Judith, 'Gender Trouble, Feminist Theory and Psychoanalytic Discourse' in L. Nicholson (ed), *Feminism/Postmodernism*, New York and London, Routledge, 1990b.

Clover, Carol J. *Men, Women and Chain Saws: Gender in the Modern Horror Film*, London, BFI, 1992.

Cook, Pam and Dodd, Philip (eds), *Women and Film: A Sight and Sound Reader*, London, Scarlet Press, 1993.

Cranny Francis, Anne, *Feminist Fiction: Feminist Uses of Generic Fiction*,

Cambridge, Polity Press, 1990.

Creed, B. 'Hottot and the Monstrous Feminine: An Imaginary Abjection', in J. Donald (ed) *Fantasy and the Cinema*, London, BFI, 1989.

Curti, L. 'Genre and Gender' in *Cultural Studies*, vol. 2, No. 2, May 1988.

De Lauretis, Teresa, 'Film and the Visible' in Bad Object Choices (eds), *How Do I Look? Queer Film and Video*, Seattle, Bay Press, 1991.

De Lauretis, Teresa, 'Guerrillas in the Midst: Women's Cinema in the '80s, *Screen*, vol. 31, No 1, Spring 1990.

Doane, Mary Ann, *The Desire to Desire*, London, Macmillan, 1987.

Doane, Mary Ann, Mellencamp, S., and Williams, L. (eds) *Re-Vision: Essays in Feminist Film Criticism*, AFI, Frederick, MD, University Publications of America, 1984.

Dollimore, Jonathan, *Sexual Dissidence: Augustine to Wilde, Freud to Foucault*, Oxford, Clarendon Press, 1991.

Donoghue, Emma, *Passions Between Women: British Lesbian Culture 1668–1801*, London, Scarlet Press, 1993.

Duncker, Patricia, *Sisters and Strangers. An Introduction to Contemporary Feminist Fiction*, Oxford, Blackwell, 1992.

Dyer, Richard, *Gays and Film*, London, BFI, 1977.

Dyer, Richard, *Now You See It: Lesbian & Gay Film*, London, Routledge, 1990.

Echols, Alice, *Daring to Be Bad: Radical Feminism in America, 1967–1975*. Minneapolis, University of Minnesota Press, 1989.

Epstein, J. and Straub, K. (eds), *Body Guards: The Cultural Politics of Gender Ambiguity*, Routledge, 1991.

Faderman, Lillian, *Odd Girls and Twilight Lovers. A History of Lesbian Life in Twentieth Century America*, New York, Penguin, 1992.

Faderman, Lillian. *Surpassing the Love of Men*, London, The Women's Press, 1985.

Foucault, M. *The History of Sexuality*, vol. 1. New York, Random House, 1978.

Franklin, S., Lury, C., and Stacey, J. (eds), *Off-Centre: Feminism and Cultural Studies*, London, HarperCollins, 1991.

Frith, Simon, *Music for Pleasure*, London, Routledge, 1988.

Fuss, Diana, *Essentially Speaking: Feminism, Nature and Difference*, London, Routledge, 1989.

Fuss, Diana (ed), *Inside/Out: Lesbian Theories, Gay Theories*, London, Routledge, 1991.

Gaar, Gillian. *She's a Rebel: The History of Women in Rock and Roll*, Seal Press, 1992.

Gamman, Lorraine and Marshment, Margaret (eds), *The Female Gaze*, London, The Women's Press, 1988.

Gans, Herbert, *Popular Culture and High Culture*. New York, Basic Books, 1974.

Gledhill, C. (ed) *Stardom: Industry of Desire*, London, Routledge, 1991.

Greig, C. *Will You Still Love Me Tomorrow: Girl Groups from the 50s on*. London, Virago, 1989.

Griffin, Gabriele (ed), *Outwrite: Lesbianism and Popular Culture*, London, Pluto Press, 1993.

Hall, Radclyffe, *The Well of Loneliness*, London, Virago, 1982.

Hamer, Diane, 'The Invention of the Dildo: Lesbianism and Legal Discourse' in *Australian Gay and Lesbian Law Journal*, vol. 2, Spring 1992.

Hayward S. and Vincendeau, G. (eds), *French Film: Texts and Contexts*, London, Routledge, 1990.

Henderson, Lisa, 'Justify our Love: Madonna and the Politics of Queer Sex' in Schwichtenberg, Cathy (ed), *The Madonna Connection: Representational Politics, Subcultural Identities & Cultural Theory*, Oxford, Westview Press, 1993.

Hennegan, Alison, 'On Becoming a Lesbian Reader', in Radstone (ed), *Sweet Dreams: Sexuality, Gender and Popular Fiction*, London, Lawrence & Wishart, 1988.

Hinds, H., *Oranges are Not the Only Fruit*: Reaching Audiences Other Lesbian Texts Cannot Reach, in S. Munt (ed), *New Lesbian Criticism: Literary and Cultural Readings*, London, Harvester Wheatsheaf, 1992.

Hobby, Elaine and White, Chris (eds), *What Lesbians Do in Books*, London, The Women's Press, 1991.

Hoberman, J. 'Fantastic Projections' in *Sight and Sound*, May 1992.

Jardine, Alice, *Gynesis: Configurations of Woman and Modernity*, New York, Cornell University Press, 1985.

Jay, Karla and Glasgow, Joanne (eds), *Lesbian Texts and Contexts: Radical Revisions*. New York, New York University Press, 1990. London, Onlywomen Press, 1991.

Jeffreys, Sheila, *The Spinster and Her Enemies: Feminism and Sexuality 1880–1930*, London, Pandora, 1985.

Joyce, J. *Ulysses*, London, Penguin, 1971.

Knight, Stephen, *Form and Ideology in Crime Fiction*, London, Macmillan, 1980.

Kitzinger, J. and Kitzinger, C. 'Doing It: Representations of Lesbian Sex', in G. Griffin (ed) *Outwrite: Lesbianism and Popular Culture*, London, Pluto Press, 1993.

Kuhn, A. *Women's Pictures*, London, Routledge, 1982.

Lacan, J. *Ecrits: A Selection*, New York, W.W. Norton, 1979.

Lacan, J. *The Four Fundamentals of Psychoanalysis*, New York, W.W. Norton, 1979.

Lewis, Lisa, *Gender Politics and MTV: Voicing the Difference*, Temple, 1990.

Lorde, Audre, *Sister Outsider*, NY Crossing Press, 1984; London, Sheba, 1986.

Lury, C., Franklin, S. and Stacey, J. (eds), *Off-Centre: Feminism and Cultural Studies*, London, HarperCollins, 1991.

Madonna, *Sex,* photographs by Steven Meisel, New York, Secker and Warburg, 1992.

Medved, M. '*Hollywood vs America*', New York, HarperCollins, 1992.

Merck, Mandy, *Perversions: Deviant Readings*, London, Virago, 1993.

Modleski, T. *Loving With a Vengeance: Mass Produced Fantasies for Women*, London, Routledge, 1990.

Mulvey, L. 'Visual Pleasure and Narrative Cinema', *Screen*, 16/3, 1975.

Munt, Sally (ed), *New Lesbian Criticism: Literary and Cultural Readings*, London, Harvester Wheatsheaf, 1992.

Musto, Michael, Cathy Schwichtenberg (ed), *The Madonna Connection: Representational Politics, Subcultural Identities & Cultural Theory*, Oxford, Westview Press, 1993.

Navratilova, Martina (with George Vecsey), *Being Myself*, New York, Fawcett Crest, 1985; London, William Collins, 1985.

Nestle, Joan, *A Restricted Country*, New York, Firebrand Books, 1987; London, Sheba Feminist Press, 1988.

Nicholson, L. (ed), *Feminism/Postmodernism*, London, Routledge, 1990.

Paglia, Camille, *Sex, Art & American Culture*, New York, Vintage Books, 1992.

Palmer, Paulina, 'The Lesbian Feminist Thriller and Detective Novel', in E. Hobby and C. White (eds), *What Lesbians do in Books*, London, The Women's Press, 1991.

Penley *et al.* (eds), *Close Encounters: Film Feminism and Science Fiction*, Minnesota University Press, 1991.

Radstone, Susannah (ed), *Sweet Dreams: Sexuality, Gender and Popular Fiction*, London, Lawrence & Wishart, 1988.

Radway, Janice A. *Reading the Romance*, London, Verso, 1987.

Russo, V. 'The Celluloid Closet', N.Y, Harper and Row, 1987.

Schwichtenberg, Cathy (ed), *The Madonna Connection: Representational Politics, Subcultural Identities & Cultural Theory*, Oxford, Westview Press, 1993.

Sedgewick, Eve Kosofsky, *Epistemology of the Closet*, Hemel Hempstead, Harvester Wheatsheaf, 1990.

Segal, L. and Macintosh, M. (eds), *Sex Exposed: Sexuality and the Pornography Debate*, London, Virago, 1992.

Sessums, K., 'Stone Goddess', in *Vanity Fair,* April 1993.

Snitow, A., Stansell C, and Thompson, S. (eds), *Powers of Desire: The Politics of Sexuality*, New York, Monthly Review Press, 1983.

Stacey, J. 'Desperately Seeking Difference', in *Screen*, 28/1, 1987.

Stein, Arlene (ed), *Sisters, Sexperts, Queers: Beyond the Lesbian Nation*, Plume, 1993.

Steward S, and Garratt, S. *Signed, Sealed and Delivered: True Life Stories of Women in Pop.* London, Serpents Tail, 1992.

Studlar, Gaylyn, *Fabrications: Costume and the Female Body*, London, Routledge, 1991.

Tallis, R. *In Defence of Realism*, London, Edward Arnold, 1989.

Tomlinson, A. (ed), *Consumption, Identity and Style*, London, Routledge, 1990.

Wilson, E., 'Borderlines' in *New Statesman and Society*, 2 November 1990.

Winterson, J. *Oranges are Not the Only Fruit*: The Script, London, Pandora, 1990.

Winterson, J. *Oranges are Not the Only Fruit*, London, Pandora, 1991. First published in 1985.

Yates, P. 'The Good Bad Girl' in *Sunday Mirror Magazine*, February 1993.

Zimmerman, B. *The Safe Sea of Women: Lesbian Fiction 1969–1989*, Massachusetts, Beacon Press, 1990.

INDEX